Defending the Guilty

Alex McBride is a criminal barrister. He is the author of the 'Common Law' column in *Prospect* magazine and has contributed to the *New Statesman* and various BBC programmes, including *From Our Own Correspondent*.

Defending the Guilty

Truth and Lies in the Criminal Courtroom

ALEX MCBRIDE

VIKING
an imprint of
PENGUIN BOOKS

VIKING

Published by the Penguin Group

Penguin Books Ltd, 80 Strand, London WC2R ORL, England

Penguin Group (USA) Inc., 375 Hudson Street, New York, New York 10014, USA

Penguin Group (Canada), 90 Eglinton Avenue East, Suite 700, Toronto, Ontario, Canada M4P 2Y3
(a division of Pearson Penguin Canada Inc.)

Penguin Ireland, 25 St Stephen's Green, Dublin 2, Ireland (a division of Penguin Books Ltd)

Penguin Group (Australia), 250 Camberwell Road, Camberwell, Victoria 3124, Australia
(a division of Pearson Australia Group Pty Ltd)

Penguin Books India Pvt Ltd, 11 Community Centre, Panchsheel Park, New Delhi – 110 017, India

Penguin Group (NZ), 67 Apollo Drive, Rosedale, North Shore 0632, New Zealand
(a division of Pearson New Zealand Ltd)

Penguin Books (South Africa) (Pty) Ltd, 24 Sturdee Avenue, Rosebank, Johannesburg 2196, South Africa

Penguin Books Ltd, Registered Offices: 80 Strand, London WC2R ORL, England

www.penguin.com

First published 2010

1

Set in 12/14.75 pt Bembo Book MT Std
Typeset by TexTech International
Printed in Great Britain by Clays Ltd, St Ives plc

A CIP catalogue record for this book is available from the British Library

ISBN: 978-0-670-91830-0

www.greenpenguin.co.uk

For my parents
and in memory of
my great friend
Harry Brack (1928–2009)

A lawyer is to do for his client all that his client might fairly do for himself.

— Samuel Johnson

Contents

Acknowledgements

In researching this book, I have interviewed some very eminent people who have been generous enough to give me their time. They are Professor Andrew Ashworth of Oxford University; Bobby Cummines, founder of the charity Unlock; Professor Jonathan Glover of London University; David Ramsbotham, former Her Majesty's Inspector of Prisons; Professor John Spencer QC of Cambridge University; David Thomas QC; and Professor Tim Valentine of Goldsmiths University. In addition, I would like to thank David Ormerod, law professor and barrister, for the incredibly useful references to the academic papers and books which kick-started much of my research. Thanks also to the librarians on the Social Sciences wing of the British Library and at Inner Temple Library, and to James Dewar at Lincoln's Inn and Marion Howard at Middle Temple.

I am also indebted to the many judges and barristers who have spoken to me both formally and informally. Unsurprisingly, they wish to remain anonymous and therefore I thank them without naming names. Special mention must go to my former head of chambers, pupilmasters and clerks. And not forgetting AB, TH, CJ, PK, HLW, JM, CR, HR, SR and TW.

There are two lawyers who have permitted me to mention them by name. They both make vital contributions to the book. The first is Graham Cooke, who patiently and repeatedly explained the mysteries of DNA and statistical analysis to me despite my obvious intellectual limitations. The statistical examples used in the DNA chapter are his and his alone. The second lawyer is District Judge David Cooper who, apart from me, is the only 'character' appearing in the book whose name is unchanged. I thank him for his devil-may-care attitude in permitting me to use his real name.

At Penguin, I would like to thank Venetia Butterfield, Andrew Smith and, most of all, Will Hammond, my editor, for his brilliant editing, supreme clarity of thought, and for plucking the book's title out of a morass of sub-standard alternatives at the very last gasp. Thanks also to Bela Cunha for her eagle-eyed copy-editing.

Heartfelt thanks to my agent, Zoë Pagnamenta, for setting me on the writing road and for her extraordinary verve and confidence in leading me along what would have been an otherwise un-navigable path.

I am also extremely grateful to *Prospect* magazine and in particular the editor, David Goodhart, and his former deputies, Alex Linklater, Jonathan Ford and Susha Lee-Stothaman, for giving me the column which was the springboard for this book.

Thanks as well to my brother, Nathaniel McBride, and to Allan Pimentel, both of whom assured me that things would turn out all right.

Lastly, I want to thank Nina Raine, who supplied brilliant ideas and loving support. I can't begin to say how much it meant.

Prologue

Temple Church's bell strikes one: lunchtime at the bar. From alleyways east and west of Inner Temple come barristers of all ages, striding confidently across the courtyard, expensively buttoned-up stomachs rumbling. They cut past the dawdling tourists, fifty-something Mid-Westerners in burgundy windcheaters and grey baseball caps, and swerve around war parties of Italians engrossed in maps. Looking down from the sun-filled room on the second floor of chambers, I marvel at the ease these barristers radiate; pleased to be there, yes, but comfortable as if they own the place. I am amazed that the bar has given me a shot at joining their ranks, joining the entitled-looking men and women in the courtyard below en route to their lunches.

Ah, lunch. I stretched my arms up, loosening my shoulders in their sockets. I had been looking forward to lunch. I had a particularly fine sandwich – pink slivers of leftover lamb, moistened with mint jelly, slapped between two slices of upmarket bread. I sat back down and hunched over the trial papers that I was reading and started to eat. My pupilmaster and I were due to meet the protagonist in the case, our client, later that afternoon. I ate gingerly as I read, trying not to drop any of the sandwich on the starchy white pages of the brief. I was hurrying to catch up on the facts of the case, eager to find out how much trouble our client was in. It didn't take long to discover that the answer was plenty.

Eric, our client, had gone down to his local gay bar. The regulars earmarked him as a bit of 'rough trade'. He was behaving oddly, throwing karate poses and jumping around. It was at the bar that he met a young rabbi, a wallflower by all accounts, whom he lured back to his nearby flat. Once they got there, Eric knocked the rabbi unconscious, strangled him and chopped him up.

Dismembering a body is hard work. Just try cutting your way through a thigh. Most 'chopper uppers' do a hack job. Not Eric. He cut beautiful straight lines. The police were faced with two possibilities: either he was a butcher by trade or he wasn't a first-timer and had done it before.

There are quite a few unsolved murders out there. Sometimes people just disappear. Eric might never have been caught if it hadn't been for the fact that he got the rubbish collection day wrong. For a whole week in high summer, the rabbi, carefully divided into six Tesco's bags and a black bin liner tied with electrical flex, sat in Eric's flat's communal rubbish bins slowly beginning to smell. Angry calls were made to the building manager. There's something off in the bins, they complained, as if something's died. Badgered into action, the manager went round to investigate. He discovered the residents weren't exaggerating. He couldn't even get near the bins – they smelt so bad. From a wary distance he spied the black bin liner lying next to the communal rubbish. That must be the source of the trouble, he concluded. Specialist equipment was required. He came back armed with a pair of yellow Marigold gloves and a towel soaked in Lynx deodorant tied around his face. Now he was ready to make his advance on the bin liner. As he got closer, he saw something was peeking out from a tear in the plastic. In his witness statement, the building manager said that he'd decided it must be a dead dog.

I took another bite of my sandwich and turned to the photos. There are always photos. Swallowing became difficult. The picture of the bin liner showed no dog but a curve of pink flesh that could only have been the rabbi's buttocks.

The building manager, unaware of what lurked in the main bins, was faced with an unpleasant dilemma. A dead dog found in the flats, which were private property, was his responsibility, but a dead dog found on the road was up to the council. But this 'dog' wasn't going to go sniffing down to the road on its own. To get it there he'd have to drag the thing. Slowly he inched it across the lawn, emptying the deodorant into the towel, which he'd now wrapped Lawrence of Arabia-like around his head, leaving only one eye to guide him. Once he'd got the bin liner to the road, he abandoned it. Before the manager could alert the council, a young police officer walking his beat came across the stinking black bin liner. A cursory inspection revealed that this was no dog but a human torso. He radioed it in.

'You're not going to believe this, sarge, but ...'

Before long the place was crawling with uniformed officers and local CID. One poor cop had to climb into the bins and, gagging, root around bag by bag for the rest of the body. While this was being done police cordoned off the whole block of flats so they could search it unit by unit. Eric was found in his flat, stripped to the waist and surrounded by cleaning products. The flat was spotless. Naturally suspicious, the detective sergeant cast an especially careful eye around and noticed a fleck of blood on the ceiling, which later tests confirmed to be that of the rabbi. The police had found their man.

Reading the trial papers, I recalled a question I had been asked by a pretty young woman whom I had been sat next to at a wedding dinner the weekend before. It's the question barristers are always asked: 'How can you defend someone who you know is guilty?'

I gave her the perfectly valid but stock answer: someone is innocent until proven guilty. No matter what they might have done nor how formidable the case against them might be, in a democratic society based on the rule of law they are entitled to a fair and just hearing. The only way they're going to get that is if they are robustly defended by committed defence barristers. Remember you never really *know* whether someone is guilty because you weren't there when the alleged crime was committed. The advocate's opinion is irrelevant. It's what the jury thinks that counts. Rather than recognize me as an irresistibly attractive paladin of justice, she started mashing up the salmon on her plate with the flat of her fork. It was clear that neither criminal barristers, nor my argument, impressed her.

Later that afternoon I met my pupilmaster at the entrance to the Bailey cells.* A line of barristers, all in battle dress – wig (a Parisian fashion craze made popular by Charles II), gown (designed to mourn Charles II's death), starched collar and white floppy things called 'bands' (replacing the ruff), double-breasted pinstripes, even the occasional fob watch – waited to get in. We waltzed by.

'I say,' said a plummy voice, 'there's a queue.'

'Cat A,' replied my pupilmaster smoothly. There is no comeback to that. Cat A is a separate part of the cell area, which is reserved for those who pose a serious risk to the public (i.e. Eric), or who have a habit of escaping.

We knocked on the small oak door that led to the cells. A set of eyes sized us up through a tiny grated window. The door opened. We walked down a narrow corridor, squeezing past a portly barrister waiting for an interview room to become free. At the end of the corridor we came to a locked steel-barred gate.

'Go on, then,' said my pupilmaster. He knew I would like this bit.

'Jailer! Jay-ler!' I called, trying not to snigger. There was silence. Then in the distance we heard the rattle of keys. I was expecting a Quasimodo-like figure dragging a useless foot but a few moments later a woman with a ginger crew cut and meaty arms appeared.

---

* The Old Bailey deals with most of the really terrible murders and murderers. People in the criminal justice industry never refer to the Old Bailey as the 'Old Bailey' just as posh people never refer to horse-riding or fox-hunting. It's either riding or hunting. Horse, fox and Old are redundant. What else could riding, hunting and Bailey possibly be?

'Cat A?' she asked.

'Cat A,' we replied.

She opened the gate and we followed her down the corridor to another gate; once that was opened, we found ourselves climbing up a twisting stairway encased in what looked like reinforced chicken wire. At the top, we came to a gate. She unlocked it, pushed us through, and then, rather disconcertingly, locked the gate behind us. I shuffled reluctantly after my pupilmaster towards an ordinary-looking door at the end of the short corridor. I was nervous. What would we find through the door? A dungeon full of psychopaths chained to the wall? My pupilmaster opened the door. I tensed as I stepped after him only to find that Cat A is surprisingly pleasant. There aren't any bars or the disturbance of other defendants shouting for a fag.

Eric, though he didn't know it, was a star. He had three lovely middle-aged female 'screws' all to himself. They treated him like a grandson.

'Are you the legal for Eric?' asked one of them, a set of keys in one hand and a cup of tea for Eric in the other.

'We are,' said my pupilmaster.

'Come with me,' she said, leading us to a room in the corner of the waiting area. It didn't look like a cell at all. It had a large window set in one of its walls, which let the light in, giving it an airy quality quite different from most of the cells I'd seen.

'Eric, love, your legal's arrived,' she said, passing him the cup of tea.

We crowded into the little room. There, finally, was Eric sitting at the other side of the desk, his hands in his lap. He had a tight half-smile and hard-to-read eyes. I was the last to extend my hand: he took it with a limp handshake as one would expect from a proper psychopath. Sitting down for a cosy chat with a young man accused of slicing up another human being for his own gratification is a peculiar way to spend a Wednesday afternoon. Eric scared me.

I felt terribly sorry for the rabbi's family. It must have been unbearable for them. Surely anyone who could commit such a bestial crime should be swiftly and permanently locked up. He might do it again.

Sitting there looking at Eric, I mulled over the pretty young woman's response to my stock answer. 'Isn't there something morally obscene in knowingly defending a guilty person? How can you sleep at night having got someone off who may go out and commit more crime, hurt more people?'

I glanced at my pupilmaster and our instructing solicitor. They weren't thinking about 'moral flaws' or sleepless nights. I certainly wasn't. We weren't making any judgement at all. It doesn't matter that the evidence is overwhelming – or whether he did it or not. All we're interested in is, 'How can we get him off?'

Why? In Britain, we have an adversarial system of justice (two opposing sides each asserting its version of events to be correct) which we've proudly exported around the world. The only way it works is if defence advocates put their all into representing their clients and able prosecution advocates put their all into presenting the evidence. Otherwise, why have a jury trial? Let a judge consider the evidence and pronounce judgement as they do in France. Defending was our job. In order to do it, to defend somebody, you have to accept their side of the story. You accept it emotionally and intellectually. It's a mental and ethical trick. You stand in their shoes and believe. No matter how repugnant they might be.

There's something else. Something no one mentions but is essential if the adversarial system is to work. You want to get defendants off because winning feels good – in fact, winning feels great. At the end of a trial you want to look the prosecutor in the eye and say, you thought you had a stone bonker of a case, did you, pal? Well I shoved it up your arse, cocksucker. You want to leave the courtroom, calmly go to the lavatory and dance madly around in victory.

Part of this exultation is pure relief. Barristers have no power. You go up against the police, the state and the court every day with nothing except your voice and your wits. The odds are against you and you exist in a state of anxious uncertainty, with only your skill to rely upon. Winning bolsters your confidence; it feeds your ego and keeps you going until the next trial. Soon you can't live without it. Winning becomes an addiction. You don't merely want to win but to win audaciously – facing the appalling odds and beating them in style. Barristers are motivated by the notion of serving justice but also by the delight of beating the other guy.

Does the admission that my pupilmaster and I sleep soundly in our beds expose us as morally bankrupt and incapable of facing up to our actions? On one level we don't have a choice. The 'cab rank' rule, set out in the Code of Practice which governs what a barrister can and can't do, dictates that a barrister must represent anyone who asks for his services providing that he is available and has the necessary level of skill and experience to take the case. In practice, the 'cab rank' rule is routinely broken, not because barristers are trying to take the cases they find the most palatable, but because they're looking for better ones, whether it be higher profile, better paid or more egregious – more Eric. It's professional pride.

In the end, diaries clashed and we could not represent Eric. At trial, he offered the partial defence of diminished responsibility, which would have made him guilty of manslaughter rather than murder. Diminished responsibility would be found if Eric was judged to be suffering from 'an abnormality of mind' which 'substantially impaired' his mental responsibility in killing the rabbi. The jurors were not persuaded. As far as they were concerned, he knew what he was doing and had control over his actions. Psychiatrists, giving evidence at trial, concluded that Eric's psychosis was untreatable. He was sentenced to a 'whole life tariff' and is unlikely ever to be released. Realistically, Eric was never going to win; even if he'd been convicted of manslaughter the judge could still have stuck him with a life sentence. But it's worth considering what Eric might have got up to had he, through a series of near-impossible events, walked free.

Let's go forward in time. Eric has long since been convicted of murder and consigned to spend the rest of his days, potentially another sixty years or more, in prison. I'm no longer under my pupilmaster's wing but have for some time been 'on my feet', that is taking cases in my own right, unsupervised and out of my depth.

I'm defending Arthur Sykes, who's accused of burning down an office complex to cover his criminal tracks – in this case, drops of his own blood. Baz, the prosecution's star witness, sits in the witness box looking as though he's been volunteered for anaesthetic-free root canal treatment. His white schoolboy shirt and the sick pallor of his face make him look translucent, as though he might disappear before our eyes. The prosecutor has just steered him through his account of the fire. From their point of view, he has done pretty well. In a halting, credible style, Baz has fingered Arthur Sykes, my client, as the man who set it. Grassed him up good and proper. It's my turn to cross-examine.

The jurors, mostly pleasant-faced ladies from the local university's faculty of arts, look at me expectantly as I stand up wiping my palms on my gown. I am Arthur's champion, the hired gun charged with righting the grievous wrong that Baz has done to his old friend. Get it right and Arthur will walk free. Get it wrong and he'll do five years in jail.

Standing at my lectern, I pretend to pause – a false display of confidence, masking my search for the first question, which I had written in capitals in my notepad. I had written out all my questions. I would flounder without them. The pad is my life-preserver. I grip it tightly and clear my throat. I am ready to do my job, to demolish Baz, and leave his account looking like nothing but a collection of badly thought-out lies. Make him sorry that he had had the temerity to mess with a client of Alex McBride, barrister-at-law, and think that he could get away with it. My hands jump and twitch with fear.

If Baz wasn't looking forward to my cross-examination, how did he think I felt? A few days earlier I had been expecting to defend an electrician who'd knocked his boss into a waterlogged hole on a building site. The boss, weighed down by his best suit and a mohair coat, couldn't get out. He kept crawling up the sides and sliding back in. None of the labourers on the site helped him.

Then there had been a last-minute change of plan. The preceding trial of the barrister who was supposed to represent Arthur had overrun so he was no longer available. My clerk had phoned me late on Friday afternoon, 'Mr McBride, sir. I've got a better case. Always on the look out for a better job for you, sir.' This blandishment really meant, 'There's no one else. We're desperate. Here's a hospital pass. Catch!' So now I was representing Arthur who had been charged with arson, a much more serious matter. The prosecution case was that Arthur had burned down the complex of Portakabin offices in order to break the evidential link between himself and a burglary.

I found my first question, the terror and adrenaline sluicing around the back of my mouth: 'You and Arthur were good friends, weren't you?'

Baz replied, 'Yes.' So far so good.

In cross-examination, you ask closed questions that elicit a 'yes' or 'no' answer. They should be short statements that the witness can either agree or disagree with. What you don't do is ask 'open' questions which allow the witness to stray from the path you want to push him down. It's best to avoid 'what', 'why', 'when'. This was the reason I had written all my questions out. I wanted to make sure I not only asked each and every one but phrased them right, too. Having got away with one question, I asked another, and another, and another. After a while I started to sound fluent. I was beginning to enjoy myself.

Baz's account, as is often the case, was very similar to Arthur's, my client. They had been good friends for a while; some weekends, after a few drinks, Baz would accompany Arthur on his trips to steal diesel for his van. On the Saturday in question, after a particularly boisterous night in the pub, the two young men with a few other friends went down to an industrial estate where they knew some mechanical diggers were parked. After climbing on and falling off several diggers, it dawned on Arthur that all their petrol caps were locked. But he wasn't to be deterred. He'd come to steal something and, by God, he wasn't going to go home empty-handed.

He turned his drunken attention to the half-built industrial estate itself. The first office he came upon was a lone Portakabin deputizing as the security department. Arthur broke in by putting his elbow through the window, slicing his arm in the process. He came out clutching a fire extinguisher, leaving a Hansel and Gretel-like trail of blood that followed him as he closed in on the office complex's nearest window. The other boys were laughing now, half-nervous, half-excited. Would he do it? You bet he would. Arthur swung the fire extinguisher at the window, shattering the pane. The alarm started to bleep hysterically but he didn't run. The industrial estate was miles from anywhere; it would take the police an age to arrive. Arthur climbed in and, working quickly, went through the complex, his blood doggedly marking his route. He collected up all the computers and passed them out to his waiting friends, who stacked them in his van. Off in the distance a siren wailed. Was it the police? Arthur leapt through the broken window, jumped in the van with his mates and sped off down the estate's dirt track to watch for their arrival. Five minutes went by, then ten, but no one came.

Up to this point Arthur's account tallied with Baz's. Yes, he'd come to steal diesel. Yes, he'd broken into the office complex – he could hardly deny it: the police had found the computers, still spattered with his blood, neatly stacked up in his flat. It was when they got to the lay-by that the two stories sheared. In his witness statement, Baz claimed that while they were looking out for the police, Arthur said, 'I'm going back to torch the place.' This 'verbal', Arthur's alleged declaration of intent, underpinned the prosecution's case. The defendant, in his own words, was confirming their case theory, namely that he 'torched the place' to eradicate the bloodstains linking him to the burglary. It was a devastating piece of evidence.

Except it wasn't. There was one problem. Just because Arthur's 'confession' was in Baz's witness statement did not make it evidence. For it to be evidence, Baz had to say it in oral testimony before the court. Baz, for whatever reason, had failed to do so and therefore, as far as the jurors were concerned, the 'confession' didn't exist because they hadn't heard it being said.

My cross-examination was going so well that I hadn't identified this gaping hole in the prosecution's case. I pressed on. I forced Baz to agree that he was a willing participant in the burglary. He'd helped in loading the computers into the van, making him in law just as guilty as Arthur. Then I moved on to the fact that Baz had been arrested and interviewed for the burglary but not charged by the police. I suggested that he hadn't been charged because he'd offered officers a much better 'collar' by giving up his old friend. I implied that he'd done this not only to avoid the burglary charge but perhaps the arson, too. Was he betraying Arthur because he was guilty of setting fire to the offices himself? This tantalizing possibility was the apotheosis of my cross-examination. It was to be a long but swift way down because things were about to go very wrong.

There is a golden rule in criminal defence: the less evidence the better. Sticking too closely to my notes, which assumed Baz would have given Arthur's 'verbal' to the jury right between the eyes, I picked up a copy of Baz's statement and broke the golden rule.

'Mr Sykes never said, "Let's go back. I am going to torch the place," did he?' I asked. As the words left my mouth I knew it was bad. I felt giddy, as if I were standing on the edge of a precipice. The jury sat saucer-eyed, staring at Arthur. My instructing solicitor looked at me as if I had just been exposed as a child-murderer. The prosecutor covered her mouth. The judge sniggered. He was a former solicitor and there was nothing he liked better than watching members of the bar blow it.

The mistake I had made was to cross-examine into evidence the most damning thing against Arthur. I had been too wedded to my notes and I had not listened to the witness carefully enough. I had done the prosecution barrister's job for her. There was nothing to do but brazen it out. I suggested to Baz, to anyone who might still be listening, that he had dreamed it all up.

'Was it the case that you couldn't remember which lie you'd told last?' I asked. 'You put one thing in your witness statement and say another thing in court. Two-Lies Baz, using the one that suits you, when it suits you.' It was desperate bluster.

When the court rose, I turned to face Arthur. 'It's been an up and down day, hasn't it?' he said. I couldn't tell him that I, his own barrister, had just got him convicted. I couldn't let him drop his head, not now. 'It'll be better when the jury have heard your side of the story,' I lied. He managed a smile and told me that he'd spend the evening with his three-year-old daughter. 'She means everything to me.'

I walked home aghast. There was nothing to do but work all night. Sleep was out of the question. Every time I nodded off I saw Arthur's little girl crying for her father. Her daddy was in jail and it was all my fault. That's one of the awful things about being a barrister: if you make a mistake it's your client who ends up paying.

The next day the omens were not good: my solicitor had decided not to return for the denouement and the officer in charge of the case had become very chatty. It's unseemly to be 'matey' with the police when you're defending but I had to keep on friendly terms because he was the last prosecution witness and he would be my foil. In some situations, cross-examination is not about undermining a witness but using that witness to set out your case. I wanted to get the investigating officer to confirm the parts of the prosecution evidence that were helpful to Arthur and build a narrative which I could then develop later in my closing speech. The reason I wanted to do this was that the prosecution case contained an oddity.

There were two Portakabin office complexes on the industrial estate, divided by an eight-foot gap: a green one, which had been burnt to a crisp, and a white one, that Arthur had burgled, which remained untouched. If the prosecution were saying that Arthur had set fire to the office complex to cover his tracks, then why did he burn down the wrong one? Via the officer, I used the building's plans to show the jury how far the incriminating bloodstains were from the fire's starting point. The police had marked them out, rather helpfully, with little plastic numbers. It looked like a crazy-golf course. The officer also confirmed that no propellant had been found where the fire began. Arising out of this were two key questions for the jury: can you be sure that Arthur started the fire to break the evidential link between himself and the burglary? If not, can you be sure he started the fire at all?

After all the questions have been asked and evidence has been heard, each barrister gives a closing speech summing up his case. The prosecutor, who is the first to speak at the end of a trial, pointed out the strong circumstantial evidence linking Arthur to the fire. He happened to be burgling the industrial estate and by extraordinary coincidence it just happened to catch fire right after he'd burgled it. Arthur's 'verbal', which she kept repeating, put words to his intention. He knew the police would come eventually so he torched the place. He didn't burn down both complexes because he didn't do a very good job. He set the fire and legged it. Who in that situation would hang around to see how well it caught?

Then it was my turn. I drew all the points in Arthur's favour together. I tried to rubbish the 'verbal', but its echo reverberated around the courtroom.

After the jury retired to consider the verdict, I beat a cowardly retreat to the robing room, where the advocates get changed for court. Arthur intercepted me on the way. He wanted to introduce me to his uncomprehending parents and his stunned girlfriend. I smiled weakly and shook hands with them. I couldn't meet Arthur's stare. We both knew that I had done for him.

In the barristers' canteen, drinking tea with the prosecutor, I said mournfully, 'I've 'potted' my own client, haven't I?' ('Potted' is barrister slang for convicted. I assume its root is from snooker: if you sink the ball, you've potted it; if you sink the defendant, you've potted him.) I was hoping she'd say something comforting but she simply nodded her head. There was no getting away from the truth. What would I say to Arthur down in the cells? I'd have to come clean. I considered running for it. If I caught the Eurostar, I'd be in Lille before nightfall. From there I could disappear into central Europe, change my name and learn how to farm turnips, something straightforward that even I couldn't screw up.

After three-quarters of an hour we were all called back into court. The jurors had a question: could they hear Arthur's verbal again? Of course they could. They hadn't even said 'alleged' verbal. I flinched as the judge read out the words. The prosecutor turned to me and said, 'They're clearly thinking along the right lines.' I couldn't disagree. The statement tied the whole case together. It was the *coup de grâce* and it'd been I who had administered it. Fifteen minutes later the jury returned, averting their gaze from Arthur (never a good sign). The foreman confirmed there was a verdict and that it was unanimous.

'Members of the jury, do you find the defendant guilty or not guilty?' asked the clerk of the court.

There was a pause. I wrote a big G in my notebook.

'Not guilty,' replied the foreman.

The judge was astonished. I leapt up. 'May Mr Sykes be discharged please, your honour?' He was. The burglary sentence could wait; he wouldn't go to prison for that.

I couldn't leave the courtroom quickly enough. Linger and the jurors might change their minds, say, 'Only joking! We find him utterly guilty.' Outside the court Arthur clutched me, pressing his face into my chest, his tears falling on my shirt. Even his family clung to me. No one was more relieved than I. Arthur would have his freedom, his little girl would have her daddy and I wouldn't be haunted for the rest of my days. I had blown a lifetime of luck in an afternoon. There was no better way to have spent it.

I gathered my things, flew down the stairs and stepped out of the court building into the warm September sunshine. I wanted to kiss every woman on the street. Pat the cheeks of the kids in their pushchairs. I walked briskly up the hill, weaving through a group of pedestrians, who, I realized, were the jurors. We exchanged big smiles and I nodded my head to show that I had recognized them. I wanted to kiss them too. Hold them in my arms, spin them around and cry out at the relief of it all. I hurried on, the joy pressing hard against my chest. Then something began to nag at me. What would the people I was passing on the street have made of the case and its verdict? Would they have thought that justice had been done? It would be easy to blame the prosecutor. Why didn't she hammer home to the jury that Arthur was an arsonist but an incompetent one? He set the fire assuming the two places would go up but blew it. Look at the terrible job he had done burgling the place. He was drunk. He was out of his league. Thanks to me, she had the killer line of Arthur pithily setting out his motive. The truth was that she hadn't made the mistakes. I had, and that left my victory all the more troubling: if it wasn't any mistake of hers, then did the fault lie with the justice system itself?

I remembered the pretty young woman from the wedding back when I was just starting as a barrister, who had taken her disgust at my argument out on her salmon. The real target of her dismay, I realized, was not barristers so much as the adversarial justice system itself, pitting two sides against each other and turning the deliberation of the facts into a partisan battle rather than a search for the objective truth. She was shocked because, as she saw it, for the system to work barristers had to present as true versions of events which they knew to be false. On one side, you have the defence trying to sabotage the prosecution case: it argues for important evidence to be excluded, undermines honest testimony and then uses the remnants of the facts, the helpful bits, to mislead the jury. On the other, you have the prosecution. The police have investigated what suits them in order to build a case against the defendant that will stick. Facts that point away from the defendant's guilt might be either ignored or not properly examined. Vital material exonerating the defendant might go undisclosed. Any notion of justice becomes lost beneath each side's self-interest.

Sitting on the train back to London, watching fields of sheep roll by, I wondered whether the whole system was corrupt. I started to question whether the 'us versus them', gladiators in sober suits whacking each other over the head with legal texts, was not the majestic display of justice I had assumed but a cynical licence to hoodwink the jury.

There is a set of procedural guidelines for criminal trials racily titled the Criminal Procedure Rules. The 'overriding objective' of these rules is that criminal cases 'be dealt with justly'. The most important element of this objective is for the court process *to acquit the innocent and convict the guilty*. As statements of intent go, it is unimpeachable and it's what the criminal courts try to do every day. But there's a fundamental and irreconcilable tension between these two principles. I didn't know whether Arthur was guilty or not. He *probably* was guilty but if 'probably' was what the jury thought, then it was not good enough. A jury has to be sure. I asked myself which one was more important: acquitting the innocent or convicting the guilty? I wondered where justice was to be found within these two competing aims. In the end the criminal justice system has to choose to lean one way or the other. And, in a sense, we have found a way: a defendant is innocent until proven guilty beyond a reasonable doubt. The question is whether our adversarial justice system helps the jury come to a 'just' verdict, or whether it makes things harder.

The consequences of Arthur's acquittal were not as terrible as they might have been. No one had been hurt. An insurance company would pay to replace the offices. Premiums would go up a notch and a lot of people had been seriously inconvenienced. Arthur had had the fright of his life. He wasn't going to be starting any more fires. His little daughter would have her dad. Wasn't that last fact the most important in the end? Maybe. Two things were sure from my perspective: trials were unpredictable and they were about much more than just 'guilty' or 'not guilty'.

PART ONE

Basic Training

1. Middle Temple Lane

Middle Temple Lane is the carotid artery of the bar. Narrow and cobbled, it runs from an easily missed doorway in Fleet Street down to a heavy Victorian barbican a stone's throw from the river. The flower of the bar has plied its trade from this street and its environs for nearly 700 years. At the top is a squash of rickety buildings that loom over the lane. Walking down there's the Edwardian red brick of Hare Court on the left. On the right the lane opens up on to the elegant Restoration style of Brick Court. Further down is Middle Temple, one of the four Inns of Court, whose sixteenth-century hammer-beamed hall was missed by the Luftwaffe on their runs up the Thames, and from which the lane takes its name. To the west of Middle Temple hall is the leafy calm of Fountain Court. The lower half of Middle Temple Lane is dominated by the forbidding grey of Temple Gardens. All the way down, outside the chambers that rent offices on this legal thoroughfare are the lists of their tenants' names hand-painted on cream boards like those of an Oxbridge college. It is to this roll call that I aspire.

Temple gets its name from the Knights Templar, the site's previous owners, who were kicked out in 1307. Middle Temple Lane divides their old property in half. Middle Temple owns everything to the west of the lane and Inner Temple, another Inn of Court, owns everything to the east.

The Inns (the others being Lincoln's Inn, situated to the north of Fleet Street, and Gray's Inn, to the north of High Holborn) are called Inns because that is originally what they were. In the Middle Ages the term 'inn' was much looser than it is now and meant not just a pub with rooms but a house or lodgings. Before the mid fourteenth century law students were attached to the courts, which was where they learned their trade. When these students were in London they lived around Fleet Street because it was conveniently located for the King's Court at Westminster Hall. The King's Court, however, was peripatetic. It moved around the country, stopping, sometimes for years on end, in other towns. The lawyers and the students were obliged to move with it, much to the annoyance of Fleet Street shopkeepers, whose businesses depended on the legal trade. All this changed in 1339 when Edward III decided to give up the idea of conquering Scotland and turn his attention to re-taking France.[1] His decision meant that the government's centre of gravity had to shift southwards. The law courts moved with it and Westminster Hall became the country's main legal centre. The students, not to mention the lawyers, judges and their hangers-on, had to find somewhere to live. The houses around Temple and Fleet Street were the obvious choice.

Now that they had a permanent home they began, as professionals do, to organize themselves. Their organizing principle was education. The *raison d'être* of the Inns of Court (though they were not called that until the fifteenth century) was to teach the next generation of barristers. They did this through debates of law called 'moots'. Moots were educational: by listening to qualified barristers debating before judges, the students gradually learned not only the law but also how court business was conducted. The moots – replete with bastard-son claimants, rods of land and monks 'deraigned by reason of precontract' (i.e. kicked out of holy orders for having made a contract to marry before becoming a monk) – were fiendishly complicated, and therefore very effective at weeding out those who were not up to the job.

The expression 'being called to the bar' has nothing to do with court. Its root comes from the Inns. Moots were presided over by judges and senior barristers who were known as 'benchers'. The hall in which the moots took place was designed to look like a real court of law, with a wooden 'bar' separating the benchers, as if they were judges.* Students worked their way up until they had attained the requisite level of skill to be 'called' to this wooden bar in the Inn's hall to deliver a legal argument.

To become a barrister you still have to be 'called' by an Inn but it is less intimidating than it was. You have to pass your law school exams, join an Inn as a student and then 'do your dinners', which means eating in your Inn's hall, mixing with the old-stagers. The number of dinners required has come down in recent years from a gut-busting thirty-six to a more digestible twelve.

Back in the late fourteenth century being a student barrister was such a popular calling for well-to-do boys that Temple, in order to manage the weight of numbers, divided itself into Middle and Inner Temple. The students were not all hard-working lawyers-to-be. Many came to glean a veneer of metropolitan sophistication before going back to manage their parents' estates. Hard-working or not, the students, known as 'apprentices of the court', were extremely rowdy. In 1326 apprentices from York and Norfolk (north *vs* south) fought a bloody pitched battle on Fleet Street which left several dead.[2] Fighting was a popular pastime. Quite a bit of what is known about the period comes from investigations into apprentices going up before the authorities, often having killed someone.

Women were another vice. The strict rules that banned apprentices bringing them into Temple in the evenings were ignored. Unsurprisingly in an area full of young men with disposable income, the brothels in and around Chancery Lane – one, enticingly, was called the Green Lattice – did an exceedingly profitable trade.[3]

---

* Students started off at the same side of the bar as the benchers. Once called to the bar, this made them 'outer' barristers because with this new rank they now sat outside the bar.

In the centuries leading up to the English Civil War the high point of the Inns' social calendar was a three-month period of feasting between the beginning of November and the end of January called 'Revels'. The Inns held pageants and put on plays. Shakespeare wrote *Twelfth Night* for Middle Temple and premièred it in their hall. Occasionally, Revels was even used for high politics. In 1561 Robert Dudley, appointed to preside over Inner Temple's festivities as a reward for wresting Lyon's Inn from Middle Temple, staged a play about a mythical English king called Gorbuduc. Gorbuduc is a wise and good king but his realm is destabilized because he doesn't have an heir. Dudley was, of course, urging Elizabeth I to marry and, more to the point, urging her to marry him. Dudley might have thrown a spectacular party but he didn't get the girl.

For the students Revels was a licence to behave even worse than usual and the Inns egged them on. During Revels, the Inns and even the king appointed from the student body 'Lords of Misrule' who, aside from play-acting and drinking, walked the streets blowing trumpets, demanding money and getting into fights. Inevitably, deaths followed. Middle Temple still holds Revels in their hall but it's a staid affair more reminiscent of the Cambridge Footlights than the bacchanalian wildness of the sixteenth and early seventeenth centuries.

The Inns might be good at teaching but they've never handed out the work. Barristers are self-employed, though they group together in order to pool their resources to pay for offices, staff, heating and so on. These pools, called 'chambers', are the vehicles that get in the work that barristers do. Confusingly, chambers are also referred to as 'sets' (a common ice-breaker question is, 'What set are you in?'). My chambers are what is known as a 'Treasury set', which means that they have supplied, in an unbroken chain, generations of Treasury Counsel, the elite band of prosecutors based at the Bailey who are charged with prosecuting the most serious and notorious cases. This isn't to say that we don't defend, too. Like all barristers, we take sides for money.

It's a flash place, my chambers. The entrance stairs are calibrated like those of a great country house, effortlessly floating you up to the front door. Our reception room is spacious and comfortable. There are big leather sofas, squared off by delicate side tables sporting back issues of *Country Life* and *Hello!*. Walking into chambers is like walking into a Harley Street clinic, except we don't deal in IVF and tummy tucks – we deal in crime. The reception room is designed to dazzle your average detective sergeant coming in for a 'con' – short for conference – with his barrister. Middle Temple Lane conspires with us in this marketing seduction. Before he has even arrived your average DS is softened up by Temple's exclusive hush, by the barristers in expensive suits and the unobtainable cars – the blue-grey Aston Martins, the glistening Jags and top-of-the-range Mercedes. Footballer cars. Cotswold cars. By the time he gets to chambers, whatever South London nick he's come from, with its cells smelling of pee and vomit, feels about as close as Easter Island. Coming to chambers is meant to be a pleasure. We want you to like it because we want you to come back – with more work.

Araminta, the prettiest and poshest of receptionists you're ever likely to meet, is on hand to greet you. 'Tea or coffee, sergeant?' she asks in her cut-glass accent, fixing him with her deep, dark eyes. She brings biscuits, delicious chocolate ones in little foil wrappers. He notices the large vase of freshly cut flowers that Araminta, just turned twenty-seven, has arranged so prettily. The only plant at the police station is the dead yucca in the chief super's office. How nice to be away from all that, stretching out on a comfortable sofa admiring the bare-throated, patrician-jawed receptionist.

The reception room's *mise en scène* conveys a subliminal message. Our customers – from the DI in the terrorist squad to the teenage rapist – see right away that they are dealing with winners. Chambers asks a rhetorical question: would we have all this plush swag if we didn't have what it takes? Plainly the answer is no. Araminta is not by chance. She's been hand-picked not merely to blend into the surroundings but to enhance them. We are a barristers' chambers posing as a Mayfair hedge fund, and we do it, if I may say so, brilliantly.

The best thing about Araminta is that she is nice to me. I time my sweeps through reception for early afternoon when it is quiet so I can flirt with her for a quarter of an hour undisturbed.

'Hello there, Alex,' she says when I pop my head around the door. She knows how to sparkle, does Araminta. She laughs at my jokes and tut-tuts at my lame indiscretions. Often when I am lingering by her desk, she says, 'Now, Alex, would you like a cup of tea?' I always want a cup of tea, especially when it's made by Araminta. She brings it to me in my favourite mug with a stack of chocolate biscuits. I eat them hungrily.

'Alex, that's your *third* one,' she says, making my gluttony appear naughtily alluring. The only thing she remains firm on are the chocolate biscuits wrapped in foil. 'You're not allowed those ones, Alex.'

'Is that because I don't matter to you?'

'Of course you do. It's just that they're reserved for people who actually contribute to chambers.'

The rest of chambers is kitted out in the *faux*-Regency vernacular, known in the antique trade as the 'brown stuff'. So as not to spoil this one-colour monotony, chambers have even hidden the computers in brown cabinets. What do they want our clients – the solicitors, police and crims – to think? That we use inkwells and quills? Well, almost. The brown stuff is part of the image too, part of our front, which we all buy into. It is a fogeyish way of not having to apply your mind to interior design. It is a timid but sound policy. The few chambers that go for a modern style end up looking about as snappy as a mid-range Frankfurt business hotel.

Another peculiarity of the criminal bar is its dismaying weakness for legal kitsch. A picture of a Rumpole lookalike cross-examining a whimpering pooch hangs next to a *Punch* cartoon in which a spats-wearing barrister assists two ladies of the night into a hansom cab. The cartoon wasn't funny in 1902 when *Punch* first ran it and it isn't funny now. This might all look a bit *passé* but it works. The skill is to come across as formidable but unobjectionable. Never show any sharp edges, apart from in court. Clients come in to be reassured. We aren't going to swap the *Country Lifes* for a pool table or exchange our suits for 'engineered' jeans and five o'clock shadow. We'd lose all our business if we did.

The engine room of chambers is the clerks' room, situated off a corridor that runs from the reception room. Barristers' clerks operate like theatrical agents. They get you work, negotiate the fees, manage your diary and then chase up the cheques when, as is usual, they fail to materialize. Clerks, almost exclusively working-class Essex boys and girls, are the antithesis of la-di-da barristers. Different we may be but that doesn't mean we don't depend upon each other. Barristers pay the clerks but without them we'd last about as long as mayflies. Mug in hand, I wander down the corridor and glance through the door. All their faces are pressed up against computer screens. They are organizing the diary for the next day. The stress is beginning to show and it's still early. Keith, the senior clerk, sitting at the rear of the room, leans back in his chair. I can hear his voice over the din.

'If I can't move this trial back, then I'm fucked. Completely fucked. Someone find Binnsy. That cunt owes me a favour and I'm calling it in.'

Keith's most pressing daily problem is covering all the work. He might have sixty-plus barristers fanned out around the country but all the while work is coming in from instructing solicitors, the Crown Prosecution Service (CPS), Revenue and Customs, the Department of Work and Pensions, the General Medical Council and so on, all of which needs to be covered. Every day he has to fight a losing game of 'pin the brief on the barrister'. If he has more work than he can handle, then the junior clerks ring around to other chambers in the hope that they have a barrister available to pick it up. It's all about maintaining relationships. When a desperate solicitor who usually sends chambers lots of work calls up at 6.30 in the evening looking for someone to cover a last-minute matter for the next day, the senior clerk wants to be able to say 'yes, your problem is solved and I'm the one who has solved it'. You hope the favour will be remembered and repaid with more cases. Added to this daily scrabble is the anything-can-happen variable of the 'late return'. A 'return' is when a barrister, often at the last minute, is not able to do work that is in his diary. A trial might have overrun or a better case might have come in which that barrister wants to take on. The returned case, which can be anything from a remand hearing at Alton Youth Court to a conspiracy to murder trial at the Bailey, goes back into the pool. Someone, somewhere, will have to pick it up.

There is a strict hierarchy in chambers. The tenant barristers – those with permanent jobs – reside in elegant rooms on the upper floors with views of quads and Temple Church. We pupils, the trainee barristers, are crammed into one sweaty room in the basement. For us Middle Temple Lane is a stream of ankles and feet. Our room is dominated by a large table, which we sit around like poker players down on our luck.

Pupillage, a year-long 'boot camp' for barristers, really is a floating game of poker: all compete against all with players coming and going, either promoted upstairs to be tenants or, more usually, out of the back door as busted flushes. Having exhausted the entertainments of the ground floor, I descend the narrow stone stairs to the basement. I slowly push open the door to the pupils' room. Five pairs of eyes turn towards it, hoping against hope it's not some tenant coming to give them work. My face peers around the door.

'Oh, it's only fucking Alex,' says Harriet dismissively, sliding a half-smoked cigarette between her lips, thickly covered with 'Most Wanted' red Mac lipstick, and taking a deep drag. Exhaling the smoke through her nostrils, she turns back to filleting a brief, her hands moving with the insouciant speed of a 1970s French bank teller counting 200 franc notes. Harriet is slim and elegant with dark hair that falls in long curls over her shoulders. She and Jane, a voluptuously curved woman with razor-straight blonde hair, have been in the pupils' room for eighteen months. They're old hands and their tenancy decision is looming. They've been deferred once already. This time it'll either be up or out. The next longest serving, and Harriet and Jane's best friend, is Wordless Will, who not being able to get a word in edgeways, has given up speaking at all. He is also a candidate for the high jump. One of them can go, two of them can go – they can all go. There is no logic to it. Getting tenancy is like drawing lots.

It's 2002, and the three constants in the pupils' room are the pressure, the mess and the fags: dirty cups and half-eaten bits of food surround the overwhelmed ashtray that is the table's centrepiece. No one cleans up because, if you do, then that is your job for ever. I push away the remains of a sausage and egg sandwich – halfway through the third bite the eater had clearly realized the error of his or her purchase – and settle down to do some paperwork. Everyone in the pupils' room smokes. Even if, like me, you don't actually smoke, you do, because there is always a cloud of stale cigarette smoke twisting above your head. Harriet and Jane lead the charge. They smoke obsessively, egging each other on: if one lights up, then the other follows suit. Will is the next to weaken, until the whole room is puffing away. Smoking at the criminal bar is *de rigueur*; barristers need nicotine as they need their wig and gown.

I sit next to Liam (who along with Mamta joined chambers at the same time as I), a tiny, red-haired Scotsman, who'd come to the bar purely so he could pick fights. Liam sits counting his cheques. 'One, two. Oh no, I must have miscounted. Let's try again. One, two. Something's going wrong here. Alex, how many cheques do I have?' He holds them up, a cheque in each hand.

'Two,' I say.

'Well, fuck me, that must be a mistake because I've been on my feet for two and a half fucking months and I've only received two poxy fucking cheques. One for £45 and one for £47. How am I supposed to live on that?'

'I'll give you a fiver, if you clean the table,' says Harriet.

'I'm never cleaning the table,' says Liam. 'On second thoughts, I'll do it for £100.'

'Listen, you chiselling little Jock. *I'd* do it for £100.'

Starting out at the bar is an uncertain venture: not only is there never a guarantee of tenancy but the pay is dire, if it comes at all. It can take months, sometimes years, to get paid. The CPS, solicitors' firms and Legal Services Commission sit on our wages as we scrabble ever higher up our personal mountains of debt. This uncertainty doesn't encourage sensible financial planning. You end up spending your wages three times over: once when you put in the bill, once when you get the list of money owed (known as 'age debt') and once when you finally get the cheque. The rule, universally ignored, is to open two accounts. You pay half your income into one account for spending and the other half into another account for your tax bill. Tax is the invisible killer. Twice a year when the bill comes in, you go cap in hand to the bank manager, who, naturally, is more than happy for you to increase your overdraft. Pensions, savings, something for a rainy day are things that other people have. At the criminal bar the best you can expect is to tread water, knowing that, if you tire and falter, then you are going to drown.

I tune out from the pupils' room noise and start to endorse my brief's back sheet. Every brief, no matter how small or how large, has a back sheet on which you are supposed to record what happened in court and what work needs to be done for the next hearing. This way the barrister who picks up the brief after you knows exactly what has happened and what to expect – or at least that's what's supposed to happen in theory. In practice, the barrister who has gone before you writes something so illegible that it looks more like an ancient Arabic curse, which, of course, it will be once the judge has screamed at you.

'Ooh, look. Alex's endorsing his brief,' says Liam, crowding over my shoulder and pointing at the page. I have written the date, the type of hearing – in this instance it is a trial – a very brief summary and the verdict.

'That's a verdict on your client, Alex, not you,' says Liam, jabbing at the page. 'We already know the verdict on you is that you're guilty of being shite.'

Mamta comes in slightly out of breath. A box of 200 Marlboro Lights sticks out of a brand-new handbag whose glossy black folds make it look as though someone has attached a strap to a monster prune.

'Great day!' she says. 'I was babysitting a VAT fraudster at Blackfriars Crown Court and after he was acquitted, he gave me these.' Mamta waves the cigarettes excitedly. 'Then I got a cheque and blew it in Miu Miu.'

'VAT fraudster? Has the duty been paid on those fags?' asks Liam.

Mamta, ignoring him, opens a packet of cigarettes and passes it around. All the smokers except Harriet take one. Marlboro Lights are too puny for her. She prefers the heavy tar of 'proper smokes' such as Dunhill and Benson & Hedges.

'Do you like my new bag?' asks Mamta. Course everyone likes it – they're smoking her cigs.

After the excitement of free fags we settle down to work. The smoking rate is always at its highest as people try to jolly themselves through the mid-afternoon slump. Around 5 p.m., the clerks start phoning down with work for the next day. As we are so junior, the bulk of cases we get last a day, if that. Harriet and Jane are already doing jury trials in the crown court. Will is on the cusp of them. The rest of us, the babies, are left at the mercy of the magistrates' court. Every once in a while we might be sent to the crown court to try on our wig and gown in front of a real judge. We jockey to get those cases. The crown court usually starts at 10.30 in the morning. If you have a central London listing, you can turn off the alarm clock, have a leisurely breakfast and stroll to court just in time for your hearing. We aren't trusted with anything important. All we get are put-your-wig-and-gown-on-and-take-them-off-again jobs. Jobs where all you're required to say is 'I'm grateful, your honour' or 'yes'.

On most Thursdays and Fridays we go for a drink. Trooping out of chambers *en masse* to the pub looks bad so we slip out by the back door unseen and double back through Pump Court. It's called Pump Court because it was here that the first pump in Temple was installed in 1622. It provided great entertainment for the students. Pumping passers-by was a favourite boisterous game. In 1628 Edward Heron leading thirty other students fell upon the King's Messenger, 'pumped him, shaved him and disgracefully used him'. They compounded their crime by 'boasting and glorying in it' around the Inn. When Middle Temple's benchers tried to discipline Heron and his friends, they rioted, smashing up the furniture in the Inn's hall. No less a figure than the Lord Chief Justice held a formal inquiry and Heron, along with the other ringleaders, was sent for a spell in the King's Bench Prison.[4]

From Pump Court it's then but a short walk down to Middle Temple bar, a pub situated inside the Inn but run independently by three delightful women. It is one of Temple's great secrets: even though it's open to anyone, most nights the place is packed with pupils and junior tenants, engaging in what Australians call the 'six o'clock swill'. The place is dirt-cheap but has a million-dollar view.

On a warm summer's evening you can stretch out on Middle Temple lawn and look out over the river. The criminal bar has the reputation of being the hardest-drinking and Middle Temple bar is where we proudly polish up our reputation. Going there is like looking in the mirror: everyone wears a dark suit, drinks too much, too quickly and smokes as if it's 1953. They are my colleagues and my friends. The people I'll be growing up with for the next forty years.

2. Meet the Clients

Cell etiquette

When I first started in the pupils' room I was ignored. I had not yet acquired the right to appear in court and therefore didn't count for much. All I did was follow my pupilmaster around like a duckling. Pupillage formally lasts twelve months. It's broken down into two six-month blocks known as 'first six' and 'second six'. The first six months of pupillage are the non-practising part of your training year. The idea is that you pick things up by watching other barristers in court. Once you've completed this first six, you get temporary rights of audience for all the courts in England and Wales, up to and including the House of Lords. In reality, you become a denizen of the magistrates' court. At first, there isn't much defending to do. It's more fighting a losing battle of trying to keep heroin and crack addicts out of jail. They'll try anything to dodge it.

On my first day I found myself in Horseferry Road Magistrates' Court cells with a junkie thief pretending to be crazy.[1] Who could blame him? If the choice was between HMP Wandsworth and a nice psychiatric hospital, I know which one I'd choose. He was wearing his trousers on his head and speaking gibberish. I was too green to realize that he was trying it on. I was on the way to get him an appointment with the psychiatric team for assessment when he popped out of his cell for one of his many visits to the lavatory. He came out just as a very beautiful long-legged female barrister was bending over to pick up her pen. He broke off in mid-gibber and enquired, eyes twinkling, 'Can I be represented by her instead?' His spell was broken. Even I could tell he was perfectly lucid. Fifteen minutes and one doomed bail application later, he was on the van to Wandsworth, the beautiful long-legged barrister nothing but a fading memory.

My next client was in the cell opposite. As with many addicts, what he really liked to do was talk about himself; he lowered his trousers to show me the huge brown hole in his thigh where he injected. 'It's the only place I can find a vein. Go on, Alex, put your finger in it.'

Going from one hopeless case to the next you pick up some important rules about cell etiquette. Number one: assess the cell before you walk into it. I learned this, just missing the hard way, when on one occasion a jailer opened my client's cell door and, as I stepped in, I heard an 'urp'. In the nick of time, the jailer grabbed me by the collar and yanked me out of the way before my client projectile vomited through the doorway. Once things had been cleaned up, I entered the cell much more cautiously.

He was a nice young man called Alastair who was waiting for the doctor to prescribe some Subutext, a heroin substitute, which stops the symptoms of coming off heroin. The doctor hadn't arrived and he was starting to get 'clucky' – junkie slang for the effects of withdrawal. He desperately wanted bail. I advised him that he had no chance. 'I mean, look at all your burglary convictions,' I said.

'But who will look after my hamster?' he asked despondently. 'It'll starve.' He then spent half an hour impressing upon me how much he loved his hamster, the only thing he could rely on other than the 'gear'.

Up in court I found myself exhorting the magistrates to give the young man bail because 'he was very concerned about his hamster's welfare.' The magistrates loved that. How they laughed, but not in a persuaded sort of way. No bail. (Animal lovers need not be distressed. The hamster didn't starve. A solicitor in the cells who knew the young man agreed to go round to his bedsit and rescue it.)

Number two: present yourself correctly in the cells – step in cautiously but never walk in showing fear or revulsion. Sit down in a confident fashion and lounge like a confederate. Always sit nearest the cell door (you want an escape route) and always ascertain where the alarm, known as the 'affray' bell, is located. The offence of affray, which carries a maximum sentence of two years, is using or threatening unlawful violence towards a person that would cause a person of reasonable firmness (whether present or not) to fear for their personal safety. I assume the affray bell is called that because if you press it, the jailers will come and commit an affray on your client.

Number three: you knock. Every cell door has a large rectangle cut in it called the 'wicket'; you can open and close it from the outside but not the inside. The thing not to do with wickets is to open them and shove your face in. Do that and eventually you'll get spat on, or punched in the nose. It's the defendant's private space so show some respect. Announce your status – i.e. I'm the person who may get you out – before asking permission to open the wicket's flap. Even then you don't stick your face in, but stand to the side of the wicket like a priest taking confession. There is good reason for this: you may inadvertently say something that displeases your client, who, in order to rectify the hurt, grabs you by the throat.

Bow Street bail

A few weeks into my second six, I am skulking in the pupils' room. Harriet, the only other pupil around, is searching for a cigarette. 'There must be one somewhere.' A half-smoked fag balanced on the ashtray has to do. The phone rings, the sound that chills a pupil's blood. It could be anything. Pupils, in addition to slaving for their pupilmasters and pupilmistresses, are required to do work for members of chambers, the tenants upstairs. One phone call and you could be shackled to three months of arcane legal research summarizing fifty years of Australian trademark law. As I'm more junior than Harriet I have to answer the phone every time. I'm in luck. It's a clerk telling me to get down to Bow Street Magistrates' Court.[2] I stroll from chambers with Harriet, who fancies coming along for the ride. We muse over our West End choices. 'Shall we go to the lunch dance at the Opera House, or shall we visit Alex's client in the cells over the road?' Harriet peels off at the entrance to the court building. Much as she likes Bow Street, there's a new boutique near Seven Dials and she's in the market for a summer dress.

Busy days at Bow Street are my favourite. I love the place. All human life really is there. Suspected Muslim terrorists waiting to be extradited are praying next to the drunk singing 'Molly Malone', next to the mortgage fraudster with the bag full of 'important documents that prove my innocence'. The other reason I like Bow Street is that it has decent cells with high ceilings and good light. Today I'm especially pleased about Bow Street because I've got Johnnie and Margie. Until a recent visit from the vice squad, they'd been living off considerable sums of immoral earnings generated by their four-outlet sex business. There is a huge amount of evidence against them but they, like most defendants, want bail applications made on their behalf. It's not costing them anything and, after all, you never know.

Despite my low strike rate in getting defendants bail when the prosecution objects to it, there is a presumption in favour of its being granted. Bail applications in court work like this. The prosecution outlines its grounds of objection to the proposed bail and then the defence makes the application. The three main categories of objection are: risk of committing further offences, risk of failing to appear at future court appearances and risk of interfering with witnesses. In Johnnie and Margie's case, according to the prosecution, all three categories apply. The legal test that the judge has to consider is whether there are *substantial grounds*, not a mere likelihood, that Johnnie and Margie will commit further offences, fail to attend and/or interfere with witnesses. There is a fourth unofficial category which is the seriousness of the offence: if someone's accused of having done something really terrible then a judge can refuse bail on the grounds that the music they are eventually going to face means that a remand is inevitable. The only way of persuading a doomed defendant not to go for a hopeless bail application is to point out that he might as well start serving his sentence.

I saw Johnnie first. I advised him that bail was almost out of the question. In bail applications you can propose conditions for the court to impose if bail is to be granted, and the conditions are put in place in order to allay any fears that the court might have that a defendant will misbehave. The conditions that Johnnie and I put together were that he would live and sleep at a specified address, report to a police station so the authorities could keep an eye on him, and surrender his passport to stop him leaving the country. Most persuasively, he had a brother who was prepared to stand a large security, which is an amount of money paid into the court, that would be forfeited if Johnnie failed to attend further court appearances.

Next, I saw Margie, a former 'tom' (the cop/'crim' term for prostitute, which can be used as a noun or a verb), about my age, who'd gone into management with Johnnie. There was no money in her family, which meant there was no money to pay a security. She'd have to make do with the standard conditions. Margie was sweet and careworn. She missed her fourteen-year-old daughter who'd been fostered because of Margie's one-time drug habit. She was distraught to be missing her daughter's birthday. 'I haven't been much of a mother, I know that, but I've never missed my girl's birthday before,' she said. I felt sorry for her. I always feel sorry for the sex workers.

On my way to the court, one of the vice squad officers stopped me. 'Excuse me, sir. There's something you should see.' He led me into a little room which housed a video recorder and a television. He put a video in the recorder and pressed 'Play'.

> *Video 1*: Margie, Johnnie and an unidentified female are getting it on.
>   I could hear Margie saying, 'This is a special treat for your birthday, Johnnie.'

'Sorry, sir. Not this bit.'

'Not so quick, officer,' I said, but he was already fast-forwarding the tape. He pressed 'Play'.

> Margie is passed out face down on the bed. Johnnie is trying to slip his penis into her. Margie wakes up.
>   'Oi, fuck off, Johnnie. Have you drugged me?' she says woozily. 'You have, haven't you, you dirty bastard...'

> *Video 2*: Johnnie's video diary. Blood is streaming down his face.
>   'Margie stabbed me in the head with a Stanley knife. I deserved it though, cause I did spike her drink, I thought it'd be fun to give her one while ... I'm really sorry, Margie. I love you.'

If you're going to videotape your private life, then don't leave the tapes lying around for the police to find. There was enough evidence to charge Johnnie with rape and Margie with wounding with intent. Unsurprisingly, neither of them wanted to press charges.

This last-minute excitement makes me late for court so I come straight out from the cells with the defendants. I hope no one thinks I'm with them – I'm wearing a reasonably smart suit – even though I am, sort of. We're in Court 1 – the court of the Chief Magistrate of England and Wales. Johnnie and Margie shuffle into the nineteenth-century wrought iron dock set plumb in the middle of the room. This courtroom gets more than its fair share of the most notorious cases. Ronnie and Reggie Kray stopped off here on their way to life imprisonment. Oscar Wilde pitched up en route to his trial at the Bailey. Defendants from Dr Crippen, the poisoner, to William Joyce aka Lord Haw Haw, who broadcast anti-British sallies from Berlin during the Second World War, appeared here as they moved towards their respective legal fates. More recently, senior Tory perjurers Jonathan Aitken and Jeffrey Archer have had their moment in Court 1 at Bow Street.

My bail application is embarrassingly awful. I stutter, start sentence clauses that I don't end, meandering around my points hopelessly. The vice squad officer keeps pulling faces and winking at me to put me off. Bastard. Bail is refused.

Judges: the magistrates' court

There are two sorts of judges in the magistrates' court: district judges and justices of the peace (JPs). During trials they sit as both judge and jury, unlike in the crown court where a judge sits with a jury. District judges are salaried former lawyers who sit alone. JPs are unpaid non-lawyer members of the public who give up their time to pass judgement on the local ne'er-do-wells. JPs usually sit in threes. This collective is called a 'lay bench'. They are committed, earnest and often slow like molasses rolling up a hill. There is nothing more dispiriting than arriving at some godforsaken court at the wrong end of Kent with a long list of remand hearings only to find that it is being presided over by a lay bench. The suicide-inducing *longueurs* aren't entirely their fault. Every decision has to be taken collectively, which means that, in order to deliberate undisturbed, they must get up and troop out of court. It's not uncommon to have a lay bench agonizing for hours whether to give a shoplifter sixty or eighty hours' community service while you sit, head in your hands, watching your old age dodder over the horizon as the day ebbs into gloom.

It is almost always better to be before district judges, who, like pre-anaesthesia surgeons, are valued for their speed. There are far fewer of these judges, and courts guard them jealously. Some London courts are so busy that they'd seize up if you didn't have a district judge, and the great unprocessed waiting their turn down in the cells would remain unprocessed.

District judges, highly experienced lawyers who know all the ducks and dives, can run things pretty well how they like. The most distinctive become cherished local celebrities with the junior bar. There was one district judge who was reputedly dying of cancer – before going to his court you'd pray he'd be dead – but every year he'd still be there convicting your clients and looking better than ever. Then there was the former solicitor who'd done well representing Italian 'men of honour'. He would sit sleepy-eyed with his head propped against one finger, a trait I supposed he'd picked up from his former clients. My strike rate with him was as bad as it was with the cancer sufferer.

The most notorious district judge of them all was based at Greenwich Magistrates' Court, a cataract of justice through which there coursed a frothing torrent of low-level crime. On the average day Greenwich Mags had crackheads, schizophrenics, heroin addicts, petty thieves, blaggers, dippers (pickpockets), drunks, wife-beaters, knife wielders, prostitutes, harassers, weed peddlers, thumpers, kickers, gobbers, flashers, shoplifters, knock-off merchants, benefit cheats, fare dodgers, fine dodgers, junior burglars, community service breachers and bail jumpers all up for their five minutes (or less) in the full glare of British justice. This flotsam started to arrive from the prisons and police stations at about 8.30 a.m. and continued until the cells could take no more. They were all bound for the custody court otherwise known as Court 1. The workload was so heavy in Court 1 that only a district judge, and an experienced one at that, could ever get through it. When you arrived in the morning the same question was on everybody's lips: was it going to be him on the bench that day?

One client I had was a personality-disordered bomb hoaxer (among other offences) known to the local constabulary as Mad Merv. Merv had been living at a halfway house for those who struggled to cope with life. The long-suffering manager had given him a final warning but Merv just couldn't help himself when the afternoon started to drag. It was then that he liked to phone up the authorities to tell them about the bombs he'd planted.

Ring, ring.

'Hello, police.'

'I've put five incendiary bombs under Peckham Mental Health Centre. Nyaaahhh.'

'I'm sorry?'

'Bombs under Peckham nut house. Do you understand? Fucking fire bombs!'

Pause.

'Is that you, Merv?'

'No. It's not Merv.'

'Sounds like you, Merv.'

'Fuck off. S'not Merv. Fire bombs, I tell you. Fucking fire bombs. Under the nut house.'

The call was then discontinued but not before it had been traced back to the halfway house.

Merv was hoping for bail. Incredibly, the halfway house was prepared to have him back even though he'd been thrown out for unrelated misdemeanours, which he was keen to tell me about. 'It wasn't the boozing they didn't like. I had cans in the room. Drinking them. One, two, three.'

'Oh,' I said.

'They didn't mind the crack. Like smoking crack me. Hide the pipe in my hand and smoke it out the window.'

'Right,' I said.

'Didn't mind none of that. It was the tarts they couldn't handle.'

'Tarts?'

'Yeah, tarts. Two of them up in my room. Big girls . . .' Merv had blown his benefit cheque on this treat.

A jailer opened the door to the dock.

'Court stand,' said the list caller.

Mad Merv continued in his rat-a-tat-tat delivery through the dock's reinforced glass windows. A young solicitor, quite musical, started to hum the 'Ride of the Valkyries'. Merv looked up in mid-babble, stopped and said as calmly as he could manage, 'Oh fuck me, it's Custody Cooper.'

There he was! The man himself. The most feared district judge in London settling into his chair. Merv turned to me, put his palms on the glass of the dock and said something I couldn't hear but by the look on his face I knew it was despairing. My full attention was on Custody Cooper. Strapped into his high-backed wooden chair, he looked like an Edwardian fighter pilot, but this was wholly deceptive. District Judge Cooper moved like an F-22 being slung shot off an aircraft carrier and he was only getting warmed up. He waved the prosecution down, no need to hear from them, and turned to me.

'What's this listed for, Mr McBride?'

'First appearance and bail application, sir.'

'How does he plead?'

'Not guilty.'

'Not guilty!'

'He's got an address to go to . . .'

District Judge Cooper at this point dispensed with my professional services on behalf of my client. 'Stand up, Merv. How are you pleading to this bomb hoax?'

'Guilty.'

'Do you have any outstanding fines?'

Merv had no idea. The clerk checked. The answer was yes, lots.

'Right, forty-two days' imprisonment, seven days in lieu of unpaid fines, concurrent. If you behave yourself, you'll come out with the slate wiped clean. Anything to say, Mr McBride?'

'No, sir.'

'Right, who's next?'

I walked out of court and took a deep sigh. An emaciated man in a tracksuit and a baseball cap, opening the door to the court, stopped me. 'Who's on the bench, guv?' he asked.

'Cooper,' I said.

He held his chin in thought for a moment, turned on his heel and was gone. That was one trap he wasn't going to walk into. If they really wanted him, the 'old bill' could make the effort to come and nick him.

District Judge Cooper was a brilliant judge for old lags like Merv. He rolled everything up, including the fines, and stuck you with forty-two days. If you were really naughty, you got fifty-six. You came out having served half the sentence, purged of your sins – a man reborn. Judge Cooper was less amenable, however, to the first- and second-timers. They got the same treatment. Bail was withdrawn and they were left to stew in their own juice in the cells. You had to admire his consistency.

Judges: the crown court

After a few months on my feet, I had demonstrated to the clerks that magistrate courtrooms did not reduce me to a crying hysteric or make me run zig-zagging in panic when the hearing started. For the clerks that meant I passed muster for minor hearings such as bail applications in the crown court where the big boys and girls hung out. The advantage of crown court bail applications is that your client is safely tucked away in prison and therefore you don't have to deal with the tears and recriminations when it all goes wrong. The disadvantage is that inevitably his or her family comes to court with expectations you can't necessarily meet. Crown court bail applications are supposed to be better prepared – a written application is submitted to the court a day beforehand – but often things are just as last minute as they are in the magistrates'.

I was sent down to Inner London Crown Court, a musty old place next to Elephant and Castle, to get Lily out of jail. The solicitors had told me that her mother would be there. The mother was essential. Time ticked by and our slot in court was fast approaching but Mum still hadn't appeared. Nine tenths of the law is hanging around. You wait for the judge, you wait for Serco, the crim deliverers, to produce your client, you wait for a court and often you wait in vain – but if you're not ready when it all goes up, then no one's going to wait for you, not so much as a second.

'Where is she?' I asked, nervously looking at my watch.

'I don't know. She's not answering her phone,' said the solicitor's rep.

The usher came out of court. 'Judge is waiting.'

'I'm not ready. Can't you give him something else to do?'

'He's finished the something else, dear. He wants to consider your client's bail.'

'I've got no Mum. I'm screwed without Mum.'

It was a shame. Even with Mum, getting Lily bail was going to be an uphill struggle. Until a week ago, Lily had been doing really well. She'd turned her life around, got a flat, a good job as an administrative assistant and started going to college in the evenings. Lily's next-door neighbours kept a parental eye on her – she was not yet twenty and a good kid. The one thing they couldn't protect her from was her on-again, off-again boyfriend, Murray. They'd told her not to let him in but he was so charming, so funny, she just couldn't resist him.

One night, as Lily was going to sleep, her bell rang. Murray was at the door. He'd brought Chinese takeaway and some weed. She ate sparingly, had a few puffs on a spliff and went to bed, leaving Murray in her living room. It wasn't the bangs that woke her up but the shouting. She came out of her bedroom and found Murray in the corridor, blood pumping out of him in little squirts.

'I've been shot,' he cried, glassy-eyed and unsteady on his feet. Lily ran out of the flat screaming, her dressing gown flapping in her wake.

'Help! Murray's dying! Help me!'

Murray, somewhat at a loose end, staggered after her. The neighbours, who had heard the gunshots, found him slumped on the landing. He wasn't dying but he didn't look too good either.

A quick once around Lily's flat by the police soon located the source of the trouble: on a coffee table in the living room, they found a pile of cellophane wraps of heroin and crack cocaine along with a stack of bloodstained cash. Murray had been using Lily's flat to conduct his business affairs. A dispute had arisen with a visitor, which, considering Murray was still breathing, appeared not to have been satisfactorily resolved. Quicker than you could say 'rival drug dealers', Lily and Murray were arrested, and jointly charged with possession with intent to supply class A drugs, namely heroin and crack. Unsurprisingly, Lily's bail had been denied at the magistrates' court. If bail were now refused in the crown court, then she'd stay inside until trial which meant she'd lose her flat, her job and be back at square one. Without Mum, I was Lily's only hope of getting out and I didn't fancy my chances.

Bail applications are held in private. Prosecuting counsel began by outlining the facts of the case – the mixture of guns and drugs played very badly with the judge. Since the offence was charged as a joint enterprise, in law, Lily tucked up in bed was just as culpable as Murray sitting in the living room cutting up the crack. The prosecutor's spin was that Murray and Lily had been running a crack den. Bail should be denied because there was a *substantial risk* that if she was released she would commit further offences and fail to attend court. I swallowed hard and stood up feeling like the tone-deaf child being summoned to sing the third verse of Aled Jones's 'I'm Walking in the Air' at school assembly.

'This is a very serious case, Mr McBride,' said the judge, which was code for 'Why are you wasting my time, numb-nut?' I hadn't even opened my mouth and things were already going badly. On the face of it Lily's might've been a serious case, but there was something that didn't add up. Why, I wondered, would someone who knew drugs were in the flat, in plain view on a coffee table, not hide them before the police arrived? Strictly speaking bail applications aren't the time to challenge the prosecution case but it was reasonable to infer that Lily had no idea that the drugs were there. She had got in with a bad crowd but, with only one caution for shoplifting, she was still essentially of good character. This was something the judge had to take into account when deciding whether there was a substantial risk that she would breach her conditions of bail. It seemed unfair that she should be tarred with the same brush as Murray. I reminded the judge of Lily's progress, pointed out that if she were remanded in custody she'd lose everything, even though there was a real chance that she would be found not guilty.

'This is all very well, but if I were to release her where would she go? And who will stand surety to guarantee her attendance at future hearings?'

I had to admit he'd got me there: Lily's flat was a crime scene and crawling with cops. My mouth opened and closed, sounds came out but none of them satisfied the judge. While I was failing to answer his questions the door banged open and in walked Lily's mum.

'Who are you?' asked the judge.

'I'm Lily's mum,' she replied.

'Call her as a witness, Mr McBride.'

I did. After that the judge completely ignored me. He and Lily's mum danced around the court in mutual admiration. Lily's mum was a nurse. Everyone loves a nurse and the judge loved Lily's mum. Unlike me, she had answers to all his questions. Yes, Lily could stay with her. Yes, she would have her own room. Standing surety was no problem. She produced her bank statements, all neatly bound, no rustling for bits of paper in a plastic bag, to show that she had the £1,000 that the judge required. He not only granted bail but was happy to do so. He beamed at Lily's mum when she agreed to meet her daughter at HMP Holloway's gates.

No one was happier than I. Wins don't come around very often. It might have been Lily's mum who won it but they all count and this one certainly would – once I had exaggerated my contribution to my clerks.

Plea and mitigation

Aside from bail applications, the other staple for a beginning barrister is plea and mitigation. You give a 'plea and mit' when a defendant has done the decent thing and pleaded guilty, usually after some stern advice from their barrister. The aim is to present the defendant in the best possible light in order to secure the lowest possible sentence. There are set mitigating factors: a defendant's age, if it's a first offence, and if someone has pleaded guilty rather than been convicted after trial. With pleading guilty there is a sliding scale: if you plead at the first available opportunity, you can expect a discount in sentence of one third; plead on the first day of trial, it drops to 10 per cent. A guilty plea is powerful mitigation and it can often make the difference between going to prison and not going to prison. When mitigating, you have to work with the material you get: a junkie shoplifter with thirty-five previous convictions and four packs of Lidl's frozen chicken stuffed down the front of his trousers is heading only one way.

The nasty thing about plea and mits and bail applications is that your services can be called upon with very little notice. One morning I found myself down at Camberwell Green Magistrates' Court, lumbered with the usual hopeless trial. I offered the prosecution a guilty plea to a lesser charge, which, to my amazement, they accepted. That meant no trial. No embarrassment of trying to sell his non-existent defence to the magistrates. What happiness! It's 10.30 a.m. and the day is mine. The only snag being that as a pupil I have to go back to chambers and that puts me at risk of the dreaded late return.

The late return is a brief that no one at the English bar wants to touch. It has bounced up and down Middle Temple Lane without finding anyone dumb or desperate enough to accept it. The 'cab rank' rule at the bar requires that if a barrister is free, it is their professional duty to take the case offered to them. In practice, people can plausibly claim that they're too busy. But eventually the music stops, and if the brief lands in your lap, you have to keep it.

If I can't avoid chambers until a decent time in the afternoon, then there's no choice but to sneak back in. I consider my options. The back route is the most direct way in but it will lead me directly past the clerks' room window. Even if I dip down below the window, they'll hear me crunching on the gravel. What if Keith popped his head out of the window that very minute? 'Mr McBride, sir, what on earth are you doing crawling on your hands and knees?' It would be hard to explain that away. No matter how you said it, 'Honing my skills as a cocker spaniel' wasn't very plausible.

The only thing to do was go through the front door. High risk, it was true, but at least it kept me the furthest distance away from Keith. At the entrance to chambers, I took off my shoes and crept up the stone stairs to the front door. I put my face up against the door and peered through the glass. No Keith. The coast was clear.

Then, quiet as a cat burglar, I pushed at the door. It opened with a creak. I looked around the corner into reception, barely daring to breathe. Araminta was engrossed with the flowers. I moved forward stealthily, sliding my socked feet along the limestone floor. I was one door and ten steps from the safety of the pupils' room. A few more seconds and I'd be tucking into a bento box of sushi and looking forward to a kip under the pupils' table. I turned the last corner.

'Jesus Christ!' I called out in shock. I was close. Keith, Jesus Christ's earthly representative, was leaning by the door to the basement smoking a cigarette. I'd been ambushed.

Keith has a sixth sense. He instinctively knows where all his barristers are. If you were lost on a mountain, it wouldn't be a St Bernard dog that would find you, but Keith, and there wouldn't be any brandy in the little barrel around his neck – it would be a bloody brief.

'Mr McBride, sir, just the man I was looking for,' he said, politely ignoring my lack of shoes. 'Could you go down to Chelmsford Crown Court for a sentence? There's been a bit of a cock-up.'

Clerks may address barristers as 'sir' or 'miss', but don't let that mislead you as to who's grinding the organ and who's dancing in front of it holding a tin cup. Soon I was sitting on a train, too busy boning up on the sentence brief for sushi and napping. An hour later, I found myself ringing the buzzer to the cells. A jailer answered.

'Legal for Howard,' I said.

He buzzed me in.

'Are you Howard's brief?'

'I am.'

'Do you want us to stand outside while you speak to him?'

'Why would I want you standing outside?' I asked.

'When he was last in prison he took a prison officer hostage. Hair trigger temper, sir. Very unpredictable.'

Now I realized why his previous barrister wasn't here. The swine had made damn sure that he was doing something else. I declined the jailer's offer. A defendant has to trust his lawyer or the relationship doesn't work. Having two burly jailers staring into the interview room watching his every move didn't exactly create a convivial atmosphere of trust. The affray bell would be more than enough.

I was expecting to see a nice modern easy-to-press strip of rubber running along the sides of the cell, which, if things went wrong, would be easy to set off. I was out of luck. The bell was an old-fashioned little button set deep into a circular dip in the wall. How was I supposed to press that if Howard started throttling me? With my toe? All I could do was sit in the chair nearest the door.

As I turned back towards it, the door opened and Howard walked in and plonked himself down in the chair nearest to the door. I was left with the one wedged tightly behind the steel desk in the far corner of the cell, which, like everything else, was bolted to the floor. Even if I squeezed out from behind the table and past Howard, getting the door open would doom me. I sat down behind the desk and sized Howard up. He had a shaved head and intense dark eyes set in a heavy stare. The muscles on his neck and shoulders tightened and relaxed in little spasms. He was already in a bad mood.

'Am I going to get sentenced today?' he asked, forgoing any opening pleasantries.

I had no idea. It was coming up to 3 p.m. The court would be unlikely to run beyond 4.30 p.m. 'I don't know,' I answered.

'If I'm not fucking sentenced today, right, I'm going to cut the screw in the dock.' He meant the dock officer, who is always present when a defendant, no matter how harmless, enters the dock.

'What are you going to cut him with?'

'I've got a razor. I'll cut the cunt. I'm not pissing about.'

'Okay.' My brain was racing. Did Howard have a razor? Could he have got it on to the prison van that had taken him to court? It was possible but unlikely. The real point was whether he would use it. He had taken a prison guard hostage but, as far as I knew, the guard had been released unharmed. I was in a tricky situation. If I told the jailer, then Howard would go up to the judge hand-cuffed as a potentially violent prisoner. Howard was, in all likeli-hood, going to get a substantial prison sentence but I was there to obtain the best result possible. In handcuffs there was no way in a million years the judge would give him a non-custodial sentence. On the other hand, what about the dock officer getting a face full of razor? He'd appreciate the warning.

Conversations between lawyer and client are legally privileged but that doesn't mean you're barred from stopping a crime. The ethical response was probably to alert the dock officer. (Maybe something like, 'Look, if you don't want a big Mars Bar – a scar to you and me – across your chops, slap on the cuffs.') I remembered the very old joke that 'Ethics' to a barrister is a county east of Lon-don. Ha, ha – I wasn't laughing.

A barrister's first duty is to the court and not his client, but being a barrister requires making fine judgements. Ultimately, I didn't believe Howard. Slicing up the dock officer would have meant a lengthy sentence. There was no upside for him. I put his threat down to pre-sentence nerves.

Howard was a crack addict and career burglar. His latest crime-fest had come to an end in a medium-sized seaside town. A man peering from behind his curtains had seen him, in broad daylight, casually picking the lock of a neighbour's front door. The man, outrage rising in his throat, couldn't dial 999 fast enough. Mean-while, Howard effected his entry, grabbed a holdall lying in the hallway and dashed around the house filling the bag. It was Junkie Supermarket Sweep with the honest citizen on the phone playing Dale Winton. 'He's in the house. He's taking the DVD player and the Play Station ... He's got the camera ... He's in the bedroom. He's even taking their shoes!'

Howard managed to get away before the police arrived, and instantly swapped his bumper haul for crack. It was the apogee of his criminal career. In his haste he'd left a fingerprint, or 'dab' as it's called in the trade, on a picture frame. As he was already well known to the police, that dab led them straight to his door. The coppers linked him to four other recent burglaries in the area. Faced with an overwhelming prosecution case and exhausted by servicing a £1,000-a-week crack habit – real work that: stealing, selling, scoring, all the time worrying about getting caught or ending up dead – Howard decided to confess. Coming clean felt good and, as anyone with an addictive personality, once he had a taste for it he wanted to do it again and again. The police drove him around town and he pointed out all the places he'd done over. Once he'd finished, he asked for a further forty-five burglaries to be taken into consideration at his sentencing hearing. He'd been out of prison for six weeks.

Howard was the classic multiple-offending drug user. The list of his convictions for dishonesty was pages long. His ever-lengthening prison sentences had failed to deal with his real problem: he had a crack habit that he couldn't afford. He was, in theory, eligible for a drug treatment and testing order (DTTO), an alternative to custody which involves an intensive programme of drug counselling.[3] It might have been unrealistic but I was going to go for it all the same.

I sat outside court waiting to mitigate on his behalf and getting increasingly worried. Time was moving swiftly on. I might have been relatively sanguine about Howard's threat downstairs in the cells but now I was feeling pretty edgy. I begged for the court to hurry up. It was nearly 4 p.m. when we were finally called in. I mitigated on Howard's behalf, arguing that the extra forty-five burglaries wouldn't have been solved had it not been for his assistance and therefore he should be sentenced on the basis of the first five only. The judge was clearly conflicted. DTTOs don't have a great success rate in turning offenders away from drugs and crime. Prisons, however, are just as ineffective. They are awash with drugs. The only after-prison care an addict releasee usually gets is the £46 discharge grant, which he duly uses to score.

Once I'd finished, the judge looked at the clock. It was quarter to five. Courts very rarely sit beyond 4.30 p.m. 'This is a complex matter, Mr McBride. I'm going to adjourn this case until tomorrow morning.' I spun around to the dock ready to shout out if Howard made a move on the dock officer. Howard didn't twitch. He could tell that the judge was considering a non-custodial sentence. Coming back the next day might be a drag but it was worth it.

The next day Howard's case was first on the list. The judge came in and gave him four years – not a bad result, although I'd hoped for better. Down in the cells Howard was much more relaxed. He had his release date – a goal to work towards. It's much easier to do time that way. Soon I was back on the train. Keith would be in chambers warming up the organ; there might be a new tune but I'd be performing the same ragged dance.

3. Saturday Court is the Party Court

Friday afternoon in the pupils' room and the promise of the weekend lies heavily on everyone's shoulders. Harriet, sitting at the head of the table, has the phone, stretched to its maximum extension, locked between her chin and collarbone. She dips strips of *pain aux amandes*, wisps of dough held together by butter and *crème anglaise*, into a steaming latte.

'Do you think Harriet's going to be long?' asks Liam, squirming to use the phone.

'Search me,' I said, watching her elegantly fold another piece of pastry into her mouth.

Liam spread out his penny share tip sheet on the table. 'Harriet?' He waved to get her attention and then mimed in great detail the bones of the telephone call he wanted to make. She ignored him.

'Harriet, I need to call my broker.'

The penny shares were about as remunerative as putting 50p each way on a greyhound at Potter's Bar dog track – and about as exciting.

'Harriet?' insisted Liam, pointing to the phone, waving the tip sheet.

'Fuck off,' she mouthed. 'Stand on the windowsill.'

The windowsill was the only place in the room where you could get any mobile phone reception, and even then it was patchy. Liam was too shy to go upstairs and do his financial wheeler-dealing outside on Middle Temple Lane.

Finally Harriet put down the phone. As Liam was making for it, the phone rang. Wordless Will's mum was on the line. Every Friday Will's mum called hoping that he'd be coming home to

Gerrard's Cross for the weekend. Every Friday Will had made other plans. Gerrard's Cross would have to remain unvisited.

For two lucky pupils the possibility in the air as the weekend approached was bittersweet. Lurking in the background was the baleful prospect of Saturday court. Working the odd Saturday shouldn't be a big deal but, believe me, it is. There is a humiliation about it that is difficult to bear. The last-minute phone call from the clerks' room, trudging up the stairs, squeezing past the nattering barristers to be presented with a thin fold-over brief with something like 'SITTINGBOURNE MAGISTRATES' COURT' typed on it. Written proof that you were the piss boy who did all the crap. Walking out of the clerks' room with a Saturday court brief tucked under your arm was like walking out with a bag of warm dog shit. It induced the same sort of stabbing embarrassment as the anxiety dreams I used to have in which I walk into a packed courtroom naked from the waist down and start, inexplicably, dancing to the 'Tweety Song'.

Mamta came in looking for Liam and me. She was in charge of the Saturday court rota and was very hot that the 'screw-ups' (no prizes for guessing who they were) knew what was expected of them.

'Who's on the rota?' she asked in the way that people say, 'Who's a pretty boy, then?' to budgerigars.

She knew the answer. She'd checked. 'Liam? Who's on the rota?'

Liam had finally got his hands on the phone and was excitedly arranging for £36 of Malaysian mining stocks to be added to his portfolio.

'Li-am!'

'Isn't it you?' he said, covering the receiver with his hand.

'I don't think so. You're first on and Alex is second.' She handed him the printed off rota as proof.

Liam put the phone down and exclaimed, 'First, first! I'm always fucking first. Another weekend buggered. I hate Saturday court.'

He started pacing around the pupils' table, trying to light a cigarette, his face more gingery than ever.

'Do you know why I hate Saturday court – because it's a total
waste of fucking time. You get sent to some distant shit hole, so far
that it makes Alpha Centauri look like it's round the fucking corner. You arrive. It's closed cause the duty clerk has sent you to the
wrong court cause he's an illiterate cunt. You spend the next hour
and a half going to the right fucking shit hole. Your client's not
there cause he's still being processed by the police. Finally, he
shows up in the cells. You read the papers. He's breached his,' Liam
paused for effect, 'sixty-hour probation order. Major fucking
crime, right. I mean what a fucking bad boy gangster this lad is.
We all know the magistrates are going to release him cause it's
bollocks. It's not even the kid's fault cause, like the shit-brained
duty clerk, he can't fucking read either. And even if he could, the
probation service have sent him to the wrong office and then failed
to get his order going so he's gone home and forgotten about it
only to get arrested four months later as he's eating a kebab on
some shopping centre bench. Can't even remember what the original offence was, so the whole exercise reaches a level of pointlessness, a fucking Nirvana of pointlessness, hitherto unattained by
mankind.'

Liam sat down and gesticulated at Jane who was carefully applying her make-up. 'And to cap it all there's a chambers' party tonight
and the champagne's already on ice.'

The phone rang. Jane answered. It was the duty clerk. Liam's
Saturday brief was already waiting upstairs. He pulled himself up
from his chair and disappeared for the walk of shame.

Saturday court, the theory goes, means that defendants will be
more efficiently processed, thereby reducing the time they spend
sitting in a police cell waiting for court to begin on Monday. In
practice things don't work out quite so smoothly. Courts run a
skeleton service, other agencies are closed. If you want to find

your client a bail hostel, which is never easy at the best of times, you are usually out of luck. Often the magistrates will put the whole thing off until Monday when the rest of the staff are back at work. Everyone, including you, will find themselves in the same court replaying the same exercise forty-eight hours later.

I don't know why Liam was complaining. Being second on call was worse than being first. When you were first on you knew that you were going to get called out; if you were second you had the chance of an undisturbed weekend and the torturous guessing game of whether you were going to be called out or not began. I had decided that I wasn't going to miss the party. I was going to follow the advice of the editor of the celebrity-worship magazine *Vanity Fair*, Graydon Carter, about booze and parties: two drinks and then pace yourself. Follow Carter and I'd be as fresh as a daisy in the morning, no matter what it might bring.

The party officially started at 6 p.m. We pupils mooched around downstairs for the first half an hour. We didn't contribute financially to chambers. The tenants, from whom nearly 20 per cent of their gross income went on keeping the show on the road, paid the bills. It would be rude to arrive on the stroke of six and start guzzling their booze. I followed Harriet and Jane up the stairs. I was immediately buttonholed, given a name badge and told to circulate with the champagne. This was a good job. I could move around repeating a few pre-prepared lines and be seen to be helpful. The tenants could read my nametag and admire my champagne-pouring skills.

As I was the supplier of the champagne, they were pleased to see me, and noticed the care, reverence even, that I showed in doling out the booze.

'Sterling work,' they said. 'Have a drink yourself.'

With their benediction, I poured myself a glass. I started to enjoy myself, roaming through the crowd filling glasses, refilling my own.

The head of chambers himself noticed my efforts and praised me. 'Well done, Alex. Make sure you get yourself a drink.'

I checked my phone. Still no call from the duty clerk with a Saturday brief. I was in the clear. I made sure that I got myself that drink. I kept up my pouring duties. Chatting to the tenants, who were once distant and forbidding, became easier and easier. Soon I wasn't just talking amiably but cracking jokes. I was putting my arms around shoulders of people I'd never met and, in the spirit of the convivial evening, refilling my glass.

There's an old poker saying that if you can't see who the sucker is then it's you. This applies to drinking: I had no idea who the drunk was because the drunk was me. I gravitated to the most enthusiastic drinkers, youngish tenants and their instructing solicitors.

'God, she's really cute,' I said loudly, indicating a beautiful blonde woman standing a few feet away. 'Who's she?'

There was silence. The enthusiastic drinkers looked at their shoes. 'That,' one of them said finally, 'is your head of chambers' wife.' Boy, was I glad I was wearing that nametag.

Of the two things that make a good barrister – discretion and judgement – I had shown neither. Araminta rescued me, putting her arm around my waist and steering me out of harm's way.

A hard core of us went to the after party at Cort's, a depressing bunker of a nightclub on Chancery Lane full of pissed-up barristers. The woman/man ratio was terrible. The guys swarmed around the few girls like demented sperm. I staggered about with Araminta, pouring gin and tonics down my neck until it was time to go home.

My next conscious memory was of lying next to Araminta, my hand stroking her tanned throat. There was a breeze. A wooden raft creaked beneath us. In the distance was the sound of breakers crashing rhythmically on a deserted beach. I felt amazingly content.

Then there was a piercing electronic chirrup. It got louder and louder, blotting out the soothing noises of the waves on the beach.

I opened one eye and then another. The chirrup persisted, sending little stabs of pain through my head. I was in bed, alone. Araminta and the raft had gone, replaced by the insistent electronic chirrup. What on earth was it? And why didn't it stop?

'Phone, fucking phone,' I heard a voice call. It was Richard, my flatmate, down the corridor. The chirrup was a phone, I surmised – my phone. I sat up and pain filled my head, as if I had my own personal jack-booted Gestapo officer goose-stepping around my brainpan, kicking the back of my eyeballs.

'Phone, fucking phone,' repeated Richard.

I could hear the phone but I couldn't see it. I scanned the room, my field of vision taking in a half-finished pizza – had I eaten pizza last night? – my desk, under which a mass of computer and stereo wires wrestled with an eggy fork, and the dirty plates half-hidden by piles of dirty clothes.

'Phone, fucking phone.'

Then in the corner I saw the blue glow of my mobile. I advanced on it, my brain scorched with pain, and pressed 'answer'.

'Good morning, sir,' said the duty clerk jauntily. 'Are we ready for our trip to Skegness?'

I looked on the bright side: at least I already had my suit on.

My first trial

It's around about Grantham that the hangover really starts to take hold. Standing on the platform waiting for the connection to the coast, I realize that I need to eat something to combat the nausea. I go to the station café to discover an extensive selection of Ginster's pie products. Having not fully learned my lesson, I decide to transpose that wise old sage Graydon Carter's drinking advice to the Ginster's product range: two Ginster's pasties and then pace yourself. Just in case, I also get something that looks like an elongated scotch egg, which a friend of mine assures me is called a Ginster's 'Berserker'. Two hours and two pasties later I find myself in Skegness as the drizzle blowing in off the North Sea turns to rain.

The hearing at Skegness Magistrates' Court is blink-and-you'll-miss-it short. Matty has breached his curfew, one of his conditions of bail. He sits in the cells looking only slightly less hung-over than me. There is little to say. The breach is so minor that even if I do nothing but play the 'William Tell Overture' with a pair of spoons, the magistrates are going to release him. As I'm here, the clerk asks me to confirm the live witnesses needed for Matty's impending trial.

It's listed for Monday, the day after tomorrow, and I know, as I know toddlers love sand, that I as 'chump no. 1' will be ordered back up to Skegness to do it. But there are, including Matty, four defendants in this trial so there's no way I can represent them all. Another barrister is going to be instructed, which starts me wondering who's going to be 'chump no. 2'.

Less than thirty-six hours later, I spot the tiny ginger figure of Liam McLeish, chump of chumps, haring up the platform at King's Cross dragging the biggest trolley bag that I've ever seen. A voice comes over the public address system announcing that the train doors will lock in one minute. Liam quickens his pace, the trolley bag skittering behind him so that it looks as though the bag is chasing him down. We jump on the train, push our way to our seats and try to look forward to the prospect of two days in Skegness.

By twelve, we are both in court and ready for the first witness. Billy Kilcooley, the victim in all this, comes into court following the usher. His loose-fitting suit cannot hide his twitchiness. His eyes dart about trying to take everything in, not because he is unfamiliar with courts but because he is nervous and excited. His body is popping with expectation. Liam and I are pretty nervous and excited, too, because, unlike Billy, this is our first actual trial.

There are four defendants: Matty, Tam, Maureen and Biff, two of whom rely on me to keep them out of jail, and two of whom are relying on Liam. They all sit in a small, sealed dock. High medieval arrow slits in the glass let the air circulate and give Liam and me the chance to whisper conspiratorially to them. One thing is clear: I care more about the outcome than they do. Their liberty is at stake but it's my ego. Whatever happens, they will eventually get out; my ego may never recover.

My boys – this is the understood term among criminal practitioners: 'my boy' did this, 'my girl' said that – are in more trouble than Liam's. Matty and Tam, barely twenty, are alleged to be Billy's principal attackers. It is they who are said to have kicked him in the face.

Earlier in the pre-trial con, these two country boys told me that they shared the same sixteen-year-old girl. Tam was going out with her and Matty, as he put it, 'was giving her one on the side, like'. Inevitably she fell pregnant.

'Who's the father?' I ask.

'I dunno,' says Matty. 'Toss a coin. Hur, hur, hur.' They remain the best of friends.

It's they who are charged with actual bodily harm and, if they get convicted, they are going to jail. I tell them that 68 per cent of magistrate court trials end in conviction. I tell them that the evidence against them is quite strong. I do not tell them I have never done a trial before.

Liam's clients, Maureen and her sixteen-year-old son, Biff, played a minor role, although, according to the prosecution, they were there all the same, chipping in to Billy's beating. The Kilcooleys and the defendants were once friends. An unsuccessful holiday in Clacton led to strains, which have separated them into two warring parties swapping tit for tat violence. Everyone seems to be beating everyone else. Billy is often on the receiving end. The year before, his own brother punctured his lung during a fight. As Billy walks past us to the witness box, Liam whispers to me, 'Looking at Billy, I'd give him a good kicking too.'

Billy's experience of the criminal courts has not made him a good witness. He quickly makes the mistake of telling obvious lies. His story is that while he was walking to a club with his sister and a couple of friends, he was accosted by a group of young men. It was dark and he was frightened. Once they had finished taunting him they set about him, kicking him in the face, the legs and the ribs. Tam, Billy claims, stamped on his head. They were joined then by a twenty-strong group. Despite his injuries and being outnumbered, Billy managed to run away with the gang in close pursuit. During his escape he found the time to visit a Spar minimarket to buy a fizzy drink.

Billy also tells the court, among other things, that as a result of the 'kicking' he had 'numerous cuts' to his face. Never exaggerate your injuries if the photographic and medical evidence does not bear them out. I open the police photos and ask him to show the court where on his face exactly these 'numerous cuts' are. Billy, twitching violently, can't help as to the whereabouts of these injuries. He thinks that by recounting his story more luridly it will be more credible.

ME: Mr Kilcooley, in photo 1, show the court where these numerous cuts are?

BILLY: I was kicked in the face. There was blood coming down my face. I was kicked in the ribs ...

ME: Yes, Billy, we've heard your story. Answer the question.

BILLY: I was kicked in the face. Numerous cuts ... (*gesticulating*)

COURT CLERK: Billy, answer the question.

MAGISTRATE: Mr Kilcooley, you must answer counsel's questions.

BILLY: Tam stamped on my head. I could see his boots through my fingers. Kicked me. Stamped on ... (*by now he is shouting, standing up, sitting down, waving his arms*)

ME: Come on. In photo no. 1, show the court your numer-
                ous cuts. Show us the blood. You can't, can you? You're
                making it up, aren't you, Billy? You are telling lies.
                (*There is uproar. Billy has poor anger management skills and
                goes bananas. He is led out of court and goes to sit with his
                mum in their Vauxhall Cavalier.*)

Even in my moment of triumph, hubris is already preparing to
mock me. Back in the courtroom, it's Maureen's evidence, the witness I fear least, which causes Tam and Matty's interests not to
diverge but shear. Maureen had said in police interview that she
had not seen any violence against Billy. Specifically, she had not
seen Matty punch him in the head. All the defendants' police interviews, only just read out in court, say the same. While she's being
asked questions by Liam, who is her barrister, Maureen blurts out
that she saw Matty punch Billy and then push him to the ground.
According to her it is the push that makes him fall. At the same
time she insists Tam went home early and therefore could not have
assaulted Billy, could not have stamped on his head.

My turn to cross-examine. What do I do? Do I go for Maureen?
Her account doesn't make any sense. The push brought Billy down
rather than the punch? Do I want to start unpicking that? She's
just exonerated Tam, and indeed the defence case rests on all of
them presenting a common and honest front to contrast with the
lying deviousness of the Kilcooleys. The case is going to turn on
whom the magistrates believe and, remembering the statistic that
68 per cent of magistrate court trials end in conviction, usually the
magistrates don't believe the defendants in the dock.

I could withdraw; up sticks and say I am conflicted, which I am,
but to do that would look petulant, ridiculous. I am not walking out
of my first trial. It might be their liberty but it's my ego. The whole
thing is made worse because it's bloody Liam, whose countenance
now resembles that of a very devout junior prelate, and his bloody

client who have messed things up. I am going to have to sacrifice someone, but should it be Matty or should it be Tam? This is why trials can be such terrifying affairs: this sort of dilemma can happen at any time and no one will apologize, especially not holier-than-thou Liam McLeish. I stand up and go with Maureen's story. I get her to iterate that Matty did nothing more than punch Billy once and that it was too soft to knock Billy down. I decide if Matty is to be convicted, then it will be on *her* facts and not the Kilcooleys'.

I call Matty last. We talk, he and I, about his love for cars. He thinks it's 'pukka' that I call him a 'grease monkey'. Matty proudly tells the court of his one qualification: car spraying. My heart is broken, for he does it beautifully, as I get him to explain that the cuts on his knuckles were caused by a dropped gearbox. My heart is broken because, while it softens the magistrates and warms them to him, it will not in the end save him from another notch on his criminal record.

I make my closing speech. The magistrates retire. Waiting in the sunshine, Matty eats chocolate-glazed buns as only a kid can, ravenously, one after the other, the chocolate from the last still crusted on his lips. Liam lounges at a safe distance, managing to smoke and smirk at the same time. They call us back in. Everyone is acquitted apart from Matty. But he is convicted on Maureen's, or if you like, our facts. The Kilcooleys are not believed, which must be galling because it is certain someone gave Billy a hearty 'doing'. The point is that our facts are much less serious: a single punch, not the all over bone-dance alleged by Billy. This means Matty will get a lesser sentence. He'll not go to jail. My ego is shaken and I'm already rationalizing.

For the whole three hours home, Liam is insufferable. He sings 'one-nil' and starts pointing at me and shouting, 'loser, loser'. Then in mock pity he starts patronizing me by saying how I did 'very, very well'. I just have to take it. At the Grantham change, I treat Liam to a 'winner's purse' of three Ginster's Berserkers.

PART TWO

The Bear Pit

4. Low-quality Crime for Low-quality Advocates

There are quality courts and then there's Northampton Magistrates' Court. From the station you take the exhaust-crusted ring road, your heart sinking as you walk past the second-hand car dealership, boarded-up shops and the dying bakery. I'd been 'on my feet' for four months and I still hadn't won a trial. I just couldn't win. It was corrosive. If I were defending St Francis of Assisi, he'd go down. I hated Northampton. I hated their magistrates, whom I unfairly dismissed as small-town semi-worthies with provincial outlooks. I got convicted every time. (You see how personally we barristers take it. We refer to the defendant and ourselves both as 'I'. Syntactically we become one: I was the getaway driver, I was hitting my girlfriend when I accidentally set light to my crack pipe – I was convicted, again.) My solicitor met me outside the courtroom. He had an appealing mixture of good cheer and resignation. Despite our affable smiles, we could both see that I was already beaten. I hadn't even met my client.

Walt was a skinny, nervous-looking kid of nineteen who had more fingers on his hands than teeth in his head. His mum had left when he was nine and after a spell in care he and his similarly abandoned friends had lived together and looked out for one another. The only adults in their lives were the people who cashed their giros and the police. One hot afternoon the summer before, the police had called looking for drugs at a house where Walt and his friends hung around. Jefferson Chait, a heavy-handed brute of a cop, climbed out of the squad car. Hassling the local youth appeared to be his mission in life. He could hear voices coming from the rear of the house. In the overgrown back garden a very young mother watched over a group of kids splashing in a paddling pool. They were having a merry time. Walt and his mates, all unemployed and with time on their hands, watched them play while they chatted with the mother.

Jefferson's search of the house was hot and fruitless. He looked pretty ridiculous coming out empty-handed, wiping the sweat from his face. The boys laughed at him and whispered among themselves. They didn't even have any cannabis on them. He couldn't touch them.

'You're a funny fucker, aren't you?' said Walt, mockingly.

Now *that* really riled Jefferson. How dare they make fun of him, an officer of the law? Jefferson strode out of the garden and back to the street. He was almost to the squad car when a voice called out from the garden, 'I'm going to get you Jefferson, you dirty black bastard. You nigger.'

He wasn't standing for that. He came charging back to see a group of boys leap over the garden wall and Walt disappear into the house. Jefferson admitted that he hadn't seen who had said it but he said he was sure that it had been Walt. He'd had many run-ins with Walt over the years and he claimed that he had recognized his voice.

It wasn't hard to locate Walt. Jefferson found him uncomfortably wedged under a child's bunk bed. 'Come out from under that bed,' he ordered. Walt refused to budge. Jefferson crouched down to encourage him but Walt wasn't moving.

In his witness statement Jefferson, a stickler for detail, said that he then produced his 'PR 24' in order to effect Walt's arrest. After a quick trawl on the Internet I discovered that PR 24 is the product name for the baton used by the police. The 24 refers to its length in inches. Throughout his witness statement Jefferson always called it his PR 24 and never his baton. I began to suspect that the baton was Jefferson's fetish. The man was obsessed. In his hands, it became a deliverer of justice.

When Walt refused to come out, he hit him on the arm with the baton – or PR 24. Walt stayed put. Jefferson hit him again and finally Walt had had enough. He emerged, to be charged with Section 4A of the Public Order Act, a minor offence somewhat tarted up by being racially aggravated. Section 4A is easy to prove. All the prosecution must show is that a person intended to cause someone 'harassment, alarm or distress' and in doing so used 'threatening, abusive or insulting words or behaviour thereby causing that person [or any other person, present or not] harassment, alarm or distress'. Section 4A is a catch-all offence that is designed to finger 'scrotes' like poor Walt.

In his instructions Walt was adamant that he'd never told Jefferson that he was going to get him, or called him a nigger. What distressed him was that he wouldn't be believed. 'I might as well just plead guilty cause they're not going to believe me,' he said. It's not unusual to have defendants want to plead guilty because they think anything coming from them will be disbelieved. Walt, like me, never won. His list of convictions was endless. I might've had all the breaks in life and he might've had none, but for that afternoon we were in the same boat and fighting for each other. While the mutual bond of self-interest between the rabbi killer and me felt immoral, the job of speaking up for Walt felt right, it felt necessary. Suddenly, it was reassuring that we had a system where someone from privilege, even an incompetent like me, spoke on behalf of someone who had nothing. I could be making money in the City or saving large companies dollops of tax, but instead our justice system had me standing up for someone society is taught to despise.

A witness's effectiveness is based on three things: credibility, truthfulness and accuracy. These categories, of course, impact on each other, so if you can undermine a witness – be it a prosecution witness or the defendant – in one of them, then you can make inroads into the other categories as well. Lay magistrates are very unlikely to believe that a police officer is lying, so attacking a police officer's truthfulness is rarely the best way to start. The way to undermine Jefferson, I decided, was to scrutinize the credibility of his actions rather than his position as a police officer. Jefferson's vulnerability was his weakness for his PR 24. It would become the star of the show. The question would no longer be whether Walt was guilty but why Jefferson was so eager to beat him.

ME: You came running back into the garden when you heard the words. Yes?

JEFFERSON: That's right.

ME: All the boys except Walt jumped over the back wall, didn't they?

JEFFERSON: Yes.

ME: You weren't ever going to catch them?

JEFFERSON: Well ... probably not. I knew who they were.

ME: Walt ran into the house.

JEFFERSON: Yes.

ME: He was much easier to catch, wasn't he?

JEFFERSON: He was the one who called me those names.

ME: Answer the question, please.

JEFFERSON: Yes. So?

ME: You came charging into the house. You had your stab vest on.

JEFFERSON: Yes.

ME: You were holding your pepper spray.

JEFFERSON: I was protecting myself. I thought I could be in danger. (*Jefferson is 15 stone plus. Walt is a shade over 10 stone.*)

ME: Is that why you also had what you refer to in your witness statement as your PR 24? To protect yourself?

JEFFERSON: Yes.

ME: Please tell the court what a PR 24 is.

JEFFERSON: It's my police baton.

ME: You found Walt under a bunk bed, didn't you?

JEFFERSON: Yes.

ME: You said in your evidence earlier that you were frightened?

JEFFERSON: Yes.

ME: Walt was wedged under the bed.

JEFFERSON: No.

ME: He was under the bed, wasn't he?

JEFFERSON: Yes.

ME: Half-trapped and barely able to move.

JEFFERSON: No.

ME: Are you seriously telling this court that you were frightened by a boy half your size wedged under a bed?

JEFFERSON: He lunged at me.

ME: Lunged at you, did he? Was it an ankle strike?

JEFFERSON: He lunged.

ME: No. You just hit him, didn't you? With your PR 24.

JEFFERSON: He lunged.

ME: You hit him because you wanted to, because you'd lost your temper?

JEFFERSON: No.

ME: Big man, aren't you, hitting a boy with your PR 24?

JEFFERSON: I was protecting myself.

ME: From a boy stuck under a bed?

(*Jefferson does not answer that question.*)

ME: Come on. Own up. You hit him because you were angry.

JEFFERSON: That's not true.

ME: Because he called you a 'funny fucker'.

JEFFERSON: No.

ME: A funny fucker.

JEFFERSON: No.

ME: Did you feel ridiculous when he called you that?

JEFFERSON: He called me other things as well.

ME: You singled Walt out and beat him with your PR 24, because he was the only one there to beat?

JEFFERSON: No.

ME: Because, I suggest to you, his only 'crime' was his cheek.

For once, Walt didn't lose his temper when he was cross-examined. He gave his account that it wasn't he who shouted out the words. The magistrates, a slab-faced trio of market town hair-dos and Rotarian ties, were faced with having to choose between backing up a black police officer (thin on the ground in Northampton) and believing Walt. I expected yet another defeat but they came back an hour later and found him not guilty. I don't know who was more surprised, Walt or me. We might've both been losers but we'd won. It meant a lot to Walt. For the first time in his life he'd succeeded at something. He hadn't lost his cool and had been believed. Would he now finally discover some self-worth, even if it were only for an afternoon? Would it inspire him to turn his life around? I didn't know, but I was sure that I had not only seen justice done but helped achieve it. For the first time, I thought that maybe this was a job that I could do after all.

Back in chambers I found that my success was double-edged. My instructing solicitor in Northampton had been so shocked by my victory that he kept sending me back there. A few weeks later I bumped into Walt's prosecutor. Jefferson Chait, the cop with the baton, she told me, had been so offended by my cross-examination that he had written to the CPS complaining. It was the best – and only – compliment that I've been paid at the criminal bar. For a second I felt like Northampton police station's most feared man. Buoyed by success and praise, I thought I was clearly ready for meatier, weightier work. I thought I was ready for a jury trial.

5. The Unlikely Story of Trial by Jury

What is the big fuss about jury trials? They pay badly, they don't bring you fame and they certainly aren't going to make you any more attractive or interesting. People with starred firsts from Oxford and Cambridge don't aspire to them. They head for the top commercial sets and, God willing, seven-figure pay packets. Their time isn't spent in court: they sit in chambers beneath their massive brains, sucking in information as a basking shark sucks in plankton, which they then squeeze through their synapses until an elegant legal argument falls out of their heads with a metallic 'plink'. If they do go to court, it's to pick over banking deals gone bad in front of judges squirrelled away in hard-to-find corners of the Royal Courts of Justice. They're long-winded, too. Notoriously, one leading commercial silk* (who commands fees of up to £1,000 an hour) spent eighty days opening a trial. So that's before any evidence is heard. Eighty days! The bank that he was representing didn't need to care: the shareholders were paying. Pull that stunt before a jury and they, with the judge cheering them on, would break your legs.

The commercial and chancery (equity, trusts and wills) bars think of criminal barristers as their idiot cousins. To them we're more knockabout hacks than lawyers, adept only at low practices and sub 'Punch and Judy' dust-ups. There is one small consolation: our work, trial by jury, holds a significance and mystique that the fancier, astronomically paid commercial disputes do not.

---

* A 'silk' is a Queen's Counsel. QCs are referred to as 'silks' because they wear a silk gown.

Ask the average person in the street to describe a trial and they'll sketch out a criminal trial with a judge, a jury, barristers and a defendant in the dock. Jury trials and their trappings exist in our collective subconscious. I suspect that if a person were pushed for some detail, he'd describe a Victorian court with a judge perched high above the courtroom like a god looking down from a cloud. I'd put money on them giving a decent approximation of Court No. 1 at the Bailey – the pinnacle for any criminal trial lawyer.

I didn't get within spitting distance of Oxbridge and never impressed the examiners much, which might be why I, dumbly, aspired not to happy remunerative hours immersed in the 1986 Companies Act but to mixing it up in Court No. 1. I wasn't lured by its high Victorian splendour. Unlike most criminal barristers, bought off by the fancy dress in lieu of a proper wage, I would happily lose the frippery of wig and gown. What enticed me were the shouts from the public gallery, the telling silences, the violent outbursts, and the resigned dumbfoundment as the evidence, with its jaw-dropping twists and turns, plays out. The criminal courts are beguiling because their currency is the human condition. They pick through the half-truths, the tragedies, the awful luck, hapless lies, grinding stupidity, bottomless greed and zero self-control with a gimlet eye fixed on the revealing detail.

Many foreign jurisdictions provide a venue and a story but the masterstroke of the English common law was to bring in an audience, and not just any old audience but one with a vote.* Without the jury there would be no real drama. If it were a judge sitting alone, we'd have a few witnesses, make a legal argument or two

---

*'Common law' is the term used to describe the English legal tradition, which has set us apart, legally speaking, from the European tradition of Roman law. It's called common law because, backed up by the monarch's authority, it applies to everyone, superseding local rules and customs. Common law also means law created by judges rather than Parliament, who, in deciding cases, establish legal precedents that future courts must follow.

and a verdict would be delivered with all the heart-stopping excitement of the results of a planning application. A jury means the criminal courts have to put on a show: immerse themselves in structure, character and plot. The real splendour is not in Court No. 1's stucco and wood panelling but in the high theatre played out for twelve people randomly pulled off the street.

I became a criminal barrister for those twelve people. With a jury, I figured, even I had a chance. I'd always hankered to be a music-hall 'song and dance man', a Jimmy Cagney, but being tone deaf and clumsy, not to mention sixty years too late, meant that the last redoubt for the likes of me was the criminal courtroom. It was the closest approximation that I could find. A barrister (like any song and dance man worth his salt) must have a repertoire and a style but must also be able to improvise: turn on a sixpence, tell a joke, conjure a gasp, extort a tear and, if his back is really against the wall, argue the law with dazzling persuasiveness. To do it successfully it's essential to like a risk, a punt, because in court we are all punters, trying our hands at a game of chance. Trials are a parachute-free plunge into the unknown. You have to enjoy the sticky, unwholesome fear that commands the pit of your stomach when you stand up to address the jury. Love the allure of the unforeseen piece of evidence. Want to obey the insistent voice in your head coolly suggesting you ask that last question which could either seize victory or consign your client to defeat.

Jury trials are real-life drama played for the highest stakes before a randomly selected audience which owes you and your client exactly nothing. On the face of it, it's a crazy system. Twelve people whose only qualifications are that they have been living in Britain for five years, haven't been convicted of a criminal offence and, as far as anyone can tell, aren't mad. Can it really be better than an impartial judge considering all the evidence, the way they do in continental Europe? More importantly, is it any fairer? Any better than tossing a coin?

The truth is that much of the jury trial's mystique and power lies in the faith we invest in it. It signifies something, defines us and the society that we like to think we live in. Trial by jury has become not only our right as British (or American, Australian, New Zealand, Canadian ...) citizens, but a mysterious bulwark protecting individual liberty from the oppressive state. William Blackstone, in his 1765 book on criminal law and practice, described the importance of the jury trial like this:

Trial by jury ever has been and I trust ever will be, looked upon as the glory of the English law ... it is the most transcendent privilege which any subject can enjoy, or wish for, that he cannot be affected either in his property, his liberty, or his person, but by the unanimous consent of twelve of his neighbours and equals.[1]

Two hundred and fifty years later our quasi-religious faith in the jury trial has not been shaken. Sadakat Kadri, in his book *The Trial: A History from Socrates to OJ Simpson*, argues that the source of our faith wasn't so much the jury itself as the surrounding publicity. Jury trials, comprised of ordinary citizens, are by definition open to public scrutiny. By the seventeenth century, the exciting ones were written up in pamphlets and newspapers and pored over by the reading public. People, whole families armed with picnics, came to watch them. Justice was out in the open, done because it was seen to be done.

Pope Innocent III kicks the game off

The exact roots of trial by jury are unclear and disputed. They lie tangled somewhere in the Anglo-Saxon and Frankish past. Certainly its origins, based on the idea of a group of men swearing to vouch a piece of information as true, are extremely old. Since the

Dark Ages, juries, so-called because they swore oaths to God, have been used to settle boundary disputes, affirm numbers of livestock on given pieces of land and name suspects of crime.[2] After 1066, the Normans kept up the Anglo-Saxon jury of accusation. These juries named names but they did not decide guilt and innocence. The business end was determined either through trial by ordeal or trial by combat.

If its roots are murky, the jury's move into criminal trials is much more precisely known. In 1215 Innocent III and the Fourth Lateran Council ended trial by ordeal by formally banning the clergy, who presided over them for a fee (naturally), from participating.[*] One method was to place a red-hot poker (sometimes cooled a bit if suspicion was weak) in the palm of an alleged wrongdoer which would then be bandaged up. A few days later the hand was checked: if it were healing nicely you were in the clear; if not, your burnt palm was the least of your problems. Trial by combat, the other accepted method of determining guilt or innocence, was impractical for the vast majority of the population and already falling into disuse. It was finally removed from the English statute books only in 1819 after an obsessively well-prepared appellant claimed his right to one by literally throwing down his gauntlet.[3]

With trials by ordeal and combat dying out, a new way had to be found. Continental Europe plugged the gap with the adoption of Roman canonical law. England demurred, repelled by the evidential rule that a person could be found guilty of a capital crime only if there were either two eyewitnesses or a confession. In theory, the rule existed to guard against judicial tyranny and error. In reality, it meant that to secure convictions the judiciary sanctioned torture called *la preuve légale*. Smashing legs and pouring boiling water on the wounds was one particularly trusted method to assist

---

[*]The Council was troubled about whether humans as post-lapsarian sinners had the right to ask for God's intervention in trivial and earthly human affairs.

the prosecution in discharging their evidential burden.[4] The English alternative, announced by royal proclamation in 1219, was trial by jury. The new system wasn't necessarily less barbaric than its European counterpart. If you refused to enter a plea, meaning you did not recognize the authority of the jury and the court, you were thrown in jail and squashed under weights – known as *peine forte et dure* – until you either changed your mind or died.

A thirteenth-century jury trial was completely different from the one we have today. There were two juries: the jury of presentment (the progenitor of the grand jury, discontinued in 1933 but still used in the United States), which decided whether to bring a charge or not, and the petty jury, which deliberated at the trial. These were not two completely separate bodies and often members of the presentment jury sat at the trial as well. The jury didn't just decide upon the facts, they also investigated the crime and asked the questions at trial. As 'neighbours' of the accused, drawn from the immediate locale, the jury knew who he or she was, and they were, in a way, quite well equipped to run the criminal investigation and evaluate the accused's character. Decisions were based on the 'done thing' as much as on any knowledge of the alleged incident. Concepts such as evidence or proof didn't exist. The jurors were charged with coming to a true answer to the matter in issue. They were pretty lenient: only about a quarter of trials led to conviction.

The pendulum swings to the prosecution

At first, 'breaching the King's peace' aside, prosecutions were private matters brought by the citizenry. Private prosecutions continued well into the nineteenth century but, as early as the 1400s, the state, irked by the jury's tendency to let defendants off, increasingly took an interest in how important prosecutions (those involving the government's political interests) were conducted. The growth of the Tudor state and the concomitant extension of the royal courts in the sixteenth century gradually led to a more organized system of criminal prosecution. The key reform was the introduction of Justices of the Peace (JPs). JPs were drawn from the local gentry. Much as they do today, JPs tried minor crimes while the royal assizes moved around the country dealing with the more serious matters. Their most important role was running the pre-trial investigation, which had once been the prerogative of the jury of presentment. This meant that they no longer had to rely on the jury for 'the facts' of the case. JPs could issue search and arrest warrants, compel prosecution witnesses to attend court and remand people in custody until trial. They were not neutral investigators but assisted the private prosecutor in building a case against the accused.

Despite the semi-professionalization of the prosecution authorities, the accused did not have anyone to speak on his behalf. Compelling the attendance of witnesses to support your defence was entirely at the judge's discretion. Most defendants were on their own. They had no warning of what the charges were or who the prosecution witnesses would be until the witnesses came into court to make their accusations.

Up until the nineteenth century, the confrontation between accused and accusers was the centrepiece of the criminal trial. The jury assessed the accused's spontaneous response, in his own words rather than through the cipher of defence counsel, to the allegations made against him.* The prevailing view was that something mysterious happened when the defendant spoke, especially if he or she were innocent. The eighteenth-century jurist William Hawkins

---

*The defendant was barred from testifying under oath to save him from committing the sin of perjury and thereby condemning his soul to burn in hell fire for all eternity. This rule was not abolished until the passing of the Criminal Evidence Act in 1898.

described an accused speaking in his own defence as requiring 'no manner of Skill to make a plain and honest Defense. The Simplicity and Innocence, artless and ingenuous behaviour of one whose conscience acquits him ... is more moving and convincing than the highest Eloquence of Persons speaking in a Cause not their own.'[5]

I suspect that an accused's chances of being believed turned on how well he came across rather than any magic of 'simplicity and innocence'. An educated, fluent defendant, or a natural actor, had a better chance of presenting himself as a credible, honest person than a tongue-tied, illiterate one. Whatever your ability, you had to talk fast because, unlike today, jury trials were searingly quick: defendants were routinely tried and convicted in fifteen minutes or less. Juries often heard several trials in one go, keeping the verdicts for each one in their heads.

Judge vs. jury: a very political arm-wrestle

In the aftermath of the Civil War, battles between politically motivated judges and independently minded juries underscored an age-old structural fissure in the jury trial: namely, who had ultimate competence over the facts of a case? Was it the judge or was it the jury? Yes, juries decided the facts; the issue was whether they could be wrong. Was their decision, even if made against the weight of the evidence, unassailable, or was a 'false' verdict effectively a lie and therefore an act of perjury, punishable by the judge? Fining jurors for suspect verdicts was by no means unknown.

It was the prosecution of two Quakers – William Penn, the son of an admiral, and Thomas Mead, a draper – which resolved the contradiction lying at the heart of the jury trial. When Charles II was restored as king, his new government moved quickly to reassert the authority of the Anglican Church of which Charles was head. The most heavy-handed of their measures was the Conventicle Act of 1664, banning Nonconformists from worshipping in groups of more than four. Breaching the Act was a serious crime punishable by hanging or transportation. In August 1670 the Act was up for renewal. Penn, Mead and about 400 other Quakers planned to hold a prayer meeting in a hall on Gracechurch Street to protest against it. When they arrived they found the hall locked. Penn seized his chance and began to address the gathering in the street. The authorities swooped.

Two weeks later he and Mead stood trial at the Bailey, charged, not under the Conventicle Act, which would have given them a chance to ridicule it, but under the common law for addressing a tumultuous assembly. The case was a humdinger, pitting freedom of religious belief against authoritarian state control. The judges – the Lord Mayor of London, Simon Starling, and Recorder Sir Thomas Howel, both ardent Royalists – also acted as prosecutors. Penn's and Mead's defence was that while they had spoken in the street they had not incited violence and therefore could not be guilty of an offence.

It was a deeply unpleasant trial. Before it had even started the tone was set when Howel heavily fined Penn and Mead for refusing to take off their hats in court (a Quaker eccentricity). Penn, who had trained as a lawyer, spent most of the trial in a pit below the court into which Howel had consigned him for being impudent enough to try to set out a defence.[6] The prosecution witnesses were not brilliant. They remembered Penn and Mead preaching to the crowd but could not remember what they preached about. At the end of the evidence the jury couldn't agree a verdict. Eight were for conviction and four, led by a juror called Edward Bushel, were for acquittal. They were sent away to continue their deliberations and return the guilty verdict that the judges demanded. When they came back there was bad news for the Recorder and the Mayor. Bushel had been elected foreman. And worse, the jury had found Penn guilty of speaking in the street (not an offence under the common law) and Mead not guilty at all. The case transcript drily records the judges' reaction: 'This both Mayor and Recorder resented at so high a rate, that they exceeded the bounds of all reason and civility.'

In 1670, if a jury couldn't reach a verdict, jurors were locked up without food, water or even a candle. (The rule that a jury could not separate until a verdict had been given was not abolished until 1870.) Recorder Howel recovered enough equilibrium to say, no doubt through clenched teeth, 'Gentlemen, you shall not be dismissed till we have a verdict that the court will accept; and you shall be locked up, without meat, drink, fire, and tobacco; you shall not think thus to abuse the court; we will have a verdict, by the help of God, or you shall starve for it.'

And with that threat ringing in their ears the jurors, along with the defendants, were hauled off for a seriously uncomfortable night in Newgate jail.

When the court reconvened the next day, the jury stood firm. Penn had spoken in Gracechurch Street but no more. Not good enough, bellowed the judges. The jury and the defendants trooped off back to Newgate. The following day the jury had changed their verdict, but not as Recorder Howel and the Lord Mayor had hoped: they found both Penn and Mead not guilty at all. The two judges were incandescent. Howel imposed enormous fines on all the jurors for returning an 'unjust verdict'. Anyone who didn't immediately pay would go to prison indefinitely. Bushel and three other jurors refused to cough up; back to Newgate they went.

Newgate wasn't just incarceration but a potential death sentence. 'Gaol fever' – an exceptionally aggressive form of typhus – and dysentery were rife. Eighty years later, in 1750, during a particularly virulent outbreak a full one-fifth of Newgate's inmates awaiting trial died, along with 'two judges, various court staff, the Lord Mayor of London' and '[o]f less note, Gentleman of the Bar, two or three students ... and Forty other Persons, whom business or curiosity had brought thither'.[7] Bushel, however, didn't die.

After two and a half months inside, Chief Justice Vaughan heard Bushel's writ for *habeas corpus*, which was the way for a person held in custody to be brought to court in order for the court to test the legality of that person's detention. Vaughan's conclusion that a court may not fine a juror for his verdict if they had acted in good faith is one of the seminal rulings in the English common law. Vaughan drew a distinction between a witness who swears to what he has seen or heard and a juror who swears 'to what he can infer and conclude from testimony of such witnesses by the act and force of his understanding'. In other words, there is a fundamental difference between what a witness knows and what a juror believes.

Vaughan's ruling is so important because it stopped judges dictating verdicts through threats of punishment and therefore limited the state's ability to lock up people it didn't like. Juries in the majority of cases might agree with the judge's own view of the evidence, and they might also heed his directions as to how to apply the law, but they were not bound by them. Guilt and innocence were their preserve and their preserve alone. The ruling meant that even if the evidence pointed towards a defendant's guilt, the jury could refuse to accept it. Vaughan had handed jurors the power to dismiss cases that they found offensive to their consciences, no matter what the letter of the law or weight of evidence might say. From that point on, the idea that the jury was the bulwark protecting individuals from the depredations of an oppressive state was guaranteed. It's an article of faith that remains to this day.

The dawn of lawyers and their fiddly rules

Vaughan's ruling did not protect people from the show trials of the Popish Plot of 1678, a so-called Catholic plot to kill King

Charles II, or Judge Jeffreys's Bloody Assizes in 1685, conducted to punish supporters of Charles's illegitimate son, the Duke of Monmouth, who had led an uprising against James II. These horrors were seen as demonstrations of a corrupt, absolutist monarchy and a conniving judiciary, which in part provided the impetus for the Glorious Revolution and the reassertion of Parliament's supremacy over the monarchy. The fundamental change of the Glorious Revolution also meant reform in the courts that would have a profound, long-term impact on the criminal justice system. The Treason Trials Act of 1696, passed in response to the judicial killings under Charles and James, gave defendants, for the first time, the right to call witnesses in their defence. It also, quite importantly from my own selfish point of view, guaranteed defendants charged with treason the right to representation by defence counsel. For a long time the effect of the reforms was not at all obvious. The Act limited defence lawyers' rights of audience to treason trials alone. What it did provide was the statutory footing for the concept of defence barristers appearing in court on behalf of defendants.[8] The Act operated like a sleeper cell. Once Parliament had established the precedent in law, judges felt able gradually to extend defence counsel's right of audience to other serious felony charges. The huge majority of cases were still prosecuted and defended without lawyers. It wasn't until the 1780s that the trickle of lawyers going through the door that the Treason Trial Act had opened became a stampede.[9]

The advent of professional lawyers on both sides of the case meant that the old performers of judge and jury slowly melted into the background. The judge increasingly became a passive, though highly influential, referee, presiding over the courtroom fray. The jury, too, no longer charged with asking the questions, fell silent. Even the accused, once the undisputed star of the show, had to settle for a cameo role. Before anyone realized, partial lawyers, rather than supposedly neutral judges, were taking over the way criminal trials were conducted. It was a slow-motion putsch.

Lawyers brought rules. Up until the beginning of the eighteenth century there was no real concept of evidence. By arguing to exclude unhelpful testimony, or to include things that assisted a client, gradually a body of evidential rules, created from judicial decisions in cases, was built up. It is from this period that the rule prohibiting hearsay – 'any statement other than one made by a person while giving oral evidence in the proceedings ... as evidence of any fact or opinion stated' – was established.

Competing lawyers vigorously putting their respective cases fatally undermined the trial as a truth-seeking exercise. These lawyers did not believe, like William Hawkins, that 'simplicity and innocence' of testimony would save a defendant from conviction. They believed that a prosecution witness's evidence must be challenged and undermined. With lawyers in on the act, trials became adversarial clashes between two opposing narratives. Nothing embodies the adversarial nature of a trial better than the cross-examination of witnesses. William Garrow, the first star of the criminal bar, described the objective of cross-examination like this:

[A]ll that it is permitted to us who stand as counsel for prisoners is to endeavour, by such questions as may occur to us, to impress on the minds of the Jury observations tending to excite distrust of the evidence ...[10]

The key words here are 'to excite distrust of the evidence', in which he includes the witnesses themselves. Garrow's soft-pedalling of the power of cross-examination is wholly disingenuous. In his hands it was a devastating weapon. His exchange with William Grove, the complainant (the person complaining that he has been wronged) and also prosecutor of a highway robbery, recorded in the *Old Bailey Sessions Papers*, captures his muscular style. Grove is alleging that the defendant, James Wingrove, had robbed him. He has bolstered his story by claiming that two other men had made a complaint to the local JP that Wingrove had robbed them as well.

GARROW: Who are these two men, let us hear a little about them?

GROVE: They are not here.

GARROW: What business are they, are they not a sort of moon-light men [i.e. smugglers]?

GROVE: It was not moon-light.

GARROW: Are they not a couple of smugglers?

GROVE: They may be as far as I know.

GARROW: So they told you they had been robbed?

GROVE: Yes.

GARROW: Did they give any charge against Mr Wingrove?

GROVE: I do not know what you mean by charges.

GARROW: I believe you do, you are pretty well used to charges; did these two smugglers of yours give any charge against this prisoner?

GROVE: They are not smugglers of mine.

GARROW: They are friends of yours?

GROVE: They are no friends of mine.

GARROW: They, these two fellows, did they make any charge against Mr Wingrove for robbing them?

GROVE: Yes, they did make a charge.

GARROW: Do not shuffle, Master Grove.

GROVE: I do not know what to say.

GARROW: I will make you know directly; upon your oath, did not these two men attend the next day at [the JP's office], and say that Wingrove was not one of the men who robbed them?

Garrow forces Grove into conceding that no charge had been made by the two men. Having destroyed his credibility and exposed him as a liar, Garrow moves to Grove's motives for bringing the prosecution, namely the statutory reward one received for evidence that led to the conviction of a highwayman.[11]

GARROW: You know it's not every day that one gets forty pounds for hanging a man; had you no conversation at the *Cock* at Stains [*sic*] about the reward for a conviction?

GROVE: You ask a hundred questions, I will answer you what I know; no, not about no reward, I have been there, and there they have been asking about it, that is, we drank together, and I said to him, as I might say to you, I do not know anything about it. I did not say any such thing, I never said anything about any reward, that I can say, I have said nothing about no reward.

Grove by this point is in a death spiral of blather. His answers are irrelevant. It's Garrow's statement, dressed up as a question, about the £40 reward that is doing the damage. Garrow is not finished. He continues his line of attack with Grove's son who is also claiming that he has been robbed. 'What coloured clothes are you to have out of the reward of forty pounds?' he asks. 'Did not your father promise you a suite of new clothes, if you would stick to him?'[12]

Reading these exchanges you can hear the acid sarcasm in Garrow's voice as he pushes Grove into admissions that sink his prosecution. Lawyers like Garrow took sides for money, as they do today. Many were not reliable: if you bought them, they didn't necessarily stay bought. A contemporary solicitor complained that he'd send briefs and fees to counsel, which they'd accept but then not appear at court. The only way to guarantee the acceptance of a brief was if an up-front retainer was additionally paid. Mix these practices together with vicious cross-examinations and evidential wheezes and it's not surprising that, even before Garrow arrived on the scene, criminal barristers had already earned themselves a bad reputation. A pamphlet in 1764 warned law students of 'how ignominious the name and character of a *mere* Old Bailey Counsel may justly appear'.[13] In the mid nineteenth century the *Law Times* was blunter: 'The

world ... knows, and has long known, that "An Old Bailey Prac-
titioner" is a byword for disgrace and infamy.'[14]

I read those traducings as a compliment. Sailing close to the
wind is often the only way to secure an acquittal. The stakes in the
eighteenth and early nineteenth centuries were higher than they
are today. Misjudge things and your client didn't just go to jail,
he hanged. Garrow was more than merely a brilliant courtroom
advocate: by arguing the law he played a significant role in establishing the right to silence and the presumption someone is innocent
until proven guilty – concepts which we now regard as essential to
a fair trial.

The theme of Garrow's cross-examination of Grove had a
proper grounding. In those days thief-takers betrayed criminals
for the reward money. It was a corrupt and unscrupulous trade,
which the authorities connived in so they could get convictions.

The most notorious group of thief-takers was the Macdaniel gang
who suckered people into participating in robberies. The 'victim' of
the robbery was also a gang member. After the robbery was committed, the victim would grass the mark to the authorities and then
give evidence against the mark at trial. Once the person had been
convicted and hanged, they'd pocket the reward. Macdaniel and his
crew were eventually found out but the authorities failed to prosecute them for murder. Instead they were convicted of perjury and
put in the public pillory, where one of them was stoned to death.[15]

Counsel was a way to even things up. Not that it necessarily
helped the poor. Eleanor Eddacres, tried at the Bailey in 1757 for
forging a bond, a capital offence, when asked why she was not
represented by counsel lamented, 'I have not a six penny piece left
to pay a porter, much less to fee counsel. If I must die because I am
poor, I can't help it.'[16] She swung. Legal advice could've saved her
life. In forgery cases it was not unknown for the prosecutor to
prepare two indictments: the first one alleging forgery, which carried the death penalty; the second, passing a forged note with

intent, which carried a sentence of transportation to the American colonies. If you pleaded guilty to the second indictment, the prosecutor then offered no evidence on the first.

The nineteenth century saw a growing trend towards professionalization of the criminal justice system. Lawyers navigated their way through ever more complex rules of evidence. A newly formed police force took over criminal investigations and developed increasingly sophisticated techniques to detect crime, which in turn meant more witnesses and more paper. The knock-on effect of all this activity was that trials got longer and longer. In 1800 a Bailey courtroom could get through twenty a day.[17] Justice was swift. The lengthening of the time trials took threatened to gum the system up. It was decided that the jury trial had to be rationed. Parliament stepped in, passing a series of Acts greatly increasing the number of offences which could be tried summarily – without a jury – in the magistrates' court.[18]

The other way of keeping the wheel of justice turning was the guilty plea. Up until the 1900s, pleading guilty, other than through the occasional deal between the prosecution and defence of the sort that might have saved Eleanor Eddacres, was rare. Judges, schooled from a time when defendants were unrepresented, believed it was their duty to ensure that the accused should not be penalized for not being conversant with the law. Practical realities began to erode the old principle and by the latter part of the nineteenth century, everything had changed. Judges were literally imploring defendants to 'cough' to charges, offering inducements in the form of reduced sentences as credit to those prepared to own up to their crimes. This reward is now formalized in law. Every defendant knows that he will get a discount of one third on his sentence – potentially all the difference between going inside and staying out – if he pleads guilty. In the last 200 years we've gone from over 90 per cent of cases ending in a jury trial to today, where it's more like 2 per cent.[19]

Unless a defendant is what barristers term as 'totally stuffed', guilty pleas are arrived at through making a deal, which is known at the criminal bar as 'carving the case'. It's a brilliantly apposite expression. You can just picture an expert hand slicing through the evidence to produce the agreed apportionment. I'll give an example of how it works. A defence barrister is representing a client who is charged on indictment (the list of offences that the prosecution says the defendant has committed) with a dwelling burglary and theft of a motor vehicle. He comes to court for the first day of trial. Prosecution counsel is in the bar mess eating eggs and bacon. Defence counsel sidles up and says, 'Any chance of carving it?' Prosecution counsel responds, 'What are you offering?' 'Guilty to the burglary in exchange for you dropping the theft of the motor,' he replies. Prosecution counsel thinks about this as he mops up the remains of his egg with a piece of fried bread. 'I'll tell you what,' he says between mouthfuls, 'if he has the burglary on full facts – (Let's say in this case that there is evidence of sophisticated planning, which will 'up' the sentence) – I'll drop the theft.' Defence counsel grins and says, 'You're on.' One vital step remains. Prosecution and defence counsel have to persuade their respective clients to agree to the deal. Prosecuting counsel must sell it to the Crown Prosecution Service and defence counsel to the defendant.

There is a loose convention that when you carve a case each side must have a piece. The size of the piece each side gets varies according to the circumstances of the case and the ability of one barrister to browbeat the other. Often when you carve a case up, it means a defendant pleading to the main count in return for lesser counts against him being dropped, as described above. Another popular way of carving a case is to have the defendant pleading on a 'basis of plea', which is a document signed by each side setting out the agreed facts of the case. The judge is then invited, though not obliged, to sentence on that basis. From the defence's point of view, a basis of plea is drawn up to minimize the seriousness of the offence and thus help in reducing any likely sentence. Deals are almost always cut at the door of the court. It's amazing how the prospect of a trial concentrates the mind of advocates and defendants alike.

Fairness

Increased numbers of witnesses and ever more paper did not mean that trials suddenly became fair. More and more counsel were prosecuting and defending cases but defendants, even those charged with murder, continued to go unrepresented. Public funding for defendants didn't appear until 1903, and then it depended on the judge agreeing that in the interests of justice it should be paid. Legal aid for all criminal cases was finally introduced only in 1949.

The great advocates of the late nineteenth and early twentieth centuries on both sides of the Atlantic, such as Clarence Darrow, Edward Marshall Hall and Edward Carson, have given way to a more paper-oriented and even technocratic advocate. The trial itself has changed in the same way. Florid speeches have been replaced by expensively produced diagrams and written argument. More and more of trial work is being done outside the trial. Criminal barristers are not in any danger of becoming like their rich commercial barrister cousins up on the hill but we are more like them than we were fifteen years ago. This is not a bad thing: no one has the attention span to listen to a five-hour speech any more. The job of the criminal barrister, however, has not changed. It is the same as in Garrow's day: to try to get the client off. To do that today, as in the past, you have to take the judge and jury with you, by making them *want* to listen to you.

I like to think criminal barristers still have a reputation for infamy and disgrace, especially among the political class. We irritate the government by getting our clients acquitted and messing up the conviction rate. The government has repaid the compliment by trying unsuccessfully to curtail the number of jury trials. Despite these attempts, trial by jury has survived because its importance has endured. The public might bay for blood when terrible crimes are committed, but equally their support for juries deciding verdicts remains unshaken. Trial by jury brings a freshness and independence of mind to trials and keeps justice out in the open.

Looking for justice can be like hunting the snark — all about dispiriting process. The early twenty-first-century trial emphasizes process as the way to guarantee a fair trial. But fairness, as Lord Bingham, a former senior law lord, put it, remains 'a constantly evolving subject'. Today it represents what has been described as a 'triangulation of interests' which includes fairness between the victim and his family, the accused and the public. For true fairness you also need an equality between the prosecution and the defence. There should be well-briefed, clever advocates on both sides, a judge mediating each side's interests and, lastly, an independently minded jury, who are prepared to do a 'Bushel' and do what they feel is right rather than what they're told.

It's a myth to say that trial by jury is an ancient right of English common law, just as it's a myth to assert that in the seventeenth century the jury was a bulwark of liberty. But by participating in jury trials, I hoped I could somehow help make these myths true. I wanted to live up to the names of the great advocates such as Darrow, Marshall Hall and Carson. I might not have had their talent but I had enough of their advocate's vanity. I liked to think that as part of the barrister class I could make a positive contribution to justice. Sounds pompous? Sure. But I thought that if you possessed a bit of an ego and a pitiless will to win, conducting a trial before a real live jury was the only place to be.

6. The Shelf of Dreams

At around five in the afternoon resistance in the pupils' room began to weaken. Inevitably, Liam was the first to crack. Unlike the rest of us, he was honest about his capitulation. 'I can't stand this any longer,' he'd announce and stomp upstairs. Several minutes later he'd be back, brief-less. 'I know I'm going to Harlow Youth Court. I always go to Harlow Youth Court,' he wailed.

We'd pretend not to notice, ostentatiously punching holes in papers, retying old briefs in ever more elaborate knots, silently biding our time. Then, one by one, we made our own lame excuses to go upstairs. I'd claim anything no matter how embarrassing – 'I'm going for a shit' or 'It's wank time. Back in a mo' – rather than admit the truth, namely a recce to the post room and the shelf where the junior clerks laid out the briefs for the next day. That shelf meant everything to us. It was our shelf of dreams. How we wished that we, like the grandest silks, could be defending notorious murderers or prosecuting psychopaths.

That afternoon, I was the last to go up. I loitered by the shelf pretending to read correspondence from my pigeonhole while one eye, swivelling like a chameleon's, scoured the shelf for the work I hungered after – the murders, conspiracies and terrorist plots. To be honest, I'd settle for anything so long as it wasn't my reality of suburban magistrates' courts and petty crime. 'Please let it not be Harlow Youth Court,' I prayed. You had to run the gauntlet there, past the defendants and their families gobbing by the entrance. If your luck was really out, you were threatened on the bus back to the station.

There I was, lingering in the post room, when the briefs finally began to arrive. Mamta got two sentences at Snaresbrook Crown Court. *Two*. I could do that, I said to myself. Liam, smirking and red-faced, waved his plea and case management hearing (PCMH) brief in front of me. It was a plum job.

'Look at this, Alex. I can tell it's going to "carve". See all these papers. The fee on this brief's got to be worth £500. You'll be off to Harlow Youth Court, I expect. When you're covered in under-class spit, I'll still be in bed.'

He was right. Someone always had to go to Harlow Youth Court, which like the Angel of Death could not be denied a soul. Why couldn't I go to the crown court? What was wrong with me? I was seized with the insecurity to which all barristers, no matter their seniority, succumb: have the clerks taken against me? Do they think I'm not up to the job? They're right – I'm not up to the job. I'm a miserable failure.

At 6.30, with everyone gone, a slim folder arrived, tied in white ribbon. What was this? Defence briefs come in pink ribbon. 'Trial at Southwark Crown Court, sir. Prosecuting.' My first jury trial and I was *prosecuting*. The shelf of dreams loved a laugh. Excitement flooded every part of me but outwardly I kept my cool. Don't look grateful. Look as though it was your birthright. Then the clerks would give you more. Where was Liam? I wanted to crow. A second later he came through the door looking crestfallen. His brief had been incorrectly allocated. Liam was bound for Harlow Youth Court after all. I danced a sailor's jig in front of him, whistling the theme tune to *Captain Pugwash*, waving my crown court trial in his face.

When I got home the excitement had drained away to leave the cold reality. Getting the brief you want feels good for about thirty seconds until you remember that you have to prepare the thing, agonize over it and make sure you don't fuck it up.

It all began when the local street-level crack dealers realized that between five and six in the morning, as the day shift took over from the night shift at Shoreditch police station, Hackney lay unprotected. For a whole hour the dealers did a handsome trade in early-bird specials. Two young cops spotted this chink in the Met's service to the borough. The next morning they drew up alongside the dealers in an unmarked police car. The element of surprise was perfect. No one twigged that they were coppers until they were already out of the car and, as they're required to do, putting on their police caps. The first dealer ran in lengthening strides down the road. Soon he was nothing but a fast-moving speck; the second swallowed his stash; the third, Ollie, never top of the class, couldn't decide what to do. Run, swallow, throw? There were too many choices. He was throwing it, then he was swallowing it, all the time attempting to escape in a high-speed version of the 'twist', finally tossing his drugs towards a shuttered shop.

One of the officers spotted them land. 'What's in that bag you threw?' he asked.

'I don't know.'

Bad answer. 'Verbals', as they're called, can be very powerful evidence since they come straight from the defendant's mouth. The correct response was either to say nothing or 'What bag?' By admitting knowledge of the bag, it was but a small step for a jury to find that Ollie knew what was inside it – that is, wraps of crack ready for sale, making him guilty of possession with intent to supply Class A drugs and thus liable for a long prison sentence.

The next day, I sat in court trying to look as if I'd done this before. My opponent could spot a newbie.

'You're sitting on the wrong side of the court, virgin.' Having humiliated me, she added, 'By the way, I'm going to argue out his verbal.'

I'd spent all night preparing my opening speech, which outlines the case to the jury; it was painstakingly constructed around Ollie's verbal cum near admission of guilt. The verbal was even more important to Ollie's defence than to the prosecution. He was running a variation on the classic 'plant' defence; instead of alleging the police had planted the drugs, Ollie was saying that one of the other dealers had thrown the drugs and the police were pinning it on him.

The defence argued that the 'what's in the bag' question showed that the cop had ample grounds for suspecting Ollie might be guilty of an offence. If an officer has such a suspicion, then he must caution the suspect before asking any questions. The wording of a caution is, 'You do not have to say anything. But it may harm your defence if you do not mention when questioned something which you later rely on in court. Anything you do say may be given in evidence against you.' The failure to caution was a breach of police Codes of Practice and Ollie's verbal should be excluded from evidence.

I countered, haltingly, that while the failure to caution was a breach of the Codes, it was not a sufficiently serious one for it to be excluded from evidence as unfair. The judge, quite rightly, disagreed with me.

'Are you honestly telling this court, Mr McBride, that this alleged verbal, extracted by a self-evident breach of Code C, should not be excluded?'

'Er?' It was hard to answer as I was busy regretting inviting my mother and father to watch my debut performance. Stammering out another 'um', I could hear my mother happily saying to the officer in the case, who was relying on my sage-like guidance, 'He's never done this before.'

Without the verbal linking him to the bag, Ollie's ludicrous story, as given to police in interview, almost stood up: he had come from his girlfriend's on the bus looking for a Lucozade and finding the shop closed, he had got chatting with the two dealers outside the shop. He hadn't known about any drugs until the police arrested him. In cross-examination, the defence tried to create doubt over the police's truthfulness. One officer had seen the bag land by the shop but the other hadn't, which seemed odd, the defence suggested, since they were standing next to each other. Inconsistencies undermine a witness's credibility and sow doubt in the jury's mind. If the jury couldn't be sure, even if they thought the police were telling the truth, then they'd have to acquit. I needed a demonstrable lie and my last chance of finding one was in cross-examining Ollie. Skimming his police interview, which the jury also had in front of them, I noticed he'd said that he couldn't remember his girlfriend's house number.

ME: You can't remember her number?

OLLIE: No.

ME: Is that because you're bad at numbers?

OLLIE: Yes, very.

ME: Really? At page 7 of your interview, you give a detailed series of buses – 30, 256, 243 – you took to get to the shop. You're brilliant at numbers.

OLLIE: (*scratching his chin*) Um.

ME: You're lying because you weren't coming from any girlfriend's looking for a drink, were you?

Ollie's answer didn't matter. He was caught telling a lie and the jury would ask themselves what he was trying to hide if not the fact that he was dealing. An hour later they came back with a guilty verdict. The judge gave him four and a half years – how about that for a bloody nose? I stood there, undefeated – the Jake La Motta of the crown court.

My unblemished record wasn't to last; little did I know that the crims and the cops were lining up to shatter my glass jaw. I was about to discover the baleful seductiveness of the shelf of dreams: once you have a taste for it, like a punch-drunk boxer you'll risk a career-ending beating in the hope of one more win.

I floated back to chambers. The clerks were uninterested in my success: the phones were ringing, available barristers were being

PART THREE

Proving the Case

7. Getting Past Half-time

Jackson had a crack habit and so did all his friends. Their problem was that they didn't have the funds to maintain a regular supply. To overcome their financial difficulties they devised a plan to raid a car showroom. Jackson, a rangy fellow with long orangutan-like arms, was given the job of sledgehammer man. No one trusted him with anything too technical. A few evenings later, with his accomplices crouching behind a minivan, Jackson picked his moment. A successful operation depended on speed of execution. He leapt up from his hiding place and loped for the car showroom. He swung the sledgehammer in a looping arc over his shoulder and smashed it against the plate-glass window. Boom. The glass exploded into a thousand tiny billowing pieces. The building's alarm began to squawk. His friends sprang forward, jumping through the breach in the glass. Sudden proximity to all these top-of-the-range, freshly waxed cars befuddled them. They stared slack-jawed at the glistening bodywork. Look at those cars. What a selection! There was too much choice. They didn't know what to take. 'Get the Porsche!' someone yelled, breaking the spell. 'Yeah, the Porsche.'

Unfortunately for them, at that very moment a police van happened to be passing. The lads in the showroom were caught red-handed; handcuffed before they'd even touched the Porsche's door handle, let alone sat in its leather seats. The others, Jackson among them (with the prospect of crack fast receding), scarpered. They dived into nearby bushes and tried to crawl away. Police flashlights picked them out one by one. Jackson was the last to be found. They pulled him out from his hiding place covered in dirt and showroom glass. This was a job for forensics. Link those pieces of glass on Jackson's sweater to the car showroom and throw in the circumstantial evidence of his being in close vicinity to the premises at the time of the raid and you've got a conviction.

Jackson, an old hand at the ins and outs of police station custody suites, sensibly gave a 'no comment' interview. The prosecution would be put to proof. This is fair enough: the prosecution brings a case and the burden is on them to prove it beyond reasonable doubt. Before you can do this, however, you must first evidentially make out the elements of the offence. This is known as establishing a *prima facie* case, that is a case strong enough that it requires an answer. If you don't have a *prima facie* case then the defendant doesn't have anything he needs to answer to.

Part of a prosecutor's job is to force the defendant to defend himself, turn the jury's attention to any flaws in his case rather than the prosecution's. A defendant's case often looks strongest at the close of the prosecution and before he has gone into the witness box. Getting a defendant to speak in his defence is always a good move because there's an excellent chance his big fat mouth will do more damage to his case than you ever could.

In barrister lingo pushing a trial past the end of the prosecution's case and on to the defendant's is known as 'getting past half-time'. Half-time isn't a temporal line – the prosecution's case almost always takes a good deal longer than the defence's. It's a waypoint, the lull after the prosecution has closed its case and before the defence has begun, when the judge asks himself, 'Has the prosecution marshalled enough evidence to make a strong enough case for the jury to consider a verdict on it?'

During the trial the prosecutor continually asks himself the very same question, only more anxiously, because basic prosecutorial competence is measured by whether you have managed to cross the half-time line. If at the end of a trial the jury comes back and acquits, no one is going to blame you. You can say that the evidence wasn't there to convince them – it's not your fault. If, on the other hand, the judge chucks the case before the jury is asked to consider it, before the defence has had to defend, then absolutely it is your fault. Word gets around. Soon the rumour is that you're so incompetent that getting an under 11's football match past half-time is beyond you.

Keeping trials running is not as easy as you might think. They're like sheep – they keep coming up with novel and unusual ways to die. One minute you're bouncing along, witnesses are coming and going, the jurors are scribbling notes, and the next you're heading back to chambers after a bollocking from the judge for forgetting about some obscure but essential piece of paper. This is the fundamental point: prosecuting trials, setting out a *prima facie* case, and then proving the matter beyond reasonable doubt is a highly technical exercise in getting the evidence, in its correct form, before the jury. Your attention is elsewhere, you miss something and, before you know it, an 'open and shut' case has collapsed around your ears, leaving you looking like a prat and defence counsel beaming.

By the time the prosecutor finally stood up to open the car raid case Jackson was the lone hold-out, everyone else having long since pleaded guilty. The glass found on his sweater and glass from the car showroom window, the prosecutor told the court, had been forensically tested. They matched identically. The glass sprinkled all over Jackson could only have come from when he smashed the window. The prosecutor held up the sledgehammer to emphasize the point. Having finished his opening speech he called his witnesses, including the officer in the case. He read out a few Section 9 statements, which are statements admitted into evidence because all parties agree them, exhibiting Jackson's interview and dealing with the movements of the sledgehammer from crime scene to police store. Finally, he closed his case and sat down, his job done. I scratched my head. I knew he'd forgotten something but I couldn't think what it was. I really should have known what it was. I was a fully qualified barrister now. I might not have a permanent job as a tenant but I'd completed my pupillage year and I had a barrister's practising certificate to prove it.

'Mr McBride,' said the judge, bringing me back from my wonderings, 'Mr McBride, are you calling your client?' He was keen to get Jackson in the witness box. It was guaranteed that when giving his testimony Jackson would be an awful witness. I had not been looking forward to the prospect. Then, it dawned on me. Wait a minute, I thought, wait a minute.

The prosecutor hadn't read out any statement from the forensic scientist confirming that the glass on Jackson's clothes had come from the showroom. Nor were there any statements from the officers who took the original samples from the crime scene. A prosecution's opening speech is not evidence but a précis of the case. Evidentially, it's nothing more than assertions. It proves nothing. When opening a case the prosecutor is like the ghost of Christmas Future in *A Christmas Carol*: he's outlining what may, not will, happen. Without statements from the officers and the forensic scientist, there was no proof that the glass had come from that showroom. It was just broken glass.

When you're defending there are two basic ways of winning a trial. First, the jury finds the case has not been proved beyond reasonable doubt, which means the facts offered by the prosecution are not sufficient to convict the defendant of the offence with which he is charged. Second, there is an evidential or legal issue which snuffs out the prosecution no matter how convincing the facts might be. Both ways are good, but beating the rap with legal argument is far, far more satisfying. Why? Well, it makes you look clever, and for a fleeting moment, you have the law at your command. You have summoned the law and for once it has heeded your call, arriving like a flash flood crashing through a narrow valley, ripping up everything in its wake. Even the strongest prosecution case is swept away. Out of the thunderous displacement of legal water, out of a world turned upside down, the defendant is lifted up and gently deposited on safe ground, excused from having to answer to anybody – free.

The legal *deus ex machina* – Jackson's only hope and a prosecutor's great fear – was a submission of 'no case to answer'. A submission of no case (also known as a half-time submission because it is made at the close of the prosecution case) is a legal argument that there is not sufficient evidence against the defendant for a reasonable jury properly directed to convict the defendant. The judge should therefore direct an acquittal. My submission had the benefit of simplicity: without the statements from the police officers and the forensic scientist there was no evidence that the glass on Jackson's sweater came from the showroom. I thought I was on firm ground but you can never be sure. Part of the law's power, its excellence, is its caprice. You can call the law down on the heads of the prosecution, smack your fist into your palm, demand hotly for its intervention and be met only with silence as the law fails to break a ripple.

I stood up and set out the prosecution's evidential failings, listing the missing statements proving the origin of the glass. The prosecutor began his response. I assumed he'd apply to reopen his case to read the appropriate statements but he didn't do that because he couldn't. The officer in the case had forgotten to get them and the prosecutor had failed to spot it before the trial began. The judge, very reluctantly, had to agree with my submission. The prosecution's case collapsed. Jackson the guilty was Jackson the not guilty. He started whooping and clapping his hands. The judge's face was stony. No one likes a bad winner. Coming into the cells, I heard Jackson excitedly telling the jailers, 'I've had a touch, I have.' It wouldn't be long now before he'd be reunited with his crack pipe. When I left, he was singing.

Halfway down the road from the court I treated myself to some unsportsmanlike crowing. 'Ha, ha! That prosecutor – I whupped him. I battered him. How could he have screwed it up? What a moron! What a dumb-arse!' Even stupider than that shit-for-brains Jackson which was an uphill struggle worthy of Sisyphus. 'A cock-up like that,' I said to myself, 'could never happen to me.'

My memory, a stickler for honesty, flung me back a few months. I was in court prosecuting a man for theft, nervously watching defence counsel as he readied to drive a stake through the heart of my case.

'Can you from the accounts here,' he asked of my main witness, 'say that the amounts of money set out in the counts on the indictment have been stolen?'

Come on, you fucker, I prayed, say yes.

'No,' came the witness's response.

The investigating officer and I had spent days putting the trial together. She had criss-crossed London chasing bits of paper, rounding up witnesses and all for nothing because I had failed to notice this terminal gap in my case.

'No?' said the judge.

'No,' repeated the witness sheepishly.

The judge looked at me and, shaking her head, said with deadpan honesty, 'Mr McBride, this is the worst-prepared case that I have ever seen.'

I flinched as I recalled her words. I flinched as I remembered the pain and the humiliation as the jury began to laugh. Anyone who has seen the film *This is Spinal Tap* will hopefully remember the incompetent publicist of their US tour, Artie Fufkin, exhorting the Tap after yet another cock-up to 'kick his ass'. In court that day, I was Artie Fufkin. Go on, judge, kick my ass, kick my ass. Inside, I was dying.

8. The Evidential Burden

Evidence is the most important thing in a trial. When prosecuting you spend most of your time worrying about how to get it in and when you're defending you spend your time dreaming up ways to exclude it. Evidence is anything that ends up being admitted into the trial. Its most common form, oral testimony aside, is 'real evidence', which can be defined as any tangible object. A document, a voice recording, a baseball bat all count as real evidence.

'Members of the jury, here is a baseball bat. The prosecution contends that defendant X used this bat to hit victim Y in the testicles.'

Real evidence is a prosecutor's friend: it's straightforward, easy to understand and interactive. Juries can touch it, admire its quality, feel its weight – evaluate how much it would hurt to be smacked in the goolies with that baseball bat. The more exciting the piece of real evidence – I can guarantee that if you pulled a bazooka out from underneath counsel's table you'd have each and every juror's full attention – the more juries love it and the more you should make use of it. Trials are theatre and pieces of real evidence are the props. A prosecuting barrister, like any good performer, must assume ownership over his props, take pleasure in them and revel in their properties. In looking at real evidence – the *objets trouvés* picked up by police at crime scenes – I am going to focus on two that are often assumed to be the most 'probative' (the legal word for a persuasive bit of evidence): the crime stain and CCTV.

DNA and the crime stain

A few years back I was prosecuting a couple of teenagers, Simon and Sam, for aggravated burglary. It's quite rare to catch burglars. Crime statistics are on their side. The Met's clear-up rate for domestic burglary is a pitiful 13 per cent.[1] Meaning that your average burglar gets away with it a little under nine times out of ten. Subtract hopeless drug addicts from this pool, and these already heartening odds improve even further in favour of the reasonably competent burglar. Happily, Simon and Sam, while not drug addicts, were way short of competence. They got caught because Sam, the bonehead, had somehow managed to leave his stun gun in the flat they were burgling.

You're guilty of aggravated burglary if you commit a burglary and at the time of the commission of the offence have with you a firearm, an imitation firearm, an explosive or any weapon of offence. Simon and Sam were armed with 'his and his' stun guns that they'd ordered out of the back of some sad-sack 'soldier of fortune' magazine. In law the stun guns might have been weapons of offence but in reality they were nothing of the kind. They were rubbish. You couldn't have stopped a gerbil with one. They had all the menace of a Mr Kipling's French Fancy. Not that I troubled the jury with this self-evident fact because it didn't make them any less guilty. To be fair to the boys the stun guns were there for intimidation rather than actual deployment. They might look crap under the courtroom's tungsten lighting but, let's be honest, if Simon and Sam came into your house at three in the morning waving them around, you wouldn't be taking any chances as to their effectiveness – and nor would I.

Shoddy or not, these stun guns were my props and I was going to play them up for all they were worth. Most real evidence comes bagged up and labelled. Always get the officer to open a bag in front of the jury. It adds to the drama. A few preparatory steps should be taken first, such as making sure the officer exhibiting the piece of evidence has got something to open the bag with. There's nothing more fatal to the dignity of a prosecution than watching an 18-stone copper failing to open the bag containing some fourteen-year-old kid's lock knife. Most importantly, check that the officer's got the evidence in his possession before you ask him to produce it in court or you will both look like clowns.

ME: Officer, where did you find the counterfeit banknote?
OFFICER: Under the defendant's bed, your honour.
ME: Did you seize the banknote?
OFFICER: I did, your honour.
ME: Can you produce that banknote now?
OFFICER: I can. (*The officer searches through the cardboard box in front of him containing his exhibits.*) Er? (*He turns the box upside down – no, not under there.*) Um . . . (*His hands are now in his pockets, shaking them out like a schoolboy who's lost his prize conker.*) I believe it's at Walthamstow police station, your honour.

We knew it was Sam's stun gun because it had been forensically tested and the DNA found on it matched his profile held in the National DNA Database. Profiling works like this: a DNA sample is extracted from the crime stain, which can be any piece of human matter left at the scene of the crime. A sample is then taken from the suspect. In the lab, scientists use enzymes to cut the respective DNA samples into smaller and smaller lengths. After these fragments have been sorted according to their size they are then dragged electromagnetically through gel along a track. Fragments with a smaller molecular weight travel further than heavier ones. The patterns created from this process are transferred from the gel to a membrane. Radioactive probes are then added to the membrane and an X-ray is taken to produce a radiograph recording the band pattern. The crime stain DNA and the suspect's DNA are then run in separate tracks through the gel, allowing their two radiographs to be compared. A match of a single band does not prove that the two sets of DNA came from the same source. By matching combinations of bands, however, you can gradually build up a more and more accurate comparison between the two sets of DNA. One combination band, for example, might be shared by one in four of the population, but if you then match another combination that might reduce it to one in sixteen of the population, or one in sixty-four and so on. Eventually, if the sample is good enough, you can work your way to the point where the match is so accurate that the chance of someone else having the same DNA profile has a random occurrence of one in one billion.

Opening evidence bags in front of juries works even better if the object in question has been forensically tested. The detective sergeant, a terrific old ham, knew exactly how to squeeze every ounce of drama out of the stun gun. He asked the usher to bring him the box of plastic gloves (a must for every courtroom), putting them on slowly enough to give me time to say, 'Now, members of the jury, the forensic testing process has left chemicals on the stun gun that are toxic, which is why the officer is putting on those gloves. The usher can provide you with plastic gloves, if you wish to examine the exhibit too.'

Soon the jury is passing the stun gun around with the studied nonchalance of a North London dinner party circulating the foie gras.

Sam's stun gun, sprayed with chemicals and covered in official-looking stickers, gave an extra impact to the DNA evidence. The jury could visualize him letting it slip from his hands in the heat of the burglary. The forensic investigation of the stun gun worked on a second, deeper level by demonstrating the thoroughness of the prosecution. Surrounded by forensic lab paraphernalia, we looked like professionals, like, dare I say it, experts. More than that, the reverence with which the stun gun was treated – the ritual of testing, bagging and handling – appealed to the jury's faith. We were no longer partial prosecutors selling our own twist on the facts of the case but men and women who were using objective science to solve the mysteries of a criminal investigation.

We have, thanks to shows such as *Crime Scene Investigation* and *Waking the Dead*, bought heavily into DNA evidence. I once prosecuted a man who liked to masturbate in front of teenage girls (contrary to Section 66 of the Sexual Offences Act 2003 and carrying a maximum penalty of two years' imprisonment). He'd wait in the park for them to start coming home from school, jump out and toss himself off before running away. A couple of schoolgirls to whom he had demonstrated his prowess saw where his semen landed. They instantly realized its evidential value. When the police turned up, the girls guided them to the crime stain. It was good work. The match not only identified the park masturbator but linked him to a knife-point rape that he'd committed a few months earlier.

DNA is an amazing evidential tool that has transformed criminal investigations and enabled the police to solve crimes that had baffled them for years. This has given people the impression that it's infallible. It isn't. DNA is fragile and easily damaged. Everyday things such as household chemicals, soil, even moisture, can corrode DNA making it much harder to extract an accurate profile. It is also susceptible to contamination. Ten per cent of crime scenes are inadvertently contaminated by the police's own DNA.[2] Even the laboratory is not safe. A cough, a sneeze, the droplets of moisture in your breath can all transfer your DNA and mix it with that of the suspect's. Risks like these have grown as DNA tests have become ever more sophisticated. It's now possible to make what is called a 'Low Copy Number' profile from as few as five to ten cells, which is equivalent to the deposit you'd leave from picking up a pen. The danger is that because DNA is sexy and cutting-edge, we accept the findings without thinking critically about them. During the Omagh Bombing trial it emerged that lab technicians had failed to wear gloves, masks and hats. Labels on the samples fell off. The police didn't use protective clothing when collecting the samples at the crime scene and then claimed in court that they had. The trial judge was horrified by these basic failings. What really got him, however, were the DNA Low Copy Number profiling techniques that amplified tiny amounts of genetic code to construct a 'match'. He found that the conclusions that the scientists confidently drew were, at best, speculative. What had looked so convincing at first glance was in the judge's opinion 'valueless'.

To ensure a fair hearing for a defendant it's vital to be able to analyse the DNA evidence properly. DNA cases, which combine forensic science and probability statistics, can baffle even experienced barristers. And if the barristers don't understand the ramifications of the evidence, how are they supposed to explain them to the jury? The first thing to say is that a DNA match doesn't necessarily prove that the sample came from the same person: it merely provides circumstantial evidence tending to show that the two samples came from the same person.[3] A problem that the courts have wrestled with is how best to express the likelihood, referred to by statisticians as the 'random occurrence ratio', that the two samples came from the same source.

I have never passed a maths exam in my life. Whenever someone has asked me if I have a maths qualification, I'm embarrassed to say, I have lied. I am, therefore, indebted to Graham Cooke, barrister and mathematician, for his excellent chapter on DNA evidence in *Rook and Ward on Sexual Offences*, which explains with admirable clarity why easy assumptions about DNA evidence are so dangerous.

Cooke sets out the key principles in DNA evidence by way of a fictional example. A left-handed male who wears glasses attacks a woman. Twenty-five per cent of men wear glasses and 10 per cent are left-handed. Therefore 2.5 per cent of the male population share both characteristics. This means the random occurrence ratio or rarity is one in forty. The suspect is left-handed and wears glasses. This does not mean that the chance of him being innocent is one in forty but simply that the suspect and unidentified attacker share a characteristic along with one out of every forty men.

This might seem obvious but it's a surprisingly easy mistake to make. The two principal reasons for this are that forensic scientist witness statements can be pretty confusing and the numbers involved extremely large.

Here's how such witness statements read in real life:

If the DNA had in fact originated from Mr X then I would have expected to obtain matching profiles.

If, however, the DNA had not originated from Mr X but from another unrelated person, then his profile must match by chance. It has been estimated that the probability of obtaining such a match with Mr X if the DNA had originated from another unrelated person is one in one million.

An equivalent way of expressing this assessment is that this result would be in the order of one million times more likely to occur if the DNA had originated from Mr X than if it originated from some other unrelated member of the population picked at random.[4]

Not very clear, I know. But what this does *not* mean is that the DNA has only a one in a million chance of being from someone other than Mr X. To assert such a conclusion is to commit the 'Prosecutor's Fallacy', so-called because it tempts the prosecutor into thinking that the one-in-a-million chance is correct. In fact, assuming the male population is 20 million, then the one in one million would mean that around twenty people had the same

DNA profile. On the strength of the DNA evidence alone, the chance that it is Mr X's DNA is one in twenty.[5]

These days when there's a full profile match the figure is now 'in the order of one in one billion'. Unlike me, Graham Cooke is not so easily fazed by such a dazzling number. Let's go back to our population of 20 million. This time the DNA random occurrence ratio/rarity is one in 1,000 million, which means there's a one in fifty (1,000 divided by 20) chance of another member of that population having the profile. If there are 200 trials in a year then in about four of those trials (200 divided by 50) there will be another candidate with the same profile. If there's nothing but DNA evidence to distinguish one suspect from another, and each man is equally likely to be guilty of the crime, then in two of the trials, the wrong man will be convicted.

Leaving aside the huge numbers in Sam's case, the DNA evidence only suggested that he had handled the stun gun, not that he had been in the flat or tried to burgle it. What really condemns a defendant is the interplay of different types of evidence. This is where Simon comes in. He's jointly charged with Sam, and the prosecution case, my case, is that they were in on it together. The boys have already accepted that they were best friends and went to the same school. In addition to these general facts of their association, Simon has managed to leave three fingerprints on a broken windowpane that, I am alleging, the boys had smashed to effect their entry into the flat.

The case is looking pretty good for me. I've got Sam's DNA on the stun gun and Simon's fingerprints on the windowpane. Fingerprints on broken pieces of glass are pretty incriminating but they don't necessarily prove Simon participated in the burglary. Simon's case was that he was a curious onlooker and he had touched the already broken panes of glass but had not gone into the flat. In law, if you haven't entered the property then you cannot be guilty of burglary. The central question therefore was: which side of the panes were Simon's fingerprints on? It was hard to tell. Forensic science might be excellent at convicting the guilty but there are other low-tech tools that shouldn't be forgotten, such as the good old diagram – real evidence par excellence. A good picture trumps a thousand words. Tucked away in the case papers I found a diagram of the fingerprint positioning on the pane of glass drawn by the scene-of-crime officer, or SOCO for short. The broken pane of glass had been stacked on one of the flat's windowsills. Her diagram reassembled the broken pane beautifully, showing that Simon had carefully picked the glass out of the window frame. Not, therefore, some kid having a look, but a burglar effecting his entry. I gave the jury a choice: was Simon practising Beethoven's Fifth Symphony on the windowsill or was he breaking into the flat?

The prosecution case is bubbling along nicely now. Simon has swirled down the guilty plughole and Sam is circling around it, getting ever closer to the edge. It would be a pity to allow him to clamber out. In order to explain his DNA on the stun gun, Sam claimed that he had touched it once, turning the thing on and off a few times. Sadly for him, we have a marvellous verbal from his mum that kills off this lie.

During the investigation the officer in charge of the case had called on Sam's mum and asked her the following question: 'Is there anything that Sam has brought into the house which you haven't been happy with?'

'Yeah,' she replied, 'a black-handled square thing with a pointed thing at the top.' This happened to be a very good description of the stun gun. His mum had unwittingly provided that little extra nudge.

The jury filed out and after an indecently short time filed back in to find them both guilty. The boys were bailed to come back for their sentence. To all intents and purposes it was their first offence so there was no chance that they would go to prison.

I came back to do the sentence. No Simon or Sam. Neither

defence counsel had a clue where they were. If they'd done a runner, where had they done a runner to? They were kids with no money. The judge issued a warrant for their arrest. A few days later the boys were located in Feltham Young Offenders' Institution. Apparently undaunted by their convictions, the boys had gone back to the drawing board. They decided that their mistake had been lack of firepower so they went out and got two real guns, loaded with real ammunition. They'd been found after an abortive robbery, hiding in a basement with the guns stuffed down the front of their trousers.

CCTV: loving the camera

Juries love CCTV. For them it's the best real evidence there is, better even than the theoretical bazooka. They love it because it's their chance to play detective. For most of a trial the jurors have to sit passively as they are spoon-fed the evidence. Once CCTV is played, however, they're in control. Free of the barristers and the judge, they can play out their Philip Marlowe gumshoe fantasy. While the CCTV is playing they can pretend to be starring in their own pitch-black film noir, smoking a Lucky Strike as a nineteen-year-old Lauren Bacall drapes herself around their neck.

Barristers should love CCTV, too. It sorts the wheat from the chaff. No more relying on the confused and unreliable witness statements of a pub-load of drunks. No more teasing out the truth from a bunch of boozed-up liars. A nice bit of CCTV and you can turn to the court and say, 'Pub fight, members of the jury, and the winners are in the dock.' Defendant X may have hit complainant Y with a glass but only after complainant Y had nutted defendant X on the bridge of his nose – six of one, half a dozen of the other.

In fact, barristers do not love CCTV because the reality is rarely so clear-cut. CCTV is a pain in the arse. If you're defending, you have to ask the prosecution for it, and if you're prosecuting, you have to hassle the police to go and get it. Officers then go down to the shop that's been turned over, or the train station where some kid's been robbed, to find that the CCTV:

> wasn't switched on;
> was broken;
> was pointing the wrong way;
> was unplayable;
> wasn't loaded with film;
> was already erased;
> was lost;
> was on a two-second stop–go frame speed which missed the crime;
> or, as is mostly the case, was of such poor quality that it showed nothing of any evidential value.

Even though Britain has more CCTV cameras than any other Western nation (there is no official estimate for the number of cameras in Britain but it's certainly many millions) snooping on all sorts of potential bad behaviour, it is estimated that only 3 per cent of crimes are solved by it.[6]

This is why, when I pushed my way into the Crown Prosecution Service room at court looking for disclosure of the evidence against my client, Giles, an alleged pub fighter, and the prosecutor said cheerfully, 'There's CCTV,' I wasn't worried. I was waiting for her to show me a collection of indistinct blobs roaming around on a fuzzy background. What were these blobs doing and to whom? Is it a pub fight? A German expressionistic dance? Mating badgers? It's anyone's guess.

The prosecutor pressed Play. The picture quality was razor-sharp. She turned to me and smiled. 'New camera.' She wasn't kidding. The camera didn't only take crystal-clear pictures, it moved, panning and zooming through the unfolding ruckus as though guided by the cinematographer Laszlo Kovacs. Whoever was operating the camera had a natural sense of composition and a genius for finding the most interesting part of the fight. Smack bang in the middle of the screen was my client, Giles, stripped to the waist and readying for action. His quarry made a break for it, but was too slow. Giles punched him in the face, triumphantly flexing his spindly arms at the hidden camera, as it filmed him in close-up. He might as well have been holding a sign saying, 'Convict me now.' Lip-readers could enjoy his post-punch exultation: 'Do you fucking want some more?' His quarry, sitting on the ground holding his burst mouth, did not.

Giles's left hook ignited the drinkers outside the pub. A dozen regulars settled their differences like gentlemen. *Crimewatch UK* was no match for this footage. It was even better than *Cops*, the American real-life crime television show that set the gold standard in the 1990s, with clips of the underclass being righteously clubbed by moustachioed patrolmen. The prosecutor turned to me, asking with her eyes whether I had seen enough. I certainly had. Why was it that the only time the CCTV was any use, it worked against me? God, life is unfair.

Pondering how to defend Giles, I remembered Reg, whom I had represented at trial on charges of actual bodily harm and affray. Reg first appeared on CCTV stepping out of a police van dressed in flip-flops, a T-shirt and summery shorts – not exactly fighting gear. His hands were cuffed behind his back and he was escorted by two police officers. What made the CCTV so interesting in this case was the gap between what was in the officers' witness statements and what I – not to mention the jury – could see with our own eyes. The police had claimed that Reg was struggling when he arrived. We could see that he wasn't. The police then alleged that he had tried to trip another officer up. It wasn't clear from the tape whether he had or not, but what the arresting officer did next was beyond dispute. He slammed Reg against a wall and then pulled the handcuffs over the back of Reg's head, doubling him over painfully. When asked why he had done that, the officer said that he had done it to stop him 'kicking out'. The CCTV was unequivocal: Reg wasn't 'kicking out'.

The footage showed things getting even livelier in the cells. Reg had been carried in like a side of beef. As soon as they unlocked one of the handcuffs, Reg used his free hand to grab a police officer and swing him around. Every time one cop broke loose, he caught another. Having been keen to get him into the cell, the police found themselves now even keener to get out. After a long struggle, Reg was still holding on to one last officer. Another cop reentered the cell and used his forearm to pin Reg up against the wall by his neck. Reg tried to push back so the cop punched him twice in the face. Stunned, Reg was manoeuvred into a corner of the cell with the cop's arm still pressed against his neck. Reg did the only thing he could do: he dipped his head and bit the cop on the shoulder. Pandemonium broke out. Police flooded the cell. Reg was battered to the floor. The police seized their chance to escape, the last officer being yanked out by his belt, as per police procedure.

To have any chance of an acquittal, I had to persuade the jury that Reg's sinking his teeth into the cop was self-defence. For this to happen, they would have to accept that the police's behaviour had been unlawful. At the very end of the tape I found something helpful: the CCTV showed the riot squad in full regalia entering Reg's cell to take his fingerprints and DNA by force. Faceless state goons versus the lone citizen was just the kind of thing that might push the jury to acquit. But the judge ruled that their entry was irrelevant to the charges and therefore inadmissible in court. Would the earlier CCTV footage be enough? All Reg could do was put his faith in the jury. Luckily for him, they came back with a verdict of not guilty.

How did any of this help Giles? The CCTV looked terminal

for him. There he was, in glorious Technicolor, smacking someone in the face. But then, recalling that it had nearly worked for
Reg, I diligently watched the whole footage. At the very end of
the tape, after the film appeared to have ended, the picture flick-
ered back to life. The police were arresting Giles's co-defendant,
Dave. An officer pinned Dave up against a shop front, picked him
up and slammed him on the floor. When Dave's girlfriend inter-
vened, they slammed her on the floor, too. She tried to get up and
the arresting officer pushed her back down with his boot. Here
before my eyes was the 'riot squad' moment. I got the other defence
lawyers to watch the clip. It directly concerned their clients. Once
they'd seen it, we demanded that all charges be dropped in return
for Dave and his girlfriend not pressing charges against the police
for wrongful arrest and assault.

There was one little problem. The couple's arrest had nothing
really to do with Giles. His arrest, under a flyover half a mile away,
had been by the book. I was worried that the prosecution might
drop charges against the couple and continue them against Giles.
He was, after all, deeply guilty. To my amazement, the prosecution agreed with our proposal and Giles and his friends were free.
The golden rule of defence is that the less evidence there is the
better – unless it is evidence that contradicts what the prosecution
witnesses are claiming under oath. CCTV is often useless but,
when it works, it's like alchemy, turning lead into gold. You just
have to sift through every frame to find it.

9. Identification: 'I'd Know Him Among a Thousand'

The December twilight was closing in around Adolf Beck who stood a few steps from the building that housed his shabby Victoria Street flat. Beck, middle-aged and greying, had had an exciting but unprofitable life. Born in Norway, he had become a seaman and, after a few years, pitched up in Aberdeen to work as a ship's broker. It was there that he developed a singing career that took him to Montevideo where he arrived in time to fight in the Uruguyan civil war, earning himself a scar on an arm. From there he went to Buenos Aires, maintaining his dual career as a ship's broker and singer. By 1874 he had relocated to Peru with plans to build a theatre in Lima. The plans never materialized. Ten years later he found himself in London and in debt.

Using a mixture of false assurances and his boundless charm, Beck had an amazing ability to persuade people to give him money. Even though he owed his landlord months of rent, he still managed to get the man to lend him £1,600 (around £100,000 in today's money). His persuasiveness, however, was not matched by business acumen. Everything he touched went bust. The final disaster was an investment in a Norwegian mine that failed to produce any ore. By 1895 Beck was penniless, but seeing him standing there on Victoria Street you would never have guessed it. He was dressed like a Victorian gentleman of means. He wore a smart coat with black silk lapels, and carried a silver-topped umbrella. Beck liked to take care of his appearance – his neat moustache and distinguished-looking grey hair were all he had left.

Coming out of the Army & Navy Store a few doors down, Ottilie Meissonier instantly recognized this 'trademark' dapper appearance. 'Sir, I know you,' she said, confronting Beck. He enquired whether she meant the dentist who worked out of the same building in which he lived. She didn't. She knew him because it was he who had swindled her out of two watches and some gold rings. On hearing this accusation, Beck took off, weaving through the traffic, with Meissonier in pursuit. They both made for a policeman, Beck getting there first. He protested that she was bothering him. Meissonier countered that three weeks earlier he had conned her out of her valuables. Smartly dressed then as now, he had stopped her on Victoria Street, the same place she'd just seen him, to enquire if she were Lady Everton. Meissonier was a humble music teacher. Beck claimed to be Lord Wilton. They fell into conversation and she invited him to visit her at home the next day.

The following day the bogus Lord Wilton arrived at the appointed time and proposed that, since she was musical and multilingual, she accompany him and some of his friends to the French Riviera. She accepted. He then said that her jewels were not good enough and suggested that he should exchange them for something better, more in keeping with his proposed trip and her new status. He wrote out a cheque for £40 to pay for the new dresses she would need for the Riviera and left with two watches (one of which he had palmed) and two rings. As soon as he had gone, Meissonier went out to cash the cheque. It didn't take her long to find out that not only was the cheque no good but the branch of the bank it was drawn on did not exist.[1]

On the strength of Meissonier's account Beck was taken to Rochester Row police station where it emerged that he fitted the description which she had given to officers three weeks earlier. Daisy Grant, another cheated woman, along with Mary Harvey, Meissonier's servant, were called in to see if they could identify him. Out of the seven-man identification parade, Beck was the only one with grey hair. Unsurprisingly, both Grant and Harvey picked him out. This was more than good enough for the police. Beck was charged and remanded in custody. The bogus peer who cheated ladies out of their valuables was too good a story for the newspapers to miss and they fell upon it. Publicity about the dapper swindler soon brought a flood of women who had been suckered – he had clearly been a busy boy – through Rochester Row's doors. They almost all picked Beck out as the con man.

Kate Brakefield, gulled in June 1895, picked him out of an eight-man line-up, saying, 'I am satisfied he is the same man.' Minnie Lewis, cheated in April, identified Beck from a crowd of fourteen. 'I had not had the least doubt in picking out the prisoner,' she later told the court. Juliette Kluth, conned in March, identified him out of a crowd of eighteen men milling about Westminster Police Yard. 'I recognized the prisoner at once, as soon as I put my foot in the yard,' she later testified. It didn't stop there. Fanny Nutt, a whole year after she'd been swindled, was so sure the con man was Beck that she told the court, 'I'd know him among a thousand.'

By the end of the investigation, Ottilie Meissonier's original Victoria Street identification was backed up by no fewer than twelve other witnesses, including a policeman, most of whom identified Beck with absolute certainty. The police charged him with ten counts of theft and obtaining by false pretences. Beck was in deep trouble. He had no plausible alibi for the dates on which he was said to have swindled the women. And anyway, how could all these witnesses be wrong?

There was something unusual about the case, however. The con man had a very distinctive style. He called himself variations on Lord Wilton, or Wilton de Willoughby. He dressed like a 24-carat swell. All the women noticed the heavy gold watch, silver-topped cane, top hat and silk-lapelled overcoat. His victims also fell into a distinctive category. They were almost always single women living on the margins – actresses, music-hall artistes, music teachers – who aspired to gentility but didn't have the means to acquire it.

His 'lordship' could spot them a mile off. They were a very clever target group because many of them supplemented their incomes, as they delicately put it in their statements, by 'seeing men for money'. Not only were they susceptible to a man who promised big but they were accustomed to talking to a complete stranger and, if it were worth it, inviting him back to their homes.

The tale that Lord Wilton spun them made him more than worth it. His opening gambit was a perfectly pitched piece of flattery: 'I beg your pardon, are you Lady Everton?', 'Didn't I meet you at the ball the other night?' or the more direct, 'What pretty feet you have. Do you play an instrument?' (She did – the mandolin.) Having got their attention, he moved on to describe his massive wealth: there was the Lincolnshire estate with ten gardeners and the land around the Brompton Road, which all put together brought in a whopping yearly income. On most occasions he said he was looking for a housekeeper, which all parties would've understood to mean a live-in, salaried mistress. The women were promised foreign travel, riding lessons and parties. It was all too good to be true.

Once he'd dazzled them, he moved on to how their clothes and jewellery would have to be improved. He asked for their watches in order to exchange them for something better, and their rings so he had the right size to buy them finer ones. Next he would write out a cheque for a bank with a copper-bottomed St James's address. He told them to expect a one-armed commissionaire from the Carlton Club, of all places, who would after an hour return their things along with the new jewellery. Finally, twirling his cane, he'd be off, sometimes even borrowing change for his cab fare.

This distinctive style is important. Long servers on the Westminster police remembered it from a trial back in 1877, when a con man calling himself John Smith used the name Lord Willoughby to swindle women with an almost identical story. If Lord Willoughby and Lord Wilton were the same person, then the con man could not be Adolf Beck because in 1877 he was in Peru failing to get his theatre off the ground and he had the witnesses to prove it.

At Beck's trial in March 1896, his barrister sought to introduce evidence of the earlier conviction. It was the only card he had to play. The judge, the second most senior at the Bailey, Sir Forrest Fulton, who, incredibly, had prosecuted the 1877 trial as a young barrister, refused to admit it on 'the grounds that it related to another and distinct issue, and one calculated to mislead the jury'. The swindled women gave their evidence and Beck, protesting his innocence to the last, was convicted and sentenced to seven years' hard labour. He was fifty-five.

From prison Beck launched a desperate letter-writing campaign, imploring the authorities to review his case. He was ignored. Two years into his sentence, the governor of the prison that had housed John Smith in 1879 reviewed Smith's file and discovered that Smith was Jewish and circumcised. Beck, without being told why, was examined. His foreskin was intact. Here was incontrovertible proof that, if the crimes had been committed by the same man, it could not have been Beck who'd committed them. The Home Office passed this information to Sir Forrest Fulton, the trial judge, asking him what he wanted to do. Nothing, was the answer. All Sir Forrest did was direct that Beck should no longer be dressed as a prisoner convicted of a second offence. The Home Office accepted his decision without a murmur.

Beck was released in 1901 and went back to his old impecunious life. In 1903 the familiar, well-crafted swindles started up again. Word got out that a well-dressed gentleman calling himself Lord Willoughby was going around town cheating women. A year later Pauline Scott arrived at Scotland Yard complaining that she'd been conned out of a ring and watch by a man she'd met on Oxford Street calling himself Lord Willoughby. The police knew who it was and set a trap. In a mirror image of the Meissonier identification of 1895, Scott, this time accompanied by a detective constable, confronted Beck on the street. 'You are the man who took my jewellery and sovereign,' she declared. Beck again denied it. 'No, I am not. I do not know you. I have never seen you in my life before.' He was arrested, charged, tried – the witnesses swore blind it was he who'd conned them – and convicted.

On 7 July 1904, ten days after his second conviction, while Beck was safely tucked up in Brixton prison, the real swindler finally surfaced. An expensively dressed, elderly gentleman calling himself Lord Willoughby, who claimed great wealth and made fantastic promises, persuaded two sisters to give him several rings and half a crown.

As he was leaving, the sisters had a pang of doubt. They got their landlord to follow the man as he went first to a jeweller's for a valuation and then to the pawnbroker's. A policeman was summoned and the man was arrested. He turned out to be the John Smith of 1877 fame, whose real name, as much as anyone could determine, was Frederick Meyer. Meyer had been quiet for some years because he had been successfully practising his trade in America.

Smith/Meyer's arrest worked like a laxative on the whole sorry affair: it all came tumbling out. More women came forward to accuse him of conning them. The evidence of his circumcision given by the prison governor to the Home Office was leaked to the newspapers. They were scandalized. How could such an injustice have been allowed to happen? And, why was it not corrected when the fact of the circumcision was discovered? Within days Beck was released and pardoned of both convictions. Initially, he was offered £2,000 compensation but pressure from the newspapers upped it to £5,000 (about £300,000 in today's money). A government inquiry was set up, led by the Master of the Rolls, the second most senior judge in the land. Everyone turned out looking bad, especially Sir Forrest Fulton, the 1896 trial judge, and the Home Office, who had done nothing to help Beck six years earlier. The scandal was such that a year later, in the light of the findings of the committee of inquiry, the Court of Appeal was established in order to review the safety of criminal convictions and correct potential miscarriages of justice.

The real significance of the case, however, is not to demonstrate bureaucratic inertia and incompetence, nor callous stupidity in the judiciary – neither of which is news – but to highlight the fact that sixteen people (coppers included), independently, picked Beck out as the swindler at the identity parades. Smith/Meyer's crimes weren't quick 'smash and grabs' where the victim catches a brief glimpse of their assailant in a dark street. These witnesses spent as much as an hour with the con man in a well-lit and relaxed setting. They had all the time in the world to make an accurate identification and they failed. It's natural to trust your own eyes – stands to reason – but what you honestly think you've seen and what has really happened can be two very different things.

To find out why this is I went to see Tim Valentine, a professor of psychology at Goldsmith's University, who specializes in the psychological process of identification. Over coffee in his office, I ask him to sketch out how memory works in relation to identification evidence. Valentine describes memory as an unintended consequence of what we see and hear because it's beyond our control. Even consciously trying to remember something such as a face or a sequence of events doesn't necessarily mean that you will. It's also easy to misremember and end up recalling things that never actually happened.

To see how memory can play tricks, says Valentine, it's important to understand how the three-stage process of memory works. The first stage is encoding, which is the processing of the physical sensory input coming into our brains. In order to have any chance of remembering something you have to be paying attention to it. For human beings the average street environment is a buzzing confusion and, in order to comprehend the input streaming into our brains, we have to apply organization to what we see and hear.

Our perception is therefore affected by what we expect to perceive because, without expectation, we could not decipher what we are seeing. Two witnesses can see exactly the same thing but encode it in two completely different ways. One witness might perceive someone as threatening and therefore encode an exaggerated version of that person's threatening movements or physical size. Another witness might perceive and encode that same person as nothing more than a passer-by rummaging for something in his pockets.

The second stage of memory – the storage – is not straightforward either. Our memories don't sit in filing cabinets waiting for us to pull them out whenever we need them. Even simple memories are immensely complex constructions that are stored in many different parts of the brain. This makes retrieval, memory's last stage, a hit-and-miss affair. Usually retrieval works from cues such as a location, the general appearance of a person, or a particular time in our lives. If you start thinking about trips to the seaside, for example, you'll start remembering details of those trips, which in turn lead to other memories. Retrieval cues work because they reconstruct the context at the time when you encoded those memories. Context retrieval techniques can pull out memories that might otherwise not be recalled. Cognitive interviews, often used by police when questioning child witnesses, try to reinstate in the child's mind the particular context of the day they are trying to remember. The idea is to get the witness to talk about the whole day. Irrelevant memories then can act as cues to dislodge important ones.

In trawling our memory we also activate dormant 'memory traces'. Memory traces – a series of connections over a network of neurones – are partial chunks of memory distributed around our brains. Memory trawls are pretty indiscriminate and the danger of recalling an event is that the memory trace we activate might lead to a misattribution, or mistrace. Let's say you're talking to a friend about the seaside and you recall that the last time the two of you went you ate scallops. Your friend says no, that wasn't the last time but the second before last. You think about it and realize your friend is right. You have been confusing two different memories because they share the same context. We do it all the time and there's no way of testing whether we've made the error or not.

Mistraces can lead to spectacular errors which underline the unreliability of identification evidence. Tim Valentine gives the example of a case he worked on where a witness to an assault outside a nightclub was asked to point out the perpetrator in court. The witness turned to the victim sitting in the public gallery and pointed to him. The judge was flabbergasted. He asked the witness to confirm the identification and again the witness pointed to the victim. The technical name for this is a 'source attribution error'. The witness, remembering two closely associated roles from the same memory, had mixed up victim and attacker. The most notorious example of this is the case of Australian barrister and identification expert Don Thomson.

One day Thomson went into a police station to see a client he was representing. The cop at the counter recognized him from an e-fit of a rapist and arrested him. Thomson was absolutely horrified. Things got worse. The police held an identity parade and the victim, who provided the basis for the e-fit, picked Thomson out as the man who raped her. Fortunately, he had a cast-iron alibi. At the time of the rape he had been with the mayor and the commissioner of police, appearing in a live television debate on, of all things, identification and miscarriages of justice. The woman had identified him because at the time of the rape she was watching him on television, and her brain transposed his face on to that of the rapist.

The woman was adamant she'd got the right man and no doubt convincing in her witness statement. It's worrying to think what might have happened to Thomson if he hadn't had an alibi, or hadn't been a well-known barrister. How could he have defended himself? Identification is so powerful and so dangerous because often it's unchallengeable, leaving a misidentified defendant with no way of defending himself other than saying, 'It wasn't me.' Three-quarters of the people on Death Row who have been proved through DNA testing by the Innocence Project in the United States to have been wrongfully convicted were put there by eye-witness identifications.

In the 1970s, following another spate of miscarriages of justice stemming from multiple witness misidentifications such as those that convicted Adolf Beck, another committee was set up, chaired by Lord Devlin, a law lord. His report concluded that trials based solely on identification evidence should be permitted only in exceptional circumstances and, if the exceptional was not present, the trial should be stopped. Devlin's committee recommended restricting identification cases because they saw that it was impossible to assess the accuracy of a purported identification. They also suggested a code of practice governing how identification procedures should be conducted, but the government ignored it. It's a rare minister who agrees to measures that will inevitably reduce the number of convictions.

In the end, the Court of Appeal settled things with a case called *Turnbull* by setting out guidelines as to how identification evidence should be treated when the defendant disputed the identification. The guidelines are given to a jury in the form of a judicial direction:

I must therefore warn you of the special need for caution before convicting the defendant in reliance on the evidence of identification. A witness who is convinced in his own mind may as a result be a convincing witness, but may nevertheless be mistaken. Mistakes can also be made in the recognition of someone known to a witness, even of a close friend or relative. You should therefore examine carefully the circumstances in which the identification was made. For how long did he have the person he says was the defendant under observation? At what distance? In what light? Did anything interfere with the observation? Had the witness ever seen the person he observed before? If so, how often? If only occasionally, had he any special reason for remembering him? How long was it between the original observation and the identification to the police? Is there any marked difference between the description given by the witness to the police when he was first seen by them, and the appearance of the defendant?

The guidelines are a classic example of how the common law, by using a judge's direction to the jury, endeavours to fix the evidence to make it 'fair'. It's the law's way of having your cake and eating it too. The jury can have the identification evidence, the reasoning goes, so long as the judge has warned them about its dangers.

It's worth considering how effective the guidelines really are in guarding against inaccurate identifications that convict the wrong person. Applying the *Turnbull* guidelines to the Beck case, what jury, having heard that direction, would be minded to acquit? The women got a good long look at Meyer as he was swindling them – a much better look than in many identification cases. There was plenty of light and no obstructions. Meissonier spotted him in the street. Beck, who looked similar to Meyer, matched the all-important first description given to police when the witnesses' memories were freshest. The *quality* of the identification was about as good as it was going to get. The women were such convincing witnesses because in their minds they were certain. As Fanny Nutt said, 'I'd know him among a thousand.' With all that weight of evidence how could a jury have any doubt? There were a few inconsistencies which Beck's defence barrister did not pick up on. When giving their first description, several of the witnesses, Meissonier included, remembered a small scar on the con man's jaw line, which Beck did not have. Some of the witnesses' first descriptions described the con man as considerably stockier than Beck. In a few instances a long time had elapsed between a witness's seeing the con man and going to the police station to identify Beck. Even if the defence had exploited these points, all the witnesses still picked him out, and who would have doubted the accuracy of such a widely corroborated identification?

Tim Valentine estimates that between 6 and 7 per cent of witnesses who make a positive identification get it wrong. This might appear to be quite a small number but that 6 to 7 per cent increases with each additional witness attending an identification parade. If you have five witnesses then the risk of one of them making a false positive identification is somewhere between 30 and 35 per cent, because each witness adds to the risk of being wrong. Even if the identification parade is as fair as you can make it,[2] take nine potential witnesses to an identification parade and the chances are one of them will identify the suspect as the person who committed the crime.

Britain might be a world leader in identification procedure but there are ways of making it better. It's easy for a policeman inadvertently to influence the result of an identity parade. Any scientific test worthy of the name should be conducted 'double blind', meaning that neither the subject nor the tester knows which the 'right' choice is. Tim Valentine has suggested this reform but it hasn't been taken up. Over the last thirty years the pendulum in trial has swung towards the defence, but it now seems to have stopped. More than anything else identification evidence shows that one of the reasons for defending the guilty is to make sure you acquit the innocent.

10. Disclosure: Friends in High Places

The hot stillness of the August morning was about to be broken. Two cops holding a stubby battering-ram known as a 'red rooster' silently counted to three, and attacked the door. On the third bang they were through, a wave of police officers washing in behind them. Linda, a black woman in her early twenties, half asleep in bed, heard the noise and sat up. A boy in his late teens called Michael was asleep on a chair beside her; he knew exactly what was happening. 'It's a bust,' he said, slipping a wedge of banknotes, his proceeds from drug dealing, under the mattress. A few seconds later the cops were in the bedroom. 'Police, nobody move!'

I met tearful Linda the next day in the cells. Her husband and two small children didn't know she was in custody, charged, as was Michael, with possession with intent to supply Class A drugs. Linda did not look like a dealer or a user. She was healthily plump, had no previous convictions and had tested negative for drugs in the police station. My initial job was to get her bail. The judge heard my application and granted her bail on condition that she surrender her Jamaican passport to the police. That was a problem. Linda couldn't surrender her passport because it was somewhere in the bowels of Lunar House – widely referred to as Lunatic House – in Croydon awaiting a visa stamp. She would have to stay put, perhaps for months or, if convicted, years.

Linda was inconsolable. It was the need for extra money that landed her in jail. Her husband, a native Brit, had been making her feel bad that she wasn't contributing to the family's finances. She cut hair part-time but it wasn't bringing in much. She had resolved to do better. It was a stroke of luck when Linda's friend Coral invited her to come and make some quick money in the provinces. Coral worked as a prostitute to feed a voracious crack habit. Without telling her husband, Linda went up for a visit. The idea, as she euphemistically put it, was for her 'to fix the prostitutes' hair'. For the first few days all had gone well and Linda made money hand over fist. She stayed with Coral at her flat, which ever-enterprising Coral let other crack addicts use in exchange for free drugs. Linda quite understandably hid her takings in her pants. On the third day, to Linda's mild surprise, Coral, a late sleeper, and her crack buddies got up early, locking the flat door from the outside as they left. Linda assumed she wouldn't be gone long and drifted back to sleep. The next thing she knew the police were standing over her asking about the drugs strewn around the room and the cash in her knickers.

The Premises Search Book, in which the police record where items have been found during a search, revealed something peculiar: the wraps of heroin and crack cocaine appeared to have been sprinkled on and around the bed like fairy dust. What drug dealer, I wondered, would leave their stash lying about like that? In someone else's crack house, you kept your drugs, like your cash, out of sight. The timing of the police's arrival, shortly after Coral's exit, was also strange. It all seemed a bit too much of a coincidence. If the police were preparing to raid the flat, why not choose a time when Coral was in? Something was fishy. There was only one conclusion: Coral was setting Linda and Michael up and the police were in on it.

In criminal trials the prosecution brings the case, and therefore must prove the case. If you're going to have a trial, the defendant has to have a fighting chance of defending himself successfully. The only way that's going to happen is if the defendant knows what the allegations and the facts surrounding those allegations are. Things have moved on from when the accused had no idea what charges they faced until the witnesses came into court to make their accusations. Without pre-trial disclosure of the prosecution's case a fair trial would be impossible. And because it's for the prosecution to run the disclosure process, they decide what is and what isn't disclosable. This doesn't mean the prosecution discloses only what it feels like. There is a legal test (there's always a legal test) for initial disclosure, which they must follow. It goes like this:

The prosecutor must disclose to the accused any prosecution material . . . which might reasonably be considered capable of undermining the case for the prosecution against the accused or of assisting the case for the accused.

Hang on a minute, you might say, don't we have an adversarial system? The prosecution assisting the defence case and potentially undermining its own case doesn't seem very adversarial at all. Well, no, it isn't. Our system has important inquisitorial features without which it could not function. A fair trial depends on the prosecution's putting the interests of justice before their own. It's a contradiction. You prosecute the hell out of someone but at the same time you not only give them the stick with which to beat you but you point out your most sensitive parts as well.

There is one important proviso: the material disclosed must be relevant to the case and to the defendant's defence. The defence can't operate like a drift-net fishing trawler dragging its net along the seabed picking up every mollusc and creepy-crawly. If the material is not relevant to the case or is merely neutral, then the prosecution is under no obligation to disclose it.

To help trials work more efficiently by focusing each party's mind on what is and what isn't relevant the last Conservative government introduced defence statements. Like prosecution disclosure, defence statements are more in line with an inquisitorial rather than an adversarial system of justice. The idea is to oblige a defendant to set out his defence early in a written signed document in order to narrow the issues to be examined during trial.

You do not have to serve one but there is a great advantage in doing so because it triggers secondary disclosure of prosecution material and allows you to ask for specific things that the prosecution have failed to hand over.

One of my jobs in representing Linda was to draft her defence statement. Her defence was 'fit up' (that the evidence had been planted by Coral with the connivance of the police) and, to have any chance, she needed to find out as much about Coral and her relationship with the cops as possible. Was Coral an informant (known in the trade as a 'covert human intelligence source', or CHIS for short)? What sort of payment was she receiving? What did the contact sheets (the logs that record what transpires between an informant and the police) say? On the face of it, if she were a CHIS, then Coral had participated in the operation. It was the prosecution's secret to divulge.

Linda found it hard to focus on all this. She missed her kids desperately and wanted to go home. Then her luck changed. I applied to the judge to reconsider the condition of bail that demanded the Home Office surrender Linda's Jamaican passport. The judge agreed that the Home Office was never going to find the passport and released her on bail. Linda was overjoyed. Mindful of her money problems, she asked if it would be okay for her or her husband to go by Coral's flat to get Michael's money stashed under the mattress. 'Are you mad?' I said. 'It would be a disaster.' The money stayed put.

The prosecution's response to Linda's defence statement was not further disclosure but notice that they were going to have a public interest immunity (PII) hearing before a judge. PII hearings, held in the absence of the defence, allow the prosecution to apply for relevant and therefore disclosable information to be withheld on grounds of public interest. If Coral were a CHIS, and it was certainly looking that way, then that was obviously relevant to Linda's defence. At the same time, police informants have to be protected or the fight against crime would be seriously jeopardized. The judge's job is to decide whether the defence can still have as fair a trial as they'd have if there were full disclosure. Without the disclosure, the judge asks himself, could the defence effectively assert that Coral was a CHIS and Linda had been fitted up?

Lack of disclosure is a common way for trials, especially big ones, to die. A serious fraud case I worked on involved a large public company in which the defendants were accused of awarding and receiving business contracts allegedly lubricated by kickbacks. One man whose company benefited from a contract had presented the woman who gave it to him with a £42,000 watch. The two of them also went on a business trip together, showering each other with little *cadeaux*, including a $60 Brazilian thong – for her, not him. Back in the Home Counties, they kept up the spending. Hundreds of thousands of pounds went into sprucing up an executive home, and thong-woman fitted out a luxury horse box with her initials painted in swirling gold letters on the side. All very rum, but the case against them collapsed because the prosecution couldn't assure the court that all the relevant papers from the company involved had been unearthed.

Linda's case was perplexing in a different way. Everyone had a secret – she was keeping her moonlighting from her husband, Michael had his hidden money, and the police were hand-in-glove with double-crossing Coral. I could guess what might be going on but I didn't know the hard facts and I never would, because when the judge ordered disclosure of the police's arrangement with Coral the prosecution chucked the case. It was a score draw. All participants got to keep their lives and their secrets. Stepping out of court, I realized there was a final nagging mystery. Who would be the first to Michael's money? There were many candidates, including the police. Perhaps no one got it and to this day it remains unclaimed. That's the thing about being a barrister – for all the confidences you're told you never know the full truth.

11. Playing the Odds

The black Mercedes X-5 slowed to a stop at the red light. A moment later a Volvo estate and a large BMW nosed in behind it. A figure in a black-and-white checked police cap pulled down tight on his head stepped out of the Volvo carrying a shotgun. In one fluid movement he snapped the gun shut and brought it up to his shoulder, aiming at the X-5's front tyre. He squeezed the trigger. There was a flash of light and then the sound of the Hatton round, specially designed for shooting out tyres, reverberating off the warehouse opposite. The driver of the Mercedes, jolted into action, popped the car into first gear and shot off from the traffic lights so quickly that the startled cop dropped his gun. The Volvo leapt after it, running over the gun. The BMW, wheels spinning, plunged into the Volvo's wake. A whole convoy of cars materialized as if from nowhere, headlights sweeping over the cop by the roadside. One by one they ran over the gun as they screamed off in pursuit. The cop, left on the sidelines, picked up his buckled gun and forlornly watched as the excitement disappeared into the darkness.

If you think this cop was feeling disconsolate, then imagine how the three armed robbers felt. One minute they're scot free and merrily driving along with £1.5m worth of gold bullion in the boot, the next a whole division of CO19, the Met's firearms unit, and Flying Squad officers, bristling with guns and attitude, were barrelling down the road after them. How, they must have wondered, had the police known?*

*The Flying Squad, which specializes in detecting armed robberies, got its name because when it was first established in 1920 its officers were given authority to operate anywhere in the Metropolitan Police District.

Twenty minutes earlier

Ryan looked at his watch. It had just gone 10.15 p.m. He turned the X-5 into the cul-de-sac that ran down one side of the site's perimeter and parked at the bottom. Craig, sitting in the back, got out first. He looked around, sniffing for danger. Everything was quiet. The cul-de-sac was reassuringly dark; the only illumination came from the glow of the lights on the plant's walls. Craig pulled a black balaclava over his head and checked his 9mm Smith & Wesson revolver. The third robber joined him at the boot of the car. All three of them wore plastic body armour under their dark boiler suits. They looked unnaturally bulky, like half-inflated Michelin men.

Satisfying himself that no one was around, Ryan pulled out a pair of bolt cutters and began to clip a large circle in the perimeter fence. No alarm sounded. High on the corner of one of the buildings, the camera that was supposed to be covering the area was angled the wrong way. The third robber, wheeling a yellow porter's trolley, joined Ryan at the fence. He walked stiff-kneed as if he were impersonating Norman Wisdom. Once the hole was cut all three climbed through, taking the trolley with them. They made their way along the side of the large brick warehouse. Two thirds of the way down they came to a door that could be opened only from the inside, but which had been left ajar. Ryan, the leader, pushed it open. He'd memorized the route they were to take from a video recording. Out of his breast pocket, he unfolded a diagram of the factory's layout, just in case. It was a treasure map setting out the path to the gold.

Knowing where you were going was essential. The factory was vast, with doors, corridors and dead ends running off in all directions. It was easy to get lost. After a few turns, past steel racks that towered high to the ceiling, the three robbers came to a security door. There was a keypad to the door's right. Ryan checked a text on the mobile phone in his pocket. He entered the numbers in the text into the keypad. It glowed green, bleeped and the door swung open.

A few minutes later, they came to the melt-shop door on the other side of which, all year round, day and night, silver, platinum and gold were extracted from bits of mechanical junk. Ryan drew his gun – a Magnum .357 loaded with 'dum dum' bullets that would break apart on impact, guaranteeing maximum damage. Craig, the most nervous of the three, followed his lead and drew his Smith & Wesson. Ryan checked the last text message on the mobile and tapped the sequence of numbers into the keypad. As the door opened the noise and heat washed over them. There was no turning back now.

Evidentially, the first we see of the robbers is when CCTV cameras pick them up walking out on to the melt-shop floor. In their boiler suits they look identical to the night-shift workers over on the other side of the room. For a moment none of them notices the robbers crossing towards them. On the CCTV you see them one by one turning to look quizzically at the three figures wearing balaclavas. Ryan and Craig are in the front, guns drawn. Norman Wisdom, walking as though following a jaunty path of crazy paving, brings up the rear with his trolley. The workers, who have only just started their shift, take in the balaclavas and the guns. One points to the robbers. They think it's the day shift playing a practical joke – smelting plant hijinx at its best. But there's something about the men in balaclavas, something wrong. The men stop laughing and look at one another. They realize that this isn't a wind-up. These guys with their guns are for real.

'Do as you're told, boys, and no one will get hurt,' says Ryan, controlled but serious, ready to do whatever is necessary.

'Over here and on the floor,' says Craig, indicating with his gun.

The men comply. One of them – a big man with a worried face – is chosen to open the precious metal store which, as it happens, turns out to be unlocked. Norman Wisdom disappears from view. Thirty seconds later he's back, hefting his trolley stacked with fifteen freshly cooled gold bars.

'Anyone moves before five minutes is up and we'll shoot you. No heroes, boys, no heroes,' warns Ryan.

The three robbers leave the way they have come. The whole job, start to finish, has taken less than eight minutes. Before the men in the melt shop have raised the alarm, the robbers are back in the car with the bullion in the boot, already thinking how they're going to spend it.

Taser, taser

Norman Wisdom flicks his eyes to the rear-view mirror. The Volvo, the robbers' lead pursuer, is gaining, its nose edging ever closer to Norman's rear wheel. He is already flat out. Gunning the car up towards the top of the hill, he steals another look in the rear-view mirror. The Volvo is now glued to his rear bumper. The X-5 hit, the top of the hill, more of a knuckle than a crest, and the three men brace themselves as the car takes off. For a second everything – the robbers, the gold, the trolley, the guns, the bolt cutters – exult in their weightlessness. A second later, gravity's laws reassert themselves. As they crash back on to the tarmac the bad news is only too apparent: the Volvo is alongside them and the game is up.

Signalling defeat, Norman slows the X-5 sharply. The Volvo, taking its chance, pulls ahead and steers it towards the kerb. The BMW, coming up fast from behind, shunts the X-5 half on to the pavement. The three cars skid to a halt. The cops come at the robbers from all directions, Hatton rounds exploding around the X-5 as the police shoot out its tyres. The cops can't get out of their cars quick enough. They swarm about the robbers, adrenaline pumping. Craig is the first to get out of the X-5. He pushes open the door and flops out on to his knees, his hands hovering around his ears, the Smith & Wesson hanging off his thumb.

'Drop the gun! Drop the gun!'

Craig lets it fall. A boot, coming from behind, pushes him face down on the floor.

'Have you got any other tools?' asks a voice, using the cop/crim slang for a gun. Craig, no longer menacing but tufty and balding, says self-pityingly that he hasn't. Replying to the police caution he offers rather pathetically, 'I wish I'd never got involved in this. I've got a lovely family.'

At the moment of capture even proper villains, 'prom noms' as they're known, cannot resist reflecting on their lot, and express, if not quite remorse, at least an admission of their human frailty.

Up front things aren't going so smoothly. Ryan has tossed the Magnum but he isn't exiting the car quickly enough. Two CO19 officers start to yank him out. Ryan isn't having that and, according to the officers, fights back against them. Four policemen instantly surround him; one kicks his legs from under him. Ryan falls to his knees but keeps up the fight, using a mixture of street-wise cunning and moves learned during a brief stint in the French Foreign Legion. It is too much for the police. They can't get the handcuffs on him.

A CO19 cop, armed with a yellow taser, rushes forward. 'Taser, taser!' he shouts.

There is no way he can use the weapon from that distance with so many other policemen about, so he switches it to 'dry stun' mode, places the taser's little blue lights on Ryan's back and gives him 50,000 volts. Ryan doesn't miss a beat. The cop looks at the taser and shakes it. This isn't supposed to happen. He doesn't know that Ryan's body armour is absorbing the electrical shock. He recharges the taser and zaps him again. Still nothing. Home Office guidelines say tasers should not be used in dry stun mode against the head or neck unless 'absolutely necessary' to save lives. It's much safer to zap soft fatty tissue which absorbs the shock better. Even though he is surrounded by armed CO 19 police officers, the cop places the taser against the back of Ryan's neck and pulls the trigger. Ryan bucks as the electricity shoots through him. The police seize their moment, pull his arms behind his back and click on the handcuffs.*

Finally, they haul out Norman. He comes without any fuss. He's seen the beating that Ryan, his best friend, has received and that isn't for him. Coming out of the car, he says, 'Thank fuck, I didn't have a gun.'

I don't know whether he said that because he'd seen the warm welcome Ryan had received from CO 19, or to minimize his role in the armed robbery. If he was trying to minimize his involvement he was wasting his time because the principle of joint enterprise says that if you throw your lot in with robbers with guns, then not having a 'tool' yourself is neither here nor there: you're just as guilty as they are.

Only Ryan managed to keep his mouth shut at the scene. A few hours later, handcuffed to a hospital bed as he came round from his tasering, he said to his police guard, 'There are only two or three people who could have bubbled me up.'

You couldn't blame Ryan for wondering if he'd been ratted on. It certainly wasn't by chance that the police just happened to be on hand as he and his robber buddies were pulling away from the smelting plant at 10.30 at night with £1.5m worth of gold bullion in the boot. I'd be curious, too.

---

*The taser used by the officer was an M26. In November 2008 then Home Secretary Jacqui Smith announced that 10,000 upgraded X26 tasers would be issued to police officers. The Metropolitan Police turned the offer down because they considered it would erode public confidence in the police.

State Amber

So what did the police know? And how? They knew that a certain commodity (the gold bars) would be targeted and they knew roughly where the robbers would strike. This tip-off intelligence had come not from a grass but by listening in on the criminals. There are two main ways you can do that: put a probe in a room or a car, or alternatively, tap their phones. Intelligence, however, is never perfect, and the gaps have to be filled in by good old-fashioned police work, which narrowed it down further until their 'best guess' was that the most likely target would be a smelting plant on the outskirts of North-east London. There were other possible venues, but the cops were confident enough of this location to concentrate the great majority of their efforts on the smelting plant site.

In operations dealing with serious crime like armed robbery, the police have three levels of command. The gold commander, in this instance a detective chief inspector from the Flying Squad, has overall charge of the operation. He has responsibility for strategy. The silver commander, a Flying Squad detective inspector, runs the operation on the ground, making the day-to-day tactical decisions. When and if he decides that the time is right to arrest the suspects, he passes control of the operation over to the bronze commander, a CO 19 sergeant or inspector, who is then responsible for nicking the crims.

In many ways the silver commander has the most important job because he has to react to events as they unfold. It is he who sifts the intelligence to get the best prediction of when, where and how the crime is to take place. Aside from probes and phone taps, there are quite a few information-gathering tools at his disposal. He can set up observation posts (OPs), tail potential criminals around, use a CHIS for information and scour police databases.

As part of their surveillance and intelligence-gathering the police had placed an OP at the top of the cul-de-sac where the robbers had cut their way into the plant. The cops had wanted to position the OP at the bottom of the cul-de-sac in order to be able to watch this whole section of the perimeter but there was nowhere to hide it. This meant that while the officer manning the OP had seen the X-5 arrive, he couldn't see where its occupants had gone or what they were doing. Remember the whole job took only eight minutes. Was that enough time to break into the plant, bypass the security apparatus, subdue the workforce and seize the gold? There was no telling if the men in the X-5 were even there to commit the robbery. They might have been only doing a recce.

There was a further complication. The police suspected that the three robbers were not acting alone and had an inside man preparing the ground. This, they decided, made it impossible to warn the smelting plant's management of their suspicions because it might tip off the inside man and therefore the robbers. Hang on a minute, you might say, isn't this all getting a bit risky? Shouldn't the police's first priority be public safety? The Met's tag line is 'Working together to make London safer'. Who's being made safer by allowing potential armed robbers, violent men, even the chance of breaking into the smelting plant? Someone might end up getting killed.

This is a difficult dilemma to square. The safest and best place to arrest the robbers would be while they're cutting their way through the perimeter fence, before they had entered the plant. But it was not a realistic option because the police didn't know for sure that the job was going to take place; they just had a pretty good idea. Taking the robbers in the plant was out of the question because not only would that alert the inside man but workers could get caught in the crossfire or taken hostage. The last thing anyone wanted was a shoot-out. A balance, therefore, had to be found between nicking armed blaggers, the Flying Squad's *raison d'être*, and the safety of the smelting plant's workforce, the police's duty of care. A compromise solution was arrived at: we might not know for sure that a robbery is going to take place and we can't watch the whole perimeter because it's too large, but we can put ourselves in the best possible position to catch the robbers with their pants down should they try to take the gold.

In a perfect world with perfect intelligence, the silver commander would arrest the robbers by using what is known as a 'fixed plot'. A fixed plot is when you concentrate your resources in one place, which means that when you come to make the intervention you've got maximum control to effect the arrest. The problem with a fixed plot is just that, it's fixed. Imagine if the Flying Squad had massed their forces at one end of the smelting plant site, only for the robbers to come and go from the other unapprehended. The only feasible option therefore was a 'mobile plot', which allows you to keep the cars of armed police moving so that you can deploy them when and where you need to. It's difficult to pull off because with a mobile plot you're shadowing the potential criminals as they move in to do the job, and, if they twig, you've blown the operation.

On the night of the robbery the silver commander was sitting in the control car having developments relayed back to him from various OPs and cars. He was aware, therefore, that the potential robbers had driven down into the cul-de-sac and that they'd been parked there for some time. Then he got a call that the X-5 was driving out of the cul-de-sac at speed with its lights off. Were they finishing their recce or were they robbing the place? He knew he had to make a decision and fast. He went with his gut feeling and radioed the bronze commander with the 'State Amber' code that signals for the arrest to be made. As things turned out, he'd made the right call.

The inside man

Ten minutes after the robbery, Freddie, the security guard, was down in the melt shop making sure the workers were all right. They were his colleagues, whom he'd worked with for three years. He put his arm around them, whispered words of support and, as it was part of his job, searched them when they left to go home. When the police arrived, Freddie went out of his way to help.

In the following days, Freddie kept his cool and continued to show up for work at the smelting plant, even discussing with his colleagues whether one of the plant's employees might've been in on the robbery. It was odd behaviour because he must have known that the net was closing in. The police had Ryan's phone and with it a series of very incriminating texts that had come from Freddie's mobile on the night of the robbery. The first read, 'How long.' The second, '10 would be a good time ok.' The third text was the most damning. It said, '21 is the code good luck see you in a few months.' The police also had the security logs, which revealed that at the time of the robbery, Freddie was in the security office sitting in front of a large bank of monitors that showed what the cameras around the site were filming.

In the end, Freddie didn't have to wait long. Three days after the other robbers had been caught, the police came for him. Freddie, bless him, had another criminal matter pending after a tempestuous visit to his girlfriend in Scotland. There had been a disagreement outside a pub and Freddie, no peacemaker, had demonstrated his general unhappiness with the state of his life by biting off another man's nose. Serious though this was, it wasn't in the same league as armed robbery. The Scots would have to wait their turn.

I'll show you mine, if you show me yours

Nicking armed robbers is all very well but it's only half the job. You've still got to prosecute them, which is where I come in. Was I leading this prosecution? Certainly not! I was third prosecuting counsel, the junior's junior, the gentleman's gentleman, a gopher in a wig.

Multi-defendant trials take lots of time to prepare. The case has to be put together and then served on the defence. Further investigations inevitably need to be made. Once these are completed the alleged robbers then serve their defence case statements. As with Linda, the statements set out each defendant's defence which, depending on what they've said, may then trigger further disclosure of prosecution material that is relevant to their stated defence. The only relevant material that would not be disclosed would be that which the prosecution applied successfully to withhold because it came under public interest immunity (PII), that is material that would jeopardize the sources and methods – intelligence and the like – that make police investigations of serious crime possible.

All four men were charged with robbery, but their defences differed:

1. Craig's defence was duress. *Archbold*, the criminal lawyer's bible, defines duress as 'a threat of physical harm to the person (including, possibly, imprisonment), which was of such gravity that it might well have caused a sober person of reasonable firmness sharing the defendant's characteristics [i.e. age, sex, IQ, etc.] and placed in the same situation to act in the same way as the defendant acted'. Craig said he was being duressed by Algie, a well-known gangster, because he owed him money, which he couldn't repay. Algie therefore gave

Craig a choice: either participate in the gold bullion robbery, or suffer serious violence.

2. Freddie's defence was duress but with a twist. He was saying that Ryan, backed up by Algie, had intimidated him into being the inside man. When Freddie had initially refused, Ryan pulled out a pistol and shot it between his legs. Freddie was also under the impression that someone had been shot dead by one of the other defendants, which gave extra oomph to the intimidation. The shooting allegation was partly true. Some years earlier, Norman had been tried for the murder of a teenager but acquitted because it couldn't be proved he had pulled the trigger.

3. Ryan and Norman Wisdom were saying something much more interesting: the armed break-in wasn't the *robbery* it looked like but a *walk-in theft* (many fewer years in prison for a walk-in theft) organized by disgruntled employees at the smelting plant. The reason Ryan had a gun was in order to make the 'robbery' look convincing in front of the CCTV cameras. Most importantly, they also claimed that the police were in on the whole enterprise, enticed by the prospect of the publicity surrounding a spectacular 'collar' of tooled-up robbers. According to Ryan and Norman, the police assertion that their knowledge of the location of the robbery was no more than a 'best guess' was a lie to conceal their involvement. The police knew damn well that a robbery was going to take place because they'd been tipped off. The lynchpin between the police and the smelting plant was none other than Algie. He was the *agent provocateur* who had set the 'robbers' up to do the job, supplying the guns in the process. The police were waiting for the 'robbers' to leave with the gold so they could spring the trap, get the arrest and bask in the excellent publicity.

This was a very clever defence for two reasons. First, Algie was a major criminal who could plausibly be accused of being an *agent provocateur*. Second, by making police knowledge of Algie's activities the heart of their defence, Ryan and Norman were putting pressure on the prosecution to reveal material that might be impossible to disclose. Failure to disclose – or even just the suspicion that something was being hidden – opened up the possibility of the trial being stopped before the jury was asked to come to a verdict. They were hoping the law just might intervene. It was a long shot, but in trials, as in life, you make your own luck, and Ryan and Norman's calculated defence was about to get all four robbers very lucky indeed.

Some of the Flying Squad's most important pieces of intelligence about the robbery came from another investigation. This investigation had recorded Algie apparently admitting that he was not only aware of the robbery but in on it. Commiserating about the robbers' arrest with one of his associates, Algie said, 'I put three into this.' Those five words went to the heart of Ryan and Norman's defence because they gave credence to the proposition that Algie was the robbery's mastermind. Whatever 'I put three into this' actually meant (was it guns, robbers or money?), did Algie's 'three' mean that he was a player in the 'job'? If it did, this would certainly have to be disclosed. Algie's words assisted the defence in a subtler way, too: with his name swirling in the background, an impression of subterfuge was created, helping them suggest, even though there was no actual evidence, that the police were involved in setting the robbers up. This was a tantalizing prospect. Entrapment might be no defence in law but police participation in a crime is permissible only if it's to obtain evidence of criminal acts, not, as one law lord put it, 'to tempt people to commit crimes in order to expose their bad characters and punish them'. If the police were involved, whether they were working with Algie or not, then the defendants would have an open-and-shut claim for the trial to be stopped as an abuse of the court's process.

It was time to call in the other investigation's prosecuting barrister and quick. There was no way this barrister could swan in through the main entrance of the court because as soon as the defence saw him they'd realize that something was afoot. So the next day, lying down in the rear seat of a police car, he was deposited at a well-hidden back entrance to the court. A waiting usher whisked him along little travelled corridors, so the first anyone saw of him was when he magically appeared at the back of the courtroom, cheeky grin plastered across his face.

At first glance, this barrister, by assuring the judge that Algie was not involved in any material way in the robbery, helped us. This meant the 'I put three into this' would not have to be disclosed to the defence for the simple reason that it didn't assist their case. The barrister wasn't really there to help us but to protect the other police investigation and he did a fine job scaring the judge into not ordering the disclosure of its other secrets. (They had a marvellous photograph of Craig and Algie walking down the street with presentation bottles of malt whisky, chatting happily together. Better still, they even had a bugged conversation of Algie encouraging the idea that Craig use him to construct a phoney duress. Sadly, we couldn't use either.) Our trial might still be on, but it wasn't going to get any easier and, fatally, defence suspicions about police collusion had not been dispelled.

The robbers' second stroke of luck was that the basis for the Flying Squad's knowledge of their plans came, in part, through phone taps. Phone taps, known in the criminal justice game as 'intercepts', are not only inadmissible in a court of law but it is a criminal offence even to suggest their existence. The reason for these strict rules is that the security services don't want people finding out what they can and cannot listen in on. This fact along with the other investigation's secrets meant that there was an endless series of unsatisfactory PII hearings, which further fuelled the defence's suspicions that the police had something to hide.

The police's line that they hadn't *known* the smelting plant was the robbers' target but that it was merely their 'best guess' didn't help either. It had taken a battering in court. Dozens of officers involved in the operation had come into the witness box repeating this best-guess mantra. Other evidence before the court appeared to contradict it. There was a video taken by a cop of the route the robbers would take from their lock-up (which the police had been watching for weeks) to the plant; the police also had a plan and aerial photo of the smelting plant. Add in the fact that the doors to the strong room storing the gold had been left open and it was easy for the defence (not to mention the jury) to conclude that the police weren't being entirely frank.

We had one remaining trump card. The judge had seen all the secret material, seen the transcripts and intelligence reports; he knew neither we nor the police were holding anything back that would assist the robbers' defence, let alone suggest the cops were in cahoots with Algie or disgruntled smelting plant employees.

The trial ground on and I finally began to feel some optimism. The prosecution case was drawing to a close and the defence case would soon begin. Focus would shift away from the police to what exactly three armed men in body armour were doing at the smelting plant if not trying to rob it. Ultimately, I figured the jury would see there was no evidence of police entrapment but lots of evidence of an armed robbery. All we had to do was call the remaining police witnesses and sit back. One of our last witnesses was the silver commander himself. Things were going swimmingly when Craig's barrister asked this apparently innocuous question, 'When did you first become aware of Algie?'

The silver commander replied, 'At the time of the robbery I didn't know who Algie was. I have become aware of him because his name was in the defence statements.'

Here was the robbers' third stroke of luck – delivered on a plate by the investigation's top cop. Claiming that he hadn't known about Algie was plain wrong. Of course the police knew who Algie was. He's a premier league villain. Surveillance logs completed during the investigation had his name all over them. The silver commander tried to correct what he'd said. He'd been giving evidence in the PII hearings for months. There were things he was allowed to say in open court and things he wasn't. I don't think he was trying to mislead anyone, he just got confused. However it had happened, it was too late and the damage was done. Things were about to unravel and even I knew it.

The silver commander's mistake was so important because he was one of the main people to explain to the judge what the police knew and when during the PII hearings, and the judge therefore had to trust him. In isolation the silver commander's error wouldn't have mattered, but when the judge put it together with the evidence contradicting the police's best-guess claim, he got spooked. The defence seized their moment, arguing that he was trying to mislead the jury by telling lies. They said the police were attempting to withhold key information about their knowledge of a person linked to the robbery and thus hide their involvement. This, the defence submitted, was blatant non-disclosure, which meant that the robbery count should be stayed as an abuse of process. We countered that everything that the police had on the robbery and Algie had been shown to the judge and therefore there was no non-disclosure or abuse of process. The judge disagreed. Put simply, he no longer trusted the police and by extension the prosecution. The robbery count was replaced with a theft instead. The robbers, or should I now say thieves, pleaded guilty to the theft and got six years in prison rather than sixteen.

The armed robbers seemingly caught red-handed came up smiling. Things were much less happy for the police and the prosecution. We had an open-and-shut case but it had slipped through our fingers. Prosecutors, rightly and fairly, have to play by the rules in a way that robbers do not. The rules that ensure defendants are able to put their best possible defence can be used by the experienced and the cunning to stymie, even sabotage, a trial. Ryan and Norman had used their defence to give themselves the best chance of attacking the prosecution's weaknesses. Prosecutions of serious crimes such as armed robberies are always particularly vulnerable. They take expert planning and a sensitive nose for where the weaknesses in a case may lie. It's easy to miss something that later rears up and kills a prosecution. The irony is that in some situations the safeguards designed to help acquit the innocent provide the guilty with a way out.

We in the prosecution might have been feeling hard done by, but it was nothing compared with the jurors. They had got the worst deal. They'd sat through four months of evidence and the only decision they'd been allowed to make was how many sugars to have with their tea.

12. Cross-examination

'I'm begging you, Gavin. Take a 20.' (I mean Section 20 of the Offences Against the Persons Act, otherwise known as causing GBH but *without* intending to do so.) 'Full facts. Every kick. Every whack.'

'I can't. Look at the papers, Alex. It's a bone dance. Jaw broken – twice. It's an 18.' (That is Section 18 of the above act or GBH *with* the intent.)

'Please, Gavin. Please. Let's not have a trial on this one.'

At this point, I'd fall to my knees if it would help persuade him to accept the lesser charge for Victor, my client. I'd kiss his boots, do anything, because I've got a bad feeling about this trial. I don't fancy it in the same way I don't fancy knocking a nail through my kneecap.

Our dispute isn't a lawyers' technical argument between sections in a statute. The outcome matters. The maximum sentence for GBH with intent is life, but the maximum for GBH minus the intent is five years. Victor won't get life but it's still going to make a big difference to his final sentence. If I can carve the case, I could reduce the time he'll have to spend in prison by more than half. The tunnel vision, the familiar blend of ego, empathy for my client and competitive professional duty, closes in around me. I'll do anything to get the result that I want.

I remember my old pupilmaster's favourite trick: like a football hooligan in a saloon bar who's had his pint spilled, he'd stand very, very close to his opponent as though he were about to head-butt him. Worked beautifully. I haven't got the presence. My forehead barely reaches the knot in Gavin's tie and my voice doesn't have the

Northern Irish menace of my old mentor's. I go back to ineffectual wheedling instead.

'Go on, Gavin. Take the 20. Please. I'm begging you. No one wants this trial.'

'What about the perverting?' asks Gavin, losing his patience. 'What do you say about that? You're not offering me anything, Alex. Do I look fucking stupid?'

Ah, that would be the perverting of the course of justice, count number two on the indictment, which, it was alleged, had taken place ten days after the initial assault. Horace got his wired-up jaw broken all over again by Barry, one of Victor's mates. The 'perverting', as it's known for short, relates to the alleged threats Victor had made to Horace, warning him not to go to the police a few seconds before Barry, defendant no. 2 in the dock, smacked him in the face. I had no idea what to say about the perverting other than it didn't help. It was a separate offence, committed on a different day, and therefore would attract a consecutive rather than concurrent sentence, further pushing up Victor's years in jail. Victor's defence to the GBH was that he had been acting in self-defence. His defence to the perverting was that 'it weren't me'. We both knew he was guilty of something. The question was what?

Victor was unlucky. He had been badly advised by his solicitor in the police station, who had allowed him to admit in interview that he had lost his temper during his argument with Horace. In order for self-defence to succeed, we would have to show that Horace had started the fight and that the defensive tactics Victor employed had been proportionate. By admitting to losing his temper, Victor – along with Eugene, his wingman in the alleged assault, and defendant no. 3 – had edged to within touching distance of a jury finding that he had not only beaten the crap out of Horace, but had formed the intent to cause 'really serious harm' before doing so. In my heart of hearts, I knew the damage limitation was not looking too good, but at least Gavin, a generous soul, was consulting the interested parties.

At this stage one thing the interested parties might like to have considered is that trials can be exceedingly unpleasant. This is especially true when a defendant like Victor has nothing left to lose. If you're going down, you might as well go down after a full-blooded courtroom bollock-kicking. In those situations, trial by jury feels more like trial by ordeal. For the witnesses giving evidence it's about as much fun as being dragged about chained to the back of a pick-up truck. The CPS doesn't usually take these realities into consideration: its test for going on with a prosecution is whether there's a reasonable prospect of conviction; the verbal spanking that Horace was going to receive doesn't come into it.

A few minutes later Gavin came back to extinguish my softening hopes of a deal. They were going for the full house. The trial was on. Half an hour later prosecuting counsel had wrapped up his outline of the case to the jury and had called Horace as his first witness. The defence barristers, Eugene's brief and I, squeezed on to counsel's row, waited in anticipation for Horace to make his entrance.

Often you will see dull-eyed barristers appear to be uninterested in the witnesses coming into court. Don't be fooled. It's an act. Beneath the cool veneer, we're desperate to see the witnesses (especially the victim) because we want to size them up. Even in the most placid of trials, the question we ask ourselves when a witness enters court is, 'Can I get the better of him, show him who's boss – knock his teeth out?' Nasty, I know.

When Horace walked into court I was aghast. He was a delicate boy of nineteen with a girlish 'afro', wearing a bright red sweater with the collars sticking out. His mother sat in the front row of the public gallery dabbing her eyes. I could smell the sympathy rising off the jury. Eugene's barrister, who like a ventriloquist could speak without moving his lips, whispered, 'We're fucked.'

The jury looked at Horace, mean and tough like Little Orphan Annie, and then at Victor and Eugene, mean and tough like George Foreman and his bigger, badder brother. It was an unequal match. Here's a tip: if you're up for GBH with intent and perverting the course of justice, don't spend your six months on remand pumping yourself up in the prison gym. Thank God, Barry, off the scale when it came to looking mean and tough, had pleaded guilty before the jury had come into court.

Appearance counts. It's not just your build that is important. Juries also evaluate witnesses by gauging their 'demeanour': do they look nervous; do they look honest; do they seem nice, and well ... innocent? We barristers want our opponent's witnesses to be brutish, shifty and palpably dishonest. My ideal prosecution witness would be a malnourished Peter Lorre who was being distracted by a man at the back of the court waving a tasty chicken leg.

The importance of demeanour, as with physique and type, is and has always been built into the criminal trial. For centuries, before lawyers were allowed to appear in the criminal courts, the 'confrontation trial' was venerated because it was believed that in the clash between accused and accuser the truth would shine so brightly as to make it unmistakable on the face of the witness telling it. In the *Duke of Dorset v Girdler*, a 1720 civil case, the judge declared that 'the other side ought not to be deprived of the opportunity of confronting the witnesses, and examining them publicly, which has always been found the most effectual method of discovering of the truth'.[1]

Faith in absolute truth emanating from the soul of our fellow man is appealing. It's a comfort to think that we as human beings are able to discern the real meaning of what others say simply from how it's presented. Certainly, I have been in court when the accused has come across as so plainly truthful that, despite the odds against him, his innocence is suddenly not in doubt. It wasn't anything they said in particular but the way that they said it. In fact, trust in the telltale signs of a witness's demeanour – their voice, expression and gesture – has stretched beyond the usual Anglo-Saxon jurisdictions. Article 6(3)(d) of the European Convention on Human Rights guarantees a defendant the right 'to examine [i.e. question] or have examined witnesses against him'. I assume the clause is there because proselytizing British drafters, steeped in the common law tradition, insisted upon it.

Unsurprisingly, America is the *ne plus ultra* believer in so-called demeanour evidence. The Sixth Amendment of the US Constitution, known as the Confrontation Clause, guarantees that 'the accused shall enjoy the right to ... be confronted with the witnesses against him ...' The Supreme Court has repeatedly reaffirmed the value of demeanour and the Confrontation Clause. Supreme Court Justice Antonin Scalia giving judgement in *Coy v Iowa* wrote that it was 'more difficult to tell a lie about a person "to his face" than "behind his back"'. Another leading American judge saw something almost transcendental happen when an accuser came face-to-face with his accused:

Demeanor is of the utmost importance in the determination of the credibility of a witness. The innumerable telltale indicators which fall from a witness during the course of his examination are often much more of an indication to judge or jury of his credibility and the reliability of his evidence than is the literal meaning of his words.[2]

Horace, looking plaintive and moist in the witness box, represented the epitome of the truthful witness and he hadn't opened his mouth. Who, aside from barristers who must persuade themselves the other side's witnesses are liars while their own are saints, could fail to warm to him?

The reality, as research has consistently shown, is that spotting deception or truth from a witness's manner and bearing is like pinning the tail on the donkey. It's pure guesswork. A humble, plain-speaking witness might be a compelling one, but it doesn't mean he's telling the truth. A stammer or a wipe of the hand proves nothing as to veracity. One American study developed a model for non-verbal behaviour separating 'tells' into three channels: face, body and voice. They discovered that when you're trying to deceive someone it's easiest to control your face, then your body and lastly your voice. So-called 'telltale indicators' such as avoiding someone's gaze or uneasily scratching your nose demonstrate nothing as to the truthfulness of the story you're telling. In fact, researchers found that body movement decreased when a high stress lie was told. Interestingly, voice is the best indicator of deception: increased hesitations, speech errors and the pitch of the witness's voice reveal more than a shaking hand.

My knowing this did not help Victor. However, I had one tool at my command which even in my clumsy hands could tease out the truth whatever it might be. The tool was cross-examination. Barristers hold cross-examination dear. It's our article of faith. We agree with the jurist J. H. Wigmore, who, back in the 1940s, wrote: '[Cross-examination] is beyond doubt the greatest legal engine ever invented for the discovery of the truth.' The downside of cross-examination, which Wigmore doesn't mention, is that that's when the unpleasantness begins.

Before Horace could be cross-examined, the prosecution barrister, as the party calling him, had to take him through his testimony. This is known as 'examination-in-chief', or 'in chief' for short. Examination-in-chief is the form of questioning used when a witness is taken through his evidence. You must not 'lead' the witness, so you ask open questions starting with words such as what, why and where. With the prosecution barrister guiding him, Horace gave lovely evidence. The story that he told flowed naturally. He was precise and confident on the facts. His account of the alleged kicking was bolstered by the speech impediment, which he will have for the rest of his life thanks to Barry punching his already broken jaw. It was like a leitmotif to the wrongs inflicted against him by Victor et al.

Horace's evidence did not vary much from what Victor had told police in interview months before. They both hung around the same estate where Victor retailed cannabis. The disagreement between them had arisen not over drugs but a gold chain. Victor had expressed an interest in buying it from Horace but wanted to verify its quality before parting with £60. He gave Horace a £10 deposit and took the chain to the local jeweller, who noticed that the clasp was broken. Victor decided he didn't want the chain, but he failed to return it. Irritated, Horace called Victor and arranged to meet him on the estate to discuss matters. It was then that the mismatch staring the jury in the face began. Horace showed up with his little brother Barnaby but Victor arrived with Eugene and four or five other fully grown lads.

Lurking in Horace's beautifully delivered evidence was a potentially fatal problem, which was that at certain important points it diverged from the statements he'd given to police at the time of the assaults. Inconsistencies and lies are not necessarily the same but they can both eat away at a witness's credibility. Cross-examination tests the evidence itself rather than the style in which it has been given. I hoped that by underlining how Horace had changed his story, it might be possible to shake the faith that the jury had in him. The question was what would the jury trust more: Horace's winning demeanour or my cross-examination – the so-called engine for the discovery of truth?

One of Horace's most damaging pieces of testimony in court, which he'd not put in his witness statement, was that Victor had boasted he'd broken the gold chain in order to humiliate him. This allegation was very important because if the jury accepted it then that would be evidence that Victor was not only the aggressor but had also set Horace up for the kicking: in other words, that Victor intended to cause Horace really serious injury. The 'lie' cannot go unchallenged, which is where cross-examination comes in. You establish the piece of evidence, you get the witness to underline its unforgettable importance and then you point out that he failed to mention it in his witness statement.

ME: You said in your evidence a moment ago that Victor claimed he'd broken your chain?

HORACE: Yes.

ME: That must have been pretty annoying.

HORACE: It was.

ME: You thought he was toying with you?

HORACE: Yes.

ME: He was humiliating you in front of all these people?

HORACE: Yes.

ME: A humiliation like that. It's not something you're going to forget?

HORACE: No.

ME: Before you came into court, you reread your statement, didn't you?

HORACE: Yes, I did.

ME: Let's have the usher pass you a copy. That's your statement, isn't it?

HORACE: It is.

ME: At the top of the first page there's a declaration to its accuracy and truthfulness, correct?

HORACE: Correct.

ME: And there's your signature at the bottom of the first page. In fact your signature is on every page, yes?

HORACE: Yes.

ME: Which verifies that it's your statement and it's accurate to the best of your recollection?

HORACE: That's right.

ME: From the date at the top, this statement was given three
          days after the alleged assault?

HORACE: Yes.

ME: When events were fresh in your memory?

HORACE: Yes.

ME: Looking at your statement, where does it say that
          Victor boasted that he broke your gold chain?
          (*Horace checks through the pages. I silently count to five and repeat
          the question.*)

ME: I've asked you a very simple question, Horace. Show
          the court where in your statement you say that Victor
          boasted that he'd broken your chain.
          (*I count to five again.*)

ME: It's not in your statement, is it? Is it?

HORACE: No.

ME: It's not there because it never happened. You're adding
          it now. Telling lies to bolster your story and get Victor,
          your friend, into trouble.

At this point the jury will be wondering why Horace added this
incriminating detail a full eight months after the alleged assault
but failed to put it in his statement a couple of days after it happened. It will also be wondering whether Horace is a liar. And it's
here, thanks to cross-examination, that Horace's demeanour, his
trump card, starts to work against him. His credibility becomes
the albatross around his neck because it looks like a cynical act.
The jurors begin to worry that perhaps he's trying to con them.
Potentially very damaging because once a jury's trust is gone, it's
very hard to get back.

Horace's evidence was riddled with 'inconsistencies' like the
above. He claimed that when he'd arrived at the estate to confront
Victor, he had tried to walk away but had been prevented by Victor's friends. This wasn't in his witness statement. He said that

once he had been pushed to the ground, he had seen Victor kick him in the face, the blow which, the prosecutor had said in his opening speech, had 'undoubtedly broken Horace's jaw'. The problem with this was that in his witness statement he had said he had been protecting his face with his arms, chin tucked to his chest. So how could he have seen who was kicking him?

I went through the two versions of Horace's evidence picking out each lie and inconsistency. It's a slow process establishing the points that you wish to make through one short statement, phrased as a question, after another. For the witness the experience is a vile one. Horace weathered the questions badly. The details of his story kept changing. He said that Victor had refused to give back the chain but then conceded that he might have. His silences grew longer, the anxiety on his face more apparent. After a while he stopped answering, failing even to deny my accusations that he was a liar.

From time to time during my cross-examination I glanced at his mother, watching me from the public gallery as I laid into her son. She was the driving force behind the prosecution. It was she who had got Horace to go to the police. She wanted justice for her son and revenge against, as she saw it, a pack of thugs. Her boy would never talk properly again. He was looking at years of surgery and pain. She was determined not to let the bullies get away with it. And now watching me humiliate her son, her Horace, standing up for his rights, must have been like watching him get assaulted all over again. Who was on trial here, she must have wondered, victim or accused? I didn't let up.

Horace might have seemed sensational in the witness box at the start of the day but by the end of it his evidence had disintegrated. Looking and sounding the part is not necessarily enough. In the 1920s Lord Justice Atkin wrote: 'an ounce of intrinsic merit or demerit in the evidence, that is to say, the value of the comparison of evidence with known facts, is worth pounds of demeanour'.[3] Surely, he was right.

The next day, I knew the prosecution were rattled when they sprang a surprise witness on the defence. For nearly a whole year, Horace's little brother, Barnaby, had refused to make a statement or come to court, but all of a sudden he'd changed his mind. In cross-examination you approach each witness differently. It paid to be kindly to Barnaby. Tone is a great way of indicating to the jury without saying anything how shocking it is that the other side is putting up a young boy to perjure himself.

Horace's mother was beginning to help, too. Sitting in the front row of the public gallery, she was no longer the concerned mother but the manipulator-in-chief bent on revenge. Horace's evidence was looking so shaky, I suggested to the jury that she felt obliged to produce an even more winsome son to shore Horace's account up. In the end Barnaby's evidence just further contradicted what Horace had said. The trial was no longer about Horace being beaten up by Victor and Eugene, but about his lies.

Things were so peachy I should have been capering around like an old peasant who's just married his son to the headman's daughter. But I was not: instead I felt a deep sense of unease. For years, I am ashamed to admit, I revelled in meting out verbal pummellings on monosyllabic witnesses. Soaring closing speeches are good. So is drawing the facts of the case together and deftly spinning them so that members of the jury, without knowing it, literally nod their heads in agreement. But they do not top a great cross-examination. My faith in questions and answers, a secular catechism, is the bedrock of my faith in the jury trial. It's the belief that defines my vocation as a criminal barrister just as the belief in transubstantiation defines a Catholic. I had trusted cross-examination's brutal efficiency in getting at the truth but now I wasn't so sure. My cross-examination exposing Horace's lies might have helped Victor but had it shone any light on what had really happened that day on the estate?

John Spencer and Rhona Flin, in their book *The Evidence of*

Children, argue that there is an inherent contradiction within cross-examination because it tries to pursue two conflicting, even self-defeating, objectives. On the one hand it aims to undermine the honesty and accuracy of a witness, while on the other attempting to extract details from that witness to assist the cross-examiner's case. Spencer and Flin are critical of the notion that cross-examination done properly should be like leading a dog on a very short leash where the witness is able to answer only 'yes' or 'no'. This constrains a witness's ability to answer questions properly, and misleads the jury. They also point out that there is a tendency in cross-examination to milk marginal points at the expense of the witness's testimony as a whole. They use the example of a nine-year-old girl who was a victim of a sex attack. The girl has picked out her alleged attacker on an identification parade. During cross-examination she is asked a series of questions she can't answer on peripheral matters such as the colour of her attacker's shoes, in order to undermine her account. I asked myself whether I was using the same sort of tricks as the barrister cross-examining the girl. Was I scoring cheap points to obscure the truth of what had really happened?

In a study by David Luus and Gary Wells children watched a story on video and then were asked questions about what they had seen.[4] Open questions, that is examination-in-chief, produced more accurate testimony from the children than closed leading questions of the sort used in cross-examination. But mock juries who were shown recordings of the children's answers without having seen the original story could not distinguish which mode of questioning had produced the most accurate and reliable answers. Extrapolate that to a real trial and you wonder how much use cross-examination really is.

Steps have been taken to make cross-examination easier for the witness. It is now possible to give evidence from behind a screen, or by video link. The old and frankly revolting practice of cross-examining a victim of a sexual assault about past sexual history for no reason other than to damage their credibility as a witness, is now prohibited. The Bar Council Code of Conduct says that '[a] barrister when conducting proceedings in Court: must not make statements or ask questions which are merely scandalous or intended or calculated only to vilify, insult or annoy'. The most effective restraint on cross-examination, however, is self-interest because to be effective when questioning a witness, as in any form of advocacy, you have to take the court with you. Duffing up a witness might be fun and make you feel like a proper barrister, but the last thing you want at the end of your cross-examination is the jury saying 'oh that poor witness'. If you vilify, you lose the jury and once you've done that you've lost the case.

At the end of the prosecution evidence and before the defence case we had a break. I nipped out of court, and nearly ran into Horace and his mum. We stared at each other for a moment. They didn't look angrily at me but surprised as though they'd been slapped in the face and didn't know why. I side-stepped them and headed for Victor in the cells. He was softly spoken and shy. I could see he was nervous about going into the witness box so I tried to reassure him.

'Never lose your temper.

'If the prosecutor calls you a liar, he's only doing his job. Don't take it personally.

'If the prosecutor suggests something that you disagree with, say no, that's wrong.

'Stick to your account of what happened.

'If you don't understand a question say so.

'And, relax.'

I tailored my last piece of advice for him especially, repeating what I had told him many times before: 'It's not a question of "guilty" or "not guilty" but of Section 18 or Section 20. In other words, it's out by Christmas or still inside come next Christmas.'

'It'd be nice to be out by this Christmas,' he said, and of course he meant it.

Victor held up fairly well in the witness box. His admissions in interview were already before the jury. Prosecution counsel tried to establish the intent but Victor resolutely maintained the line he'd given in police interview – that there had been no kicks. The prosecutor found himself with little room for manoeuvre because he'd told the jury in his opening speech that the kick was the blow which had 'undoubtedly' broken Horace's jaw. If the jury was not sure about this, then, in the prosecution's own terms, GBH with intent was not proved.

And that is how it turned out. After a few hours in retirement, the jury came back and found Victor and Eugene guilty of GBH without intent and Victor not guilty of perverting the course of justice. Gavin, the CPS lawyer who had refused my deal before the trial, was horrified. It was not the result that he had been expecting. To be fair it was not the result that I'd been expecting until Horace's evidence began to fall apart.

On balance the jury's verdict accurately reflected the facts, and cross-examination had played a central part in unearthing them. My saying this doesn't suddenly make cross-examination a magic wand. It's still easy for advocates to bamboozle witnesses, especially the young, with double negatives and questions phrased in a way that defies answering. At a recent case at the Bailey a silk asked a four-year-old witness, 'He didn't touch you with his willy, did he?' Imagine being four and trying to answer that.

Wigmore was wrong: cross-examination is not the 'greatest legal engine for the discovery of the truth'. But then trials are not oracular. Absolute truth is not a realistic outcome. Trials are there to determine guilt and innocence, not to answer every question and reveal every mystery. Oral testimony underscores the limitations of the trial, which in turn underscores the limitations of justice. Justice, guaranteed by the rule of law, might be one of the essential elements of a civilized and tolerant society but, sadly, that doesn't mean it can make everything better. Whatever the outcome, whatever its rightness, Horace's jaw is still shattered, the Portakabin offices, which Arthur may or may not have torched, are still ashes, and the young rabbi with a whole life ahead of him is still dead.

PART FOUR

Judgement

13. The Purple Lifeboat

Judging is a lonely job. Once you were down in the trenches with all your barrister mates and suddenly you're elevated to the remote eyrie of the bench. At the bar, if things go wrong and your client cops thirty years after a trial at the Bailey, you can always toddle off down the road to a wine bar and laugh about it all with prosecuting counsel over smoked salmon sandwiches and champagne. You can't do that on the bench. There is no 'Never mind, old chap' and slaps on the back. You're on your own, and besides, as a judge, you have to show a bit more decorum and restraint, which means no solace-seeking in Fleet Street watering holes.

Being a judge is scary too. If you get something wrong, you risk humiliation at the hands of the Court of Appeal, who, among other things, review judicial decisions made at trial and sentence. Really screw up and they might send you one of their infamous letters, dispatched in brown envelopes, listing your judicial failings. No fun reading one of those over the corn flakes, I'm told. Judges are not supposed to get things wrong. It's bad for morale – not to say embarrassing – if people realize the judge is a bit, you know, confused. Common law assumes judges are omnipotent and has set the rules up accordingly, giving them almost complete discretion over the regulation of their own courtroom. Within those four walls, our common law tradition turns judges into near gods.

Courtroom power, however, is poor recompense. Who'd want to sit there day after day listening to idiots like me failing to make a decent stab at things? It's no wonder so many of the judiciary succumb to judge-itis, a disease whose symptoms, constant irascibility and bad temper, can flare into hernia-splitting rage at any moment. One senior circuit judge I know starts his day red-faced and truculent. From there it's downhill all the way. Judge-itis is really just frustration, and impotent frustration at that. The reason is that while a judge might be a Rajput in his courtroom, his fiat runs out at the door. Make an order for the CPS to serve documents on a certain date and they stick two fingers up at you. You can make as many orders as you like but it's not going to make one jot of difference. All you'll get is insincere, nasal apologies. It's the same with the lemons at Serco. Ask them why they haven't produced a prisoner they were supposed to produce and you'll be met with a blank stare and mumblings about a lack of staff. In the end, rage is all you've got because no one gives a rat's arse about your orders until the trial actually starts. Then, magically, you have everyone's full attention.

Battling gross inefficiency and galling mediocrity means that satisfaction (forget about victory) is hard to come by. When the opportunity arises a judge must be alert in order not to let it slip through his fingers. One particularly thankless judicial task is passing sentence. Part of handing down a sentence is summing up the aggravating and mitigating features of the offence and the general poor character of the offender. Back in the 1990s a judge telling one burglar to whom he'd just given three years, 'You are nothing but a common criminal,' got the reply, 'Well, you're nothing but a cunt.'

The judge kept his cool. 'Bring that man back,' he ordered. The burglar, glaring defiantly, was re-seated.

'When I leave court this afternoon, I will leave in my Mercedes. Bach will be playing on the stereo. I will go home and I'll prune the roses in my garden while my wife cooks a delicious dinner. We will eat together in the conservatory and enjoy a nice bottle of claret. You, on the other hand, will be taken to HMP Brixton. For the next several years you will be locked up twenty-three hours a day. You will eat slop and defecate into a bucket, which you share with two other men. Now, who are you calling a cunt?'

Okay, being a crim is worse than being a judge, but so what? In my short time at the criminal bar, I couldn't understand why anyone would want to join the ranks of the judiciary. The answer came to me in my dreams, or sort of. One hot afternoon I was asleep under a wide-legged mahogany table in my pupilmaster's office. (I had two or three places for my afternoon siesta and this was my favourite from my early days as a beginning pupil.) I was awakened when the door opened and two pairs of feet came into the room. It was the head of chambers and another silk. Getting caught would be bad so I breathed as quietly as I could and listened in on their conversation.

'Joanna's got it. Formally leaving chambers this week.'

'Going to the bench, is she?'

'Being made up' (the expression used for someone becoming a judge) 'next month.'

'That is good news. I'm so glad. Lucky to be getting out.'

'The purple lifeboat, eh. Steady wage, holiday pay, civilized hours and, best of all, a pension.'

'God, yes, one of those. Always wondered what they were like.'

The head of chambers and the other silk, nearly seventy years of experience between them, laughed and then fell silent for a moment as they thought about the unfamiliar concept of a pension, of being paid to be retired. Finally, I understood. *That's* why barristers went to the bench. You jumped into the purple lifeboat (purple is the colour of a crown court judge's robes) for financial security because there was certainly none to be had at the bar. I lay under the table thinking about my own long-term financial prospects. Would I be pension-less as well, forced to work until I dropped dead face down in the 'Dish of the Day' at Croydon Crown Court's bar mess? It didn't seem like the most appetizing of fates – going out with a splat.

I waited for the two of them to leave and went back down to the happy fug of the pupils' room. Mamta, jacked up on a new pair of high heels, was standing on the table doing as much of a twirl as five days' worth of lunch leftovers would allow.

'What do you think, Alex? Don't they just say FMHN?'

'What's F-M-H-N?'

'Fuck Me Hard Now,' explained Liam, buried in his accounts ledger.

'They're lovely,' I said and changed the subject. 'Liam, do you ever think about pensions?'

'All I'm thinking about is two weeks in Greece this summer.'

I looked at Harriet, boss pupil, sitting at the end of the table. She arched her eyebrows, giving me an 'Are you serious?' look and slid another full-fat cigarette out of the pack.

'Okay, so Harriet isn't going to need a pension but what about everyone else? Mamta?'

'Alex, I'm wearing Fuck Me Hard Now shoes, not Fuck Me Hard Later shoes.'

'Will? Pension?'

Wordless Will looked from Mamta to me and mimed that it was time for the pub by pretending to pour a drink into his mouth. Then he pointed at my wallet, fingering imaginary notes: the drinks were on me. There was my explanation. Will had summed up financial planning at the bar. Go on a bender and stay on a bender, so that by the time the taxman comes for his reckoning, there'll be nothing left. Working as a criminal barrister is like being a gunslinger. Either you get out or you die with your boots on. You keep going because you have to. The only difference between you and an indentured coolie is that you get to wear a clean shirt.

Walking to the pub, I wondered what it would be like leaping into the courtroom fray at the age of seventy. Leaping was the wrong word. It'd be more like settling in, only instead of being on the sofa with the *Daily Telegraph* crossword, you'd be on a hard bench trying to remember your client's name. Trials are demanding at thirty-five, let alone seventy. If I was still doing it at seventy,

I'd need snooze breaks, pee breaks and someone to carry my books. A few barristers do keep going. Trialling is what they do. Stuff a hinterland, and *stuff* golf. Everyone else makes for the purple lifeboat. Getting in that long, snaking line might not be the most palatable exit strategy but as the pay and prospects at the criminal bar go down and the exigencies go up, the queue to become a judge grows ever longer.

14. Bias

In common-law countries the judiciary is drawn from litigators –
in Britain that means barristers and, to a lesser but growing extent,
solicitors. You need judges who, aside from being legally qualified, have also had experience of the courtroom and its demands
(Justices of the Peace are the exception in that anyone who has
the time and a good character can become one). This means that
most judges are white, male, middle-aged and middle class for
the simple reason that until pretty recently that was the make-up
of the professional pool from which they were drawn. Courts
presided over by such a caste are often perceived as biased (or at
the very least lacking empathy) by the young, the dark-skinned
and the marginalized. This is a real problem. The criminal justice system only works if it has public confidence, which it won't
have if certain parts of society believe they are not being fairly
treated.

Unfairness is felt most keenly in sentencing. The *Guardian*
newspaper reported in 1990 that black people were twice as likely
to be sent to prison as whites for the same offence.[1] I don't know if
that figure was accurate but accuracy wasn't really the point; what
mattered was that it seemed accurate. Disquiet among ethnic
minorities about biased sentencing led Roger Hood to conduct a
study in the early 1990s of sentencing outcomes in six crown courts
in the West Midlands. His idea was to measure to what degree
the perception of unfairness translated into reality.[2] The most
interesting thing about his findings was the lack of uniformity in
results. Birmingham Crown Court had no measurable difference
between the sentencing outcomes for white, Afro-Caribbean or

Asian defendants, but other courts such as Dudley and Coventry did. Lengths of sentences varied hugely between the judges, too.

Overall Hood found that while there was a significant racial bias in the likelihood of a defendant going to prison and the length of sentence imposed, it was not as pronounced as people perceived it to be.* Comparing like with like he found that an Afro-Caribbean defendant was about 8 per cent more likely and an Asian defendant was 5 per cent more likely to go to prison than a white defendant. In terms of length of sentence, overall Afro-Caribbeans received 3.4 months longer than whites, while Asians got nine months longer.

Ten years after his research in the West Midlands, Roger Hood looked at how judges, lawyers and defendants perceived racial bias in court. Judges, unsurprisingly, felt that their decisions weren't influenced by a person's colour or background. Ethnic minority defendants, just as unsurprisingly, weren't so sure.

---

*This is a difficult and sensitive subject. Hood found that in the West Midlands Afro-Caribbeans were more likely to be prosecuted for robbery and possession with intent to supply illegal drugs than whites or Asians. Whites, on the other hand, were more likely to be prosecuted for burglary. Robbery is an indictable only offence, which means it must be dealt with by a crown court, which has far greater sentencing powers than the magistrates' court. Possession with intent to supply is technically an either-way offence (meaning triable either in the magistrates' or crown courts) but in practice is almost certainly going to end up in the crown court. Burglary, though still a serious offence, will generally have a better chance of staying in the magistrates' court and, even if it doesn't, will attract a lower sentencing tariff. It's easy to get five years for drug dealing or robbery but you've got to try pretty hard to get that for burglary.

Another factor Hood found that might affect perception on sentence length was that black people were less likely to plead guilty. Pleading guilty at the first available opportunity leads to a discount in sentence of one third and can make all the difference in whether you go to prison or not. It should be noted that there is no evidence that black people are more likely to commit crime or that they are more likely to commit certain crimes.

The interweaving of perception and reality is impossible to unpick. Bias is complicated. Decisions are influenced by dozens of little things, many of which the person making the decision will not be aware of. The complexity of decision-making becomes unfathomable when you transpose this on to a jury. Rhona Flin says that the optimum number of people to take a decision is between three and six. Larger groups tend to be either overly cautious or overly careless. Suffice to say, whether you have a judge or a jury, you have to be aware of and accept the lottery effect.

Juries are drawn from particular catchment areas and within those catchment areas there will be a preponderance of certain classes and types of potential members of a jury. This means that the location of your court can have a bearing on the final result of the trial. A young black man being tried for a crime at Woolwich Crown Court has a better chance than he has at Kingston-upon-Thames, and a far better chance than he would have at St Albans. I have no statistical evidence to back this up but I know it to be the case in the same way that I know a certain judge at St Albans will send your client (whatever his colour or background) to jail while a certain other judge won't.

As a barrister there's not much you can do if your client insists on getting arrested, charged and prosecuted in a 'convict all the brutes' part of the country, just as there's nothing you can do about his colour, build or appearance. There are, however, steps that you can take to ameliorate the unfortunate situation in which your client finds himself. One of the rules of good advocacy is to know your tribunal (judge and/or jury) and part of that is to be aware that small details can influence the way it will behave. In this task one thing is sure – clothing counts. As a criminal barrister providing a comprehensive service, it's important to be ready with more than just legal advice: you must also have a courtroom fashion tip or two up your sleeve. Your standard 'Saturday night glass-in-the-face pub rucker' will almost always insist on wearing a suit. It's not the sort of suit the judge will be wearing and, inevitably, will be accompanied by a gold Windsor-knotted tie. To the jury he'll look like a footballer, which is, naturally, just the sort of image your client thinks he wants to convey. He loves Wayne Rooney and he loves Joey Barton. Many jurors might not feel the same way. They will assume that footballer lookalikes are violent louts who are by definition guilty. A good tactic I used with one 'glasser' client was to get his tearful girlfriend to take him down to British Home Stores to pick up a nice jumper and a spongy pair of Clark's. I wanted him walking from the dock to the witness box looking like the sort of 'douche-bag' who is dressed by his mother. Sends all the right signals.

When you're being prosecuted for an offence of dishonesty, expensive clothes are a no-no. I had a client who came to chambers for a conference wearing a blue suit from one of the trendier Savile Row tailors. He was swinging a little black bag with Prada emblazoned on it. It might as well have said 'Swag'. His huge watch, circled with diamonds, was even worse. Coupled with a February suntan (despite his bail condition not to leave the country), the effect was suicidal. He looked as though he'd just flown in from the Costa del Car Ringer, which was unhelpful as the stolen item in question was a very expensive yellow lorry. My client must have noticed me goggling at the watch because before I could say anything he said, 'Don't worry, Alex. I'll be wearing Marks & Spencer's on the day.' It's always a pleasure to work with a professional.

No one understood the powerful effect of appearance on juries better than the celebrated lawyer-scoundrel William Howe, who, with his partner Abraham Hummel, dominated the New York bar in the second half of the nineteenth century. His speciality was to present his client to the jury as the honest 'little man'. Howe liked to dress his clients, who were paying him huge sums, as paupers. He didn't stop with clothes. He sculpted a visual narrative to put his clients in the most sympathetic light. One of his favourite ploys was to create a bogus tableau of the accused's family for the benefit of the jury. On the first day of a trial, Howe would wheel in a snow-haired mother and a wife of fragile beauty, sometimes suckling a babe in arms, but always with a string of waif-like children in tow. These 'families' were kept on a retainer so they could be summoned up when required. Howe had got the idea when, early in his career, he was defending a sailor accused of murdering three of his captains, one after the other. To Howe's horror, the prosecution brought the dead men's wives and children into court. He was not going to be outplayed by a fast one like that but he had a problem. His crazy, dangerous client was single. What was he going to do and at such short notice? Then it hit him. What about his own wife and child who, as luck would have it, were sitting in the public gallery? They would do splendidly as the killer's 'family'. He was right, they did: the homicidal sailor was found not guilty. Howe and Hummel stooped much lower than even this. They bribed witnesses, nobbled juries and had many a judge and city politician in their pockets.[3]

Howe liked to dress himself up, too. It was part of the performance. When he was defending a capital case, he would start the trial nattily dressed in a loud waistcoat and purple trousers of his own design. As the trial wore on, his clothes became increasingly sombre, sepulchral even, until the day the jury was to retire to deliberate its verdict, when he would appear dressed in deathly black to underline to the jurors the horrible finality of a guilty verdict. It was very effective: Howe almost never lost a case.

Sometimes non-professional clients get it right without any help from me and there was one who got it absolutely perfectly. I first saw her adrift among the stampede of shiny tracksuits and Nike baseball caps coming through the court's doors. I wished Howe could have been there because he would have been full of admiration. I approached her tentatively. We exchanged pleasantries. I bided my time until I thought it the right moment to suggest that she take off her coat. She eased it off her shoulders without protest. She looked marvellous. Her throat was hidden by a beige polo neck, over which she wore a white, yellow and brown horizontal lined V-neck sweater. Her pleated beige skirt reached unrevealingly to her ankles. In a stroke of genius, her hair, set fast in a *demi-glace* of L'Oreal, was in the style of a Romford lady shopper. This woman was a picture of African matronhood: sombre, respectable, law-abiding.

She was accused of attempting to obtain services by deception, in this instance opening a bank account with a dodgy driver's licence. The prosecution's case was that she had entered a bank with another black woman and handed the licence, which happened to have my client's name, address and photo on it, to a teller as proof of her identity. Her defence was that it wasn't she who had come into the bank. She'd been the victim of an identity theft. The teller, a young white woman, was the prosecution's main witness. When the women had entered the bank she was immediately suspicious of them. In her evidence, she described the woman with the licence as between twenty-five and thirty and wearing a see-through green top which revealed a black bra. Her accomplice was the same age; she wore a little denim skirt and pink sunglasses. In cross-examination the teller agreed with my suggestions that the two women were 'brassy' and 'showed a bit of leg'.

When my client left the dock to take the witness box the effect on the magistrates was all too apparent. It was clear that she was not the sort of person to show a bit of anything. She hadn't given evidence, yet she was already playing a blinder.

The teller was a good witness and competent too: she'd noticed that the licence was a fake. Her checks, made from the back of the shop, had spooked the two women sufficiently that when she came back they'd vanished. But this, along with my client's brilliant wardrobe, enabled me to make the most of the fact that she wasn't twenty-five to thirty years old but forty-seven, neutralizing the teller's insistence that the woman who handed over the driver's licence was the woman whose picture appeared on it.

In a perfect world all my clients wouldn't just look respectable, but would resemble the jury or the magistrate as closely as possible. Research in the early 1970s showed that older magistrates imposed more lenient fines on older drivers and more severe ones on younger drivers than their younger colleagues did. You don't have to extrapolate far to realize that the same might apply to acquittal or conviction. Dressing your client or getting your trial listed when a certain judge is on holiday are not cynical manipulations of the process; the criminal justice system has in-built biases and your job as a criminal barrister is to combat them.

So what were the outcomes for my three clients? The jury found the club 'glasser' guilty. He had previous convictions for violence but amazingly the judge didn't send him to prison. Was it the British Home Stores sweater that kept him out? Probably not, but who is to say it wasn't a factor in the judge's overall impression of him? The lorry thief pleaded guilty on the day of trial to a different charge and therefore got the maximum discount. He was sentenced to twelve months imprisonment. The African lady, who holds a Master's degree in education and was working as a teaching assistant at the time of trial, said a man had offered to help her speed up her licence application. She filled in a DVLA form, attached a photo and paid him £30. She never saw the man again. The magistrates could not be sure beyond reasonable doubt that it was she who entered the bank and so found her not guilty. If she'd come to court with a plunging neckline the outcome might have been different. Certainly that was the impression I got when her daughter arrived at court to meet her. She, in her tight mini-skirt, looked like a twenty-year younger version of her mother.

15. Trusting the Jury

A very senior judge once asked me this question: 'If you were innocent of the crime with which you were charged would you want to be tried by a judge or a jury?'

'I'd go for a jury every time,' I reply.

'I wouldn't.'

'Why?'

'Because I'd be concerned about an irrational conviction. I'd opt for a judge because he'd have to give a reasoned judgement of why I was guilty. Then I'd have the option of taking it to appeal. With a jury, I'd be terrified they'd do something crazy.'

This very senior judge has never practised in the criminal courts but he's presided over a lot of criminal trials and deliberated on countless criminal appeals. He is, to say the least, highly experienced. His opinion has real weight. I wasn't convinced by his argument but I didn't want to discount his point about an irrational conviction without examining it properly. Had I missed something? Should I be reassessing my assumptions about the jury trial?

It was time to call a few criminal barristers and canvass opinion. I called Max, who was on his bike.

'McBride, what do you want?' said Max, one hand on the handlebars, the other holding his mobile.

'Max, I've got a question.'

'I've been drinking with P. God, he's a nancy. Three pints of lager and he needs to go home.'

Three pints? Excellent! Max – merrily bullish but not slurringly drunk – would be at the perfect level of intoxication to offer up his thoughts on the jury system. 'If you were innocent would you want to be tried by a judge or a jury?' I asked.

'I'd go for a jury every time.' Exact same answer that I had given the very senior judge.

'Wouldn't you be concerned about an irrational decision?'

'Irrational decision! What about an irrational decision from the judge? I have no faith in judges. I don't want some mad cunt like Judge M deciding my fate.'

I had forgotten about him. Max was right. Judge M was a mad cunt, perhaps the maddest cunt of them all.

Max disappeared for a moment and all I could hear was fuzz. Then he came back. 'Sorry. Going over Battersea Bridge. Raining hard. Bit of a speed wobble.'

Once he'd cleared the bridge with the rain in his face – 'it's really coming down now, I can't see anything at all' – we compiled a list of judges we didn't fancy our innocent chances with. The list, let's call it 'Maxie's Mad Cunts', got pretty damn long. More than five MCs, you ask? Way more than five.

'I would apply one caveat,' said Max (typical lawyer, always has to attach a caveat). 'Judges can be staggeringly credulous. I should know. When I'm prosecuting appeals from the magistrates' court it's amazing what crown court judges swallow. Piss-poor excuses about not having any car insurance, lame bleatings about their lack of an MOT. Still it doesn't get away from the fact that the man in the street doesn't like passing judgement. They keep their blood-curdling opinions for talk radio. But when they go into the jury room, they don't want to take the responsibility.'

Next I phoned Zoë.

'McBride! Just when I've got a screw loose.'

'I'm sorry?'

'Trying to fix the engine on my narrow boat. I've taken it apart but I can't put it back together.'

I asked her the same question. She gave the same answer that Max and I had: 'I'd go for a jury every time.'

'Why?'

'It's a numbers game. If you've got one person then you're stuck with their prejudices. But you're going to be very unlucky to get twelve racists, or twelve mean bastards. Numbers keep people honest. The only exception is heavy crime where juries will be more shocked than a judge and therefore quicker to convict. But anyway,' Zoë added, 'which innocent person in their right mind would want that mad cunt Judge M deciding their fate?'

Conviction rates in the magistrates' courts, where you are tried by either a district judge or a lay bench of unpaid volunteer magistrates, are significantly higher than in the crown court where a jury makes the ultimate decision. You can be sure the government would love to get rid of juries if they could. It would not only save lots of money but also mean more convictions – a win-win from their perspective.

Still I respected the very senior judge's opinion. I was gratified that he had the confidence to put his fate in the hands of his brother and sister judges. There aren't many barristers that I can think of who I would want defending me if I were accused of a crime.

Up until the early 1970s you qualified as a juror only if you paid rates and paid them separately. This excluded most women (in 1970 only 11 per cent of jurors were female) and most people in council housing because their rates were rolled up in the rent. Lord Devlin famously described the British jury of the time as 'predominantly male, predominantly middle-aged, middle-minded and middle-class'. Ironically, these days the middle classes are the most avid dodgers of jury service. You hear the same excuses in the same BBC newsreader voices time and again:

'My business couldn't survive without me.'

'I'm starting a new job.'

'What about my skiing holiday in Verbier that I've booked? Xanthe and Ludo would just die if I couldn't go.'

The reason I prefer juries is because they have an independence that judges and magistrates do not. I'm not saying judges and magistrates are toadies, far from it, but juries don't rely on their job as jurors. There's no career in it for them. They can make decisions without worrying about criticism or ridicule. They do it for two weeks or so and then go back to their usual work. Juries also have a freshness of mind. The case for a jury is entirely new. They can look at it on the facts, unclouded by the experience of the hundreds of similar cases spinning through a judge's head.

The other extremely important advantage of juries is that unlike lawyers they're not enslaved by the black letter of the law. Remember the not guilty verdicts passed in the William Penn trial in the seventeenth century despite the judiciary's best efforts. Juries can sniff out an injustice like no other tribunal. If they see a nasty law or unfair prosecution, juries will often refuse to play ball even if, technically, the defendant is guilty of the offence. The term for this is jury nullification. I love jury nullification, all barristers do. It's the wild card in the pack – the top trump that can spring your defendant no matter what the evidence or the law says. Jury nullification is the by-product of a jury's independent mind that predicates our trust in the twelve men and women called to sit in judgement.

I once did not put my trust in a jury. It's a mistake that still bothers me. My client was called Benedict. He'd never been in trouble with the police before and was charged with three counts of theft from his employer, Frank, the owner of three South London pubs. Benedict had been a successful bar manager. His energy and can-do attitude caught Frank's eye. Frank offered him a job managing one of his pubs. Benedict wasn't so sure. He liked his job – it paid okay. Frank made promises. The pub took between £6,000 and £8,000 a week, he said. Fifteen per cent of that would make a handsome salary. Benedict said he'd think about it. Over several months Frank persisted, eager for him to start. Benedict made a counter proposal. Since he had a young family, a wife and two kids, what he'd really like is a wage and a smaller percentage. Frank said that he'd love to help but none of his managers ever got a wage. They all worked on percentage. On the basis of estimated takings and the attractive percentage, Benedict took the job and moved his family into the cramped flat above the pub. A month or two after he'd installed himself, he discovered that there was a snag. The earnings that Frank had promised were a lie. The pub wasn't making anything like £6,000 let alone £8,000 a week. It was closer to £4,000, sometimes even less. To Benedict's credit, he threw himself into resuscitating the place. Despite his energy, it was a losing battle. The pub was dying and Benedict was stuck.

Average takings were not the only lie that Frank had told. All his other managers, including the person Benedict had replaced, weren't on pure percentage but a wage plus a percentage. Frank, by not paying his new manager a wage, kept the revenue coming in from the pub without incurring any cost.

On percentage alone Benedict found it increasingly difficult to make ends meet. He went to Frank and asked for a wage but was fobbed off with assurances that business would pick up. It didn't. Gradually, Benedict, without Frank's permission, started to dip into the pub's till. He'd take £10 here and £20 there. He took money out of the safe. The unusual thing about this is that he made no secret of it. He pulled money out of the till in front of the staff. His debt quickly ballooned to over £1,600 and depression set in. His initial enthusiasm was replaced with lethargy. Benedict retreated to the flat above the pub. When Frank realized the deficit, he offered a deal: if the money were paid back the police would not become involved and the job would remain on the table. Benedict didn't pay the money back. A week later he was arrested.

Before the trial started the judge made it quite clear that he had, to use a legal cliché, 'taken a view'. The judge thought Benedict's was a particularly unpleasant example of stealing from an employer. What had really got him was Benedict's first police interview, where he had blamed the other employees for taking the money, asserting that they used his signature on the daily takes total to cover their tracks. This was a disaster, which Benedict had corrected in a second police interview by admitting that it was he who had taken the money. The judge felt that Benedict had changed his line only because he knew his original excuse wasn't going to stack up. The judge indicated that Benedict's attempt to blame others meant that he was minded to send him to prison if convicted.

The trial had gone pretty well. Frank's lies had come out and he'd come across as untrustworthy and calculating. The evening before he was to give evidence, I advised Benedict about the possibility of changing his plea to guilty, warned him of the danger of his effective admission in police interview that he'd taken the money. The law defines theft as dishonestly appropriating property belonging to another with the intention of permanently depriving the other of it. Benedict had certainly taken property belonging to Frank and had little intention of paying it back (the money had only been paid back an hour before the trial had started). The real question was whether Benedict had been acting dishonestly. In law dishonesty can be objective – dishonest according to the ordinary standards of reasonable and honest people – and subjective – the defendant himself realizing that his taking of the property was dishonest. First, the jurors decide if the defendant objectively speaking was dishonest; if they find that he was, they go on to consider whether he was subjectively dishonest.

Benedict went home in good spirits after we had decided together that he would maintain his not guilty plea, give evidence and put his trust in the jury. If the trial had been in the magistrates' court, he would've been facing odds similar to a snowball sailing through hell's hottest dungeon. But he wasn't in the magistrates', he was in the crown court, and even if his chances were slim, they weren't entirely gone.

I discussed the pros and cons with my solicitor. What worried us was the risk of jail. The more we talked as lawyers, the more we convinced ourselves as *lawyers* that Benedict had to go guilty. The law said he was guilty and we were there to apply the law to the facts of the case and advise accordingly. The next morning Benedict was determined to continue with the trial but I talked him out of it. I used my professional authority, setting the terms of the argument to suit the conclusion that I wanted. It was his decision, but I ensured that he would exercise it the way I wanted him to. I was not being cynical, merely helping my client to get the best possible result.

In court, as soon as Benedict changed his plea, I knew I had screwed up. The members of the jury looked at each other stunned. They were never going to convict him. For them, and they were right, Benedict had been wronged. Here I was wronging him all over again. His actions may have fulfilled all the elements of theft but they judged that he had not been dishonest. It just didn't feel right to find him guilty. Benedict didn't go to prison but he did leave court with a conviction for dishonesty that would stay with him for the rest of his life – and it was my fault.

16. Doling it Out

Since revenge for its own sake cannot be justified, it will follow that the natural justice of punishment, as of every other act of man to man, must depend solely on its utility, and that its only lawful end is some good more than equivalent to the evil which it necessarily produces.

– Samuel Johnson

Prison works. It ensures that we are protected from murderers, muggers and rapists – and it makes many who are tempted to commit crime think twice.

– Michael Howard, Conservative Party conference, October 1993

The game's up. Your client's just been convicted at trial, or like Clarence, done the decent thing and pleaded guilty. You stand up and apologize on his behalf. This is known as mitigation. There are set mitigating factors, such as never having been convicted before, or having pleaded guilty at the first available opportunity, which will automatically reduce a sentence. Clarence knew he was getting 'bird', slang for a prison sentence. The only question was, how long? He arrived at court as if he were going on a cruise. He had three holdalls, two large cardboard boxes and a stereo to which he'd duct-taped his favourite CDs. 'Got to have your creature comforts,' he said. I couldn't disagree. After sentence has been passed you're not allowed to hand anything to your client because he is now a prisoner, so we checked his bags into the cells early.

'What, is he having *both* of them boxes?' asked the dubious jailer on the door.

'They are my absolute essentials,' insisted Clarence. He couldn't possibly 'go away' with anything less.

He was too likeable to refuse.

Sitting outside court, Clarence explained how it had all gone wrong. His dad had disappeared when he was a baby. He'd craved a father figure and found him in a sly old con who'd taken him under his wing. The con would dream up the wheezes and Clarence would help make them work. When he got five years for dealing the con's drugs, he loyally kept his mouth shut. No one grasses up his old man.

A guy about Clarence's age was waiting to be sentenced too. 'You can do prison hard, or you can do it easy,' he said. 'I chose hard: if the screws wanted me out of the cell, they'd have to come in and get me. If they pissed me off, I'd cover everything in shit.' (I had one client who refused to come up to court. To ward off the jailers he smeared himself in and then ate his own faeces. Worked a treat.) Hard was not for Clarence. He chose easy.

The last time he had gone inside he had been addicted to crack cocaine and, despite the fact that prisons are awash with drugs, he managed to get clean. He was a model prisoner and passed exams in computing and English. When he got out he left his old life behind. He made a good marriage, had a couple of kids and found a job driving lorries. But it's not easy to escape a past. Some years later, he received a call from his old life. The father-figure con was in jail again and needed Clarence, who was like a son after all, to do him one small favour. At first Clarence refused; he had a family. But the con wouldn't give up. Prison is hard for an old man. All he was asking for was one social visit. Was that really too much to ask? Gradually he wore Clarence down.

'This is why it's so difficult to leave that life behind. How could I say no? He was desperate. I owed him.'

This logic might seem nuts but for Clarence it was an act of love for a father who'd cared. He arrived at the prison with heroin concealed in his belt and wedged between his buttocks. He was nervous and it showed. CCTV cameras watched his every move. The whole enterprise was suicide, a *beau geste* for old times' sake. As he tried to hand the drugs over the prison guards swooped.

Defendants always ask what sentence they're going to get and Clarence was no exception. It's wise to err on the high side to avoid disappointment. The guideline case was pretty discouraging; it concerned a man who'd brought heroin into prison for his son. He had no previous convictions, unlike Clarence, but like Clarence he had entered a guilty plea at the first opportunity. In upholding a five-year sentence the Court of Appeal said that 'the supply of [heroin] to a serving prisoner is a most serious offence and a lengthy custodial sentence was required'. Until recently, four years was an important line. If you got under four, you were a short-term prisoner and served only half your sentence; over four and you served two-thirds.

Just before we were called into court, Clarence disappeared into the lavatories. A few minutes later he emerged walking like Gary Cooper in *Gunfight at the OK Corral*. I was suspicious.

'Clarence, you haven't stuffed anything up your 'batty', have you?' I asked.

'No, Alex, clean as a whistle. I've learned my lesson.'

It was packed in the courtroom; rows of barristers were squeezed into the public gallery waiting their turn. Clarence was one of many to be processed that day. Mitigation works best if you can get the judge, battle-hardened from years of sentencing, to look beyond the mechanical exercise of sticking numbers on bodies. To do that you have to tell the truth, not absolute truth but *a* truth. It was Clarence's talent for friendship, the generosity which had landed him in court in the first place, which ultimately made the difference. Along with his luggage, he'd brought his boss as a character witness. The boss, a young man about his age, told the judge about his friend. He talked about Clarence's hard work and integrity and as he did so he began to cry, unselfconsciously, in front of the crowded court. He cried because of the injustice of Clarence's life, and his triumph in spite of it. The judge was a sour old deputy but his heart was touched. He exercised his discretion, which he was entitled to do, and gave Clarence three years, far less than the Court of Appeal guideline suggested. On an electronic tag, Clarence would be out in a year.

Leniency is increasingly the exception to the general rule. The government dislikes the fact that judges use their discretion when passing sentence. They want uniformity, forgetting that every case, with its own facts, is different and that mercy often makes sense: isn't it better to have Clarence outside supporting his family and paying his taxes rather than banged up at the Exchequer's expense?

Sentences are getting longer. The public and the government like stiff sentences. Revenge is sweet, if fleeting. I am ashamed to say that when I'm prosecuting I sometimes feel a self-satisfied smile twist across my face when the jailer leads the freshly convicted defendant down to the cells. That'll teach him, I say to myself, mentally waving *bon voyage*. I don't know why punishment makes us feel better. It might be that seeing someone getting what they 'deserve' makes up for some of the injustices and unfairnesses in daily life.

For centuries the punishment end of the criminal justice system was there to make miscreants pay. It was their just desert, after all. Wrongdoers were put in the stocks, which was more than just a humiliation. They were lucky if their fellow citizens only threw rotten fruit because there was no guarantee anyone was going to step in once the rocks started to fly. The authorities had other tricks up their sleeves. Offenders were branded, had their noses chopped off, their ears clipped, and their tongues bored. Then there was hanging, which during the eighteenth century became the default punishment for more and more crimes. By the early

1800s over 200 offences, including very minor property crime – any theft over 5 shillings, theoretically, attracted the death penalty – could and did lead to a hanging. There were ways out. Some offences were 'clergyable', which meant you could claim 'benefit of clergy' and have a capital sentence commuted.

The concept of 'benefit of clergy', thought up by Thomas Beckett, established the principle that clergymen were exempt from capital punishment. This meant that a man guilty of an offence who showed himself to be in holy orders could claim benefit of clergy and be handed over to the ecclesiastical authorities whose powers of punishment were much weaker. In the Middle Ages an official called the 'ordinary' decided who he would or wouldn't 'claim'.[1] Over the years judges usurped the ordinary's role and the criteria for claiming benefit of clergy were relaxed. Deciding who was and wasn't eligible was done through a reading test. The claim took the form of the convicted felon (women couldn't claim benefit of clergy until 1624) falling to his knees to 'pray the book', which meant reading Verse 1 of Psalm 51, known as the 'neck-verse' for obvious reasons. This rule in turn was further relaxed to allow illiterate people a chance of saving their skins. To do that they had to commit the neck-verse to memory and recite it. This is what they had to remember: '*Miserere mei Deus secundum magnam misericordiam tuam, et secundum multitudinem miserationum tuarum dele iniquitatem meam.*'[2] Shouldn't be too hard you say, but then you're not trying to do it while someone is attaching a rope to a gibbet with your name on it. Hard or not, the relaxation of the rules made the neck-verse very popular for, by the end of the sixteenth century, nearly half of the convicted felons were claiming it.

The authorities' response was to make it unavailable for the more serious offences. Benefit of clergy remained a popular escape route and saved many lives but a lot of people still ended up dangling on the end of a rope. The gibbet at Tyburn (near present-day

Marble Arch), which was capable of dispatching handfuls at a time, saw heavy use.

Hangings in London, and no doubt elsewhere, were a spectator sport. All walks of life, no matter how low or high, loved them. Hanging days were *de facto* public holidays. The night before, people began to position themselves in the pubs and coffee houses along the journey's route. By the time Newgate opened its doors the next morning for the procession to Tyburn, a large crowd was waiting to accompany it. The condemned – children were not spared – rode in wagons sitting astride their own coffins.[3] Offenders of rank or fame were allowed to use private coaches. Earl Ferrers, who'd shot dead his steward, travelled to his Tyburn appointment in a landau drawn by six black-plumed horses. He wore his marriage suit because his wedding and hanging were the two unhappiest days of his life. Just about everyone dressed up – a white cockade in your hat denoted innocence, and a shroud guilt. Dick Turpin, the notorious highwayman, wore 'a new fustian frock and a pair of pumps'. Lord Derwentwater, beheaded on Tower Hill in 1746, dressed himself in a scarlet coat with black velvet and gold trim, a gold-laced waistcoat and a hat with a feather in it.[4]

Women heading for the gibbet wore white with silk scarves and threw flowers and oranges to the crowd. The procession was leisurely. If family or friends were in the crowd, it would stop to allow everyone a chat. Taverns along the route offered free 'parting cups' to the condemned, which meant by the time they arrived at Tyburn many were paralytically drunk.[5]

Hangings drew enormous crowds, often into the tens of thousands. Even tourists came to watch this peculiarly British piece of ghoulish fun. A German count, in town for George III's coronation, made time to see one and was impressed by the sang-froid with which the condemned approached their fate. Those who could afford it availed themselves of the raked seating erected alongside the gibbet (portable from 1759). A widow called Proctor owned the surrounding land and her seats, priced according to the view and the 'hangee's' fame, were known as 'Mother Proctor's Pews'. For the roiling, drunken masses squeezed into Tyburn, it was every spectator for himself.

An eyewitness described the scene before a hanging like this:

It was a ribald, reckless, brutal mob, violently combative, fighting and struggling for foremost places, fiercely aggressive, distinctly abusive. Spectators often had their limbs broken, their teeth knocked out, sometimes they were crushed to death.[6]

The crowd, considering the trouble and risk they'd gone to, wanted more than to be entertained, they wanted to be caught up in the frenzy of death. They cheered those who, standing on the cart with the noose around their necks, gave them a last-minute speech, and booed those who did not. Side-taking extended to the hanging itself. When the cart was driven away and the condemned, dropped on to their nooses, began to die, the crowd cheered or groaned at each twitch and convulsion. They shouted out insults and jokes as the dying person's family rushed forward to pull down on their loved one's legs to shorten the suffering.

Part of the tension leading up to a hanging was the chance of a last-minute reprieve. They weren't uncommon. In 1758, when a forger's death sentence was commuted at the gallows, the outraged mob rioted, smashing up the seating. As ever the crowd was fickle. After the satisfaction of a hanging had waned, they might fall into despondency. It was usual practice to lay the hanged person at their prosecutor's door (eighteenth-century trials were mostly prosecuted by the victim). One woman who had successfully done for a burglar had his body left on her doorstep. An angry crowd gathered. They broke into her house, carried out her furniture, piled it up and set it alight while they held off the troops, who had been called to protect the lady's property, until everything had been burned.

The late eighteenth and early nineteenth centuries were the high-water mark for hangings. The authorities became increasingly aware that the Bloody Code, which detailed the list of crimes that attracted the death penalty, had lost all sense of proportion. Questions began to be asked whether the spectacle of hanging was an effective way of deterring offenders from committing crimes. Hangings were public entertainments, not dreaded public warnings. The 1800s therefore saw the death penalty removed from more and more offences, including attempted murder. Hangings continued but in much reduced numbers, and after 1868 they moved behind closed doors.

Terrible public death was replaced with orderly Victorian incarceration. Until the nineteenth century prisons were little more than privately run dungeons that relied on their prisoners to turn a profit. An Italian count called Cesare Beccaria came up with the idea of locking people up to deter crime and incapacitate criminals. His book *On Crimes and Punishments* (1764) put forward the radical argument that 'the purpose of punishment is not that of tormenting ... The purpose, therefore, is nothing other than to prevent the offender from doing fresh harm to his fellows and to deter others from doing likewise.'

Beccaria's thesis was hugely influential. It was taken up and developed by the utilitarian Jeremy Bentham who envisaged penal policies that were governed by rationalism rather than the old retribution of hanging and disfigurement. Punishment, he argued, should be justified by the good that comes from that punishment rather than for its own sake. Bentham believed that people were rational actors who, having considered the costs and benefits – the pleasure versus the pain, as he put it – would choose not to offend and the crime rate would fall.

The great jail-building boom of the 1840s proved Bentham

wrong. Human beings don't behave rationally. Crime is committed for all sorts of extremely complex reasons that Bentham's
theory of imprisonment could not address. The authorities tried
refinements, emphasizing prison's corrective role by reforming
bad characters through pious and respectable living. Drawing the
criminal out of the person didn't work too well, either. These
early disappointments haven't shaken our faith in the penal system. Our love affair with incarceration has endured. In fact, we're
locking more people up than ever. In November 2008 the prison
population rose to over 83,000, an increase of 30 per cent on 1997
levels, even though the number of people being convicted each
year had barely budged.

A significant component of the increase in prison numbers has
been made up of offenders incarcerated for non-violent crime
who, as a rule, serve very short sentences. Over half of the 91,000
or so people sentenced to custody in 2007 were given six months
or less. Assuming they behave themselves, they won't serve six
months but one half of that and probably a lot less. (The situation
is even crazier with women prisoners. The average sentence being
served in HMP Holloway is twenty-eight days.) Chances are the
prison will release them on an electronic tag to make room for the
next wave of (short-term) prisoners. This massive floating number
doesn't include the 10,000-plus remand prisoners who have not
been convicted of any criminal offence, sitting in jail awaiting trial.
Eighty per cent of remand prisoners are there for property crime
and when they're finally dealt with, assuming they're convicted in
the first place, half of them will receive a community sentence.

The problem with all these short-term prisoners is that they
clog up the prison system. They're not there for long enough to do
anything useful with them so they end up being warehoused at
staggering expense. Housing a Cat B general prison population
inmate costs over £40,000 a year. On that kind of money you
could send a kid to Eton, enjoy a couple of luxury holidays plus a

blow-out weekend at a celebrity chef's hotel/restaurant and still have change left over. The very senior judge I spoke to had long since come to the conclusion that short sentences are a total waste of time.

Growth in sentence length is alive and well at the other end of the scale, too. For example, sentencing tariffs for some categories of murder have doubled. We're now in the weird situation where if you shoot someone dead the starting point is thirty years, but if you stab them to death it's only fifteen. Longer sentences attract laudatory headlines in the newspapers and please the voting public but, considering prison's unbelievable cost – the yearly bill is nearing £5bn – it's worth asking to what extent locking people up actually works in reducing crime and keeping us safe. To answer this question it's important to understand what prison is for. A common confusion is that it's there to punish. It isn't. The sentence, that is to say the loss of liberty, is the punishment, not prison. Does it follow that prisons should be like first class on the *Queen Mary*? Of course it doesn't, but they should be decent.

Prison has three primary goals: deterrence, incapacitation and rehabilitation. The difficulty is that it succeeds in all three of these things only to a limited extent. The threat of prison does, of course, deter people from committing crime, but there's a catch. There is no link between the length of sentence and the amount of deterrence that a sentence gives: doubling a term of imprisonment doesn't mean that a potential criminal will be twice as deterred from committing a particular crime. The reason for this is simple. Deterrence feeds off risk. People are deterred from committing crime by the risk of *getting caught*, and the risk is pretty small. If it's worth the chance then the downside of prison, no matter what the sentence might be, ceases to dissuade the potential criminal.

Let's take the unpopular and prevalent offence of domestic burglary, by way of an example. In the 1990s the Conservative government passed a 'three strikes and you're out' law whereby a third-time domestic burglar would get a minimum sentence of three years, unless it was 'unjust in all the circumstances to do so'. The idea was to deter potential repeat burglars from committing that crime. According to their own figures, the Metropolitan Police's clear-up rate for domestic burglary in 2007–8 was 13 per cent. If you're a drug addict, or you've lost your job and can't put food on the table for your family, is 'three strikes and you're out' going to make a blind bit of difference when you've got a great chance of not getting caught? Bumping up sentences makes us feel that something is being done when in truth it isn't. Sentencing rules like these make the rash assumption that people thinking about committing crime have an idea of what the sentencing tariff for their chosen offence will be. Your average potential third-time burglar, say hyperactive Howard, isn't going to forgo his crack pipe for a trawl through the Sentencing Guideline Council website, only to discover the bad news and decide three years isn't worth the trouble.

Proper crims, unlike law-abiding citizens, do not think about jail sentences in linear terms. A couple of years ago I was in conference with a successful money launderer (never caught) and his son, who hadn't shown the same sureness of touch as his old man, and had been snared bang-to-rights mid-burgle. We were mulling the pros and cons of the son's pleading guilty in return for a twelve-month sentence rather than the thirty-month sentence he was likely to receive after a trial. I, like a poor man's Jeremy Bentham, was all for the plea on the grounds that prison was bad and therefore as little prison as possible was good. My job is to get the best possible result and I thought that twelve months should be seized with both hands. Mr Money Launderer, leaning against his top-of-the-range Jag, still warm after the trip to court from his large detached Buckinghamshire house, disagreed. 'No, Alex, you don't understand. When you get a bird, twelve months is the same as three years. It's the same.' I didn't understand and I still don't, but then I'm not a professional burglar who needs to be deterred from doing over other people's houses.

Politicians, despite what they tell you, know longer prison sentences don't deter crime. The Halliday Report, commissioned by the Home Office and charged with examining what sort of sentencing did and didn't work in reducing crime, concluded that longer sentences had no deterrent effect whatsoever. The reason many politicians push longer sentences is that it plays well with voters, whom it pays to keep in ignorance. We feel that someone's 'getting tough' and 'something is being done'.

Sentencing expert David Thomas QC calls this sort of thing 'politics by legislation'. His favourite example is Section 51A of the Firearms Act, which, hastily passed in the aftermath of the gunning down of two young women outside a party in Birmingham, introduced mandatory sentences of five years' imprisonment for possession of a firearm.

'Section 51A,' he says, 'is the height of preposterousness. It was sold as a way of reducing violent crime, but if people aren't going to be deterred by life for shooting someone dead, then why do they think they'll be deterred by five years for possessing a firearm?'

Similarly, we're encouraged to believe that prison protects us by keeping criminals locked up so they can't commit crime. Certainly there are a lot of very unpleasant people safely in prison who can't go around hurting the rest of us but, and I know this is counter-intuitive, longer sentences have almost no effect on crime levels.[7] One study estimated that a 25 per cent rise in the prison population led to a paltry 1 per cent drop in crime. Crime rates in America have gone up and down quite independently of the ever increasing prison population. The Halliday Report concluded that there was no value in changing the sentencing framework 'for the sole purpose of increasing an "incapacitation" effect'. Longer sentences have no significant impact on levels of crime because if you take offenders out of circulation, they're quickly replaced by the next generation.

The majority of crimes are committed by young men, most of whom will grow out of criminal behaviour without any intervention from the courts because the police won't catch them.

The government has tried to improve the incapacitation effect by introducing sentences of public protection for offenders who are identified as dangerous. On the face of it, this is a great way of focusing on the most predatory offenders but the legislation succeeds and fails on the ability of the courts and probation to predict who is and who isn't dangerous. This is notoriously difficult. Professor Andrew Ashworth of All Souls College, Oxford is pessimistic about the ability of anyone to predict dangerousness accurately. He cites the Floud Committee's survey in the early 1980s, which found that no method of prediction had a strike rate better than 50 per cent and many were much lower. Floud found that clinical predictions, like psychiatric and probation reports, which judges rely on when sentencing, are less accurate than actuarial measurements based on objective criteria of selected characteristics. A Home Office report reviewed 700 prisoners' cases and followed forty-eight that were classified as 'dangerous' after their release from prison. They found that nine of the forty-eight committed offences that could be termed as dangerous, which is a prediction rate of 20 per cent. Offenders classified as non-dangerous among the 700 also went on to commit dangerous offences, albeit at a lower frequency.

Rehabilitation is not a magic bullet either: it takes a long time, a lot of coordination and is expensive. It does have one major advantage over deterrence and incapacitation in that its benefits are elastic: after a certain point the deterrent and incapacitation effect stop increasing, but with rehabilitation the more and the better you do it, the more you reduce the chance of someone going back to crime. Rehabilitation is so important because out of the current 80,000-plus prisoners, only around thirty of them are never getting out. Everyone else is going to be released at some point, and it's their reentry into society that prison should be concentrating on. Prison can be said to work only if reoffending falls. Over-crowded prisons mean that work and education programmes fail to function because there aren't enough staff to administer them. It's no surprise that, comparing like for like, the reoffending rate over the last ten years of increasing prison populations, instead of going down, has risen by 12 per cent.*

Deterrence and incapacitation have a relatively small effect on crime levels because only a tiny fraction of crimes is ever sentenced at all. Taking the Home Office's own figures along with data from the British Crime Survey (BCS), Professor Ashworth makes this fascinating and telling calculation.† He starts with the 'cautious assumption' that about 45 per cent of crimes are reported every year. Of that 45 per cent only 55 per cent are actually recorded by the police, which leaves us with 24 per cent of total crimes still in the criminal justice system. Since the detection rate for recorded crime is so low, the 24 per cent becomes 5.5 per cent of all offences. Just over half of these cleared-up offences lead to a conviction or a caution, so the figure drops to 3 per cent. Take away the offences that are dealt with by cautions and you're left with only 2 per cent of all crimes being sentenced by a court. In the end, Ashworth estimates about 0.3 per cent of crimes lead to a prison sentence. The point he makes is sobering: so few criminals are caught, convicted and sentenced in the first place that it's impossible to sentence (or imprison) enough of them to have much effect on crime.

---

*The government, as David Ramsbotham, the former Her Majesty's Inspector of Prisons, points out, has recently changed the way the reoffending rate is calculated in order to hide this embarrassing fact.
†The British Crime Survey measures the amount of crime in England and Wales by asking people about crimes they have experienced in the last year. The BCS includes crimes which are not reported to the police but excludes crimes against under-sixteens. Recorded crime is a different measure. It is crime reported to and then recorded by the police. The police for various reasons do not record all crimes. Suffice to say measuring the 'true' crime rate is probably impossible.

17. Bird

I sat in the deserted youth court waiting room sipping vending-machine coffee. Out of the corner of my eye, I spied the detective sergeant approach. He wanted to talk about Stanley, my sixteen-year-old client. I beckoned him over.

'Excuse me, Mr McBride, sir. If it's a guilty, I'm going to be asking for Stanley's bail to be revoked.'

'Okay,' I said. It was decent of him to let me know. 'What about the others?'

'Not opposing their bail. They've got mums here to take them home. Anyhow Stanley's got proper form, previous for robbery.'

Stanley was outside having a fag with his three co-defendants. The snow had been falling all afternoon and it was beginning to settle. I looked out of the window. A raucous snowball fight had broken out. Even though he was outnumbered Stanley was holding off his friends with ease. He had a fantastic arm. The snowballs he threw travelled like guided missiles. Horsing around in the car park these proto-robbers looked like kids after school rather than crims on the first rung of the crime ladder. Their trial's outcome was not in doubt. Stanley and his co-defendants were sunk.

An usher came out of court. Verdict. I called Stanley in. He jogged up the stairs rosy-cheeked and out of breath. I took him to one side and told him that if it went against him he was going to get remanded in custody. Apart from a few nights in police cells it would be his first time in prison, probably his first of many. I thought Stanley would run for it (if I had news like that, I'd have been halfway down the street by now) but he just nodded and walked into court.

Stanley and his friends' crime had been 'steaming' on exurban trains. They'd put up their hoods and walked up the carriages looking for kids they could intimidate into handing over their mobile phones. A boy at each end of the carriage would stand guard while Stanley and another accomplice sat down next to their victim to scare them into parting with their phone. Even though they hadn't used actual violence in taking the phones, they were still guilty of robbery. In law, robbery is made out if, in order to steal, you put, or seek to put, the victim in fear of being subjected to violence. It was a pathetic and doomed crime. One kid they targeted knew a couple of them from school. It didn't take long for his mum to call the police. Put that together with the CCTV of them on the train looking feral and the prosecution couldn't fail.

The three co-ds went out of the door with a promise of supervision orders (probation for the under eighteens) and their mums. Stanley, whose parents were nowhere to be seen, was led down to the cells to wait alone for the van to Feltham Young Offenders' Institution. I went down to say goodbye. I found him sitting on the wooden bench in his cell. He looked up and I could see his terror. I wished I could do something, change something, but the judge had made his decision and it wasn't going to be rescinded. Stanley said he was okay but I could tell that he was lying. He started to cry. He tried to fight the tears, show that he was a tough guy, but it didn't work. I sat down next to him, put my arm around his shoulder and pulled him tight against me. We sat there, him crying, me silent, for a long while. Finally, the van arrived. I got up, shook Stanley by the hand and, telling him that it would be okay, walked out of the door.

What did I know about it being okay? I didn't have a clue. The court was my bit of the criminal justice system and the rest of it was well beyond my purview. Sitting on the train home, I wondered how Stanley was, and what prison would be like for him. I wondered whether it would help him or the kid he'd robbed or the kid he was going to rob.

For barristers and judges prison sentences are abstract. They're notches on the bedpost, a way of keeping score. You pin the sentence on the crim and move on to the next case. As I've told myself many times, prison is somewhere your client goes but you don't, no matter how bad things get. To find out a bit more about the realities of prison, I went to see Bobby Cummines, a reformed armed robber and hit man who runs a charity called Unlock, which helps to reintegrate former prisoners back into society. Sitting in his modern office, Cummines, a small, compact man in his late fifties, looks more like a company director than a former major criminal. He is friendly and honest, as if he's on a life-long twelve-step programme to make amends for his first thirty-five years.

Cummines says that the first time you get a bird is the hardest. He spent his trial in a haze. The reality started to close in around him only when he heard the guilty verdict. Cummines's experience is the same as it is for every newly convicted prisoner. You go down the narrow stairs to the cells, the jailers take your details and bag your things. You're loaded on to the prison van thinking about the years you've just got. Stanley would have travelled in one of those Serco vans you see driving around with the darkened reinforced windows. Inside, these vans are divided up into little cubicles known as 'sweatboxes' because of how hot they get. According to Cummines, the worst trip was to HMP Parkhurst on the Isle of Wight. He had to stay in his sweatbox during the crossing, convinced that, if the ferry started to sink, no one was coming to get him. I once prosecuted a claustrophobic handler of stolen goods. The judge wondered out loud how this claustrophobic, who was in custody, had been brought to court. 'Open-top bus,' was the best answer.

These days, Cummines says, once you arrive at prison they ask you questions to gauge your physical and mental state, which is change for the good. Then after a quick visit to the showers, you are finally brought out on to the wing – which is when it really hits you, as it must have hit Stanley. People are calling out, maybe threatening to cut you up in the morning. There's the crying and the banging, often going on all night. The smell is bad. You're put in a cell, more likely than not with someone else, where the pair of you will stay locked up together for twenty-three hours of every day. At least Cummines had a cell to himself. Own cell or not, you can forget about privacy: the wicket can be opened at any time and a pair of eyes peer in on you.

The large majority of prisoners, unlike Cummines, are hardly criminal masterminds. They are people from the very bottom of society. Sixty-five per cent read and write below the level of your average eleven-year-old. Two-thirds were unemployed before they went into prison and one-third were homeless. Sixty-six per cent used drugs and 63 per cent were hazardous drinkers. Nearly three-quarters suffer from some sort of mental health disorder.[1] In short, most people in prison come from an underclass of those who have fallen through society's cracks.

Bobby Cummines got his criminal start stealing things off lorries. Before long he graduated to smashing restaurant windows and then demanding protection money and free dinners from the proprietors. It didn't take him long to achieve the prison sentence that he craved. Not yet out of his teens, he was convicted of manslaughter. For him prison was not a corrective experience. During his seven and a half years inside all he learned was how to be a better criminal. By his own admission he went in a nineteen-year-old street thug and came out a fully fledged organized criminal with a firm of his own. Most of his connections and all of his criminal knowledge were picked up inside. He swapped numbers and tips with everyone from Irish terrorists to Italian wise guys. For him prison was no different from going to university – except that instead of reading English, chemistry or maths his degree was in serious crime.

Cummines's prison education started with the 'food boat', which is the basic organizational unit for inmates with real criminal aspirations. The food boat is a group of prisoners who club together for meals. The members all chip in to make eating as good as it can be. Everyone brings something to the table. The food – fresh vegetables and the best cuts of meat – is stolen from or bribed out of the kitchen. Cummines and his fellow food boaters even employed another prisoner to do the cooking and cleaning for them. The food boat works in a similar way to Oxford University's famous Bullingdon Club. They both attract the same aggressively ambitious types with big egos. Food is a nice distraction, but neither of these self-selecting clubs is just about eating. They are vehicles for establishing one's credentials with one's network. The food boat has a jump on the 'Buller' in that it doesn't just offer high-powered networking but an education as well.

David Ramsbotham, a former Her Majesty's Inspector of Prisons, and Bobby Cummines, approaching prisons from two different ends of the system, believe that proper education and training – of the sort *not* run by the food boat – can divert prisoners from falling back into crime. The trick is to offer the chance of a trade or a qualification that a prisoner can see may lead to real paid work on the outside. Without education and training, most former prisoners are still poor, unskilled and hooked on drink and drugs. Ramsbotham cites the report written in response to the Strangeways prison riot in 1990, which concluded that the three things most likely to prevent reoffending were a home, a job and a stable relationship. Prison, argues Ramsbotham, should, and could, be helping with the first two things on that list.

Bobby Cummines is critical of the regimented life that prisoners have to lead – being told when to eat, when to wake up, when to wash – which kills off the initiative and get-up-and-go required in life on the outside. Ironically, the thriving black economy in prison reflects the realities of life on the outside much better than the usual dead-end prison jobs. Prison is a highly evolved capitalist environment. Everyone has to have a little job or a sideline to survive. Cummines's enterprise during his second lengthy stretch was money lending. He'd lend out cash at a hefty 25 per cent interest rate. If some fellow prisoner's wife couldn't pay a bill, Cummines would cover it. That prisoner would then have to pay the money back with wages from his prison job, or by payments in kind, say parcels of meat filched from the kitchens.

Cummines also lent money for treats. If someone fancied a flutter or a bottle of spirits (in the late 1980s the prison price for a bottle of spirits was £25 – the going rate these days, I'm told, is between £60 and £80) and needed cash up front, they knew where to go.

If people were not paying Cummines back, he'd pick the person who owed the least and then he or one of his henchmen would cut the person up with a blade, 'serving him up', as it's called. Word of what had happened would go around the jail and the other debtors would be falling over themselves to repay their debts. The reason you sliced up the guy who owed the least was because that person was going to hospital for a long time and writing off a fiver made more business sense than writing off a £50 debt from someone else. It might seem incredible that something as bulky as a bottle of whisky is available in prison; the truth is you can get anything you want so long as you can pay for it.

Nowhere does this apply more than with drugs. When he was Her Majesty's Inspector of Prisons, David Ramsbotham estimated, much to the government's irritation, that each prison had at least ten drug dealers, and in the big ones it was more like twenty. Several of my own clients have survived very nicely in jail by dealing heroin and crack. It's how Clarence got by before he straightened himself out. The Prison Service estimates, probably conservatively, that about £5m worth of drugs circulates through the prison system every year.

'You'd have to have a fucking big arse to smuggle in that lot,' says Cummines. His point being that the amounts are so large that there's no way all those drugs – not to mention the bottles of drink and mobile phones – are coming in stuffed up people's bums. A lot of contraband is brought in by corrupt prison officers, or as Cummines puts it, 'hooky screws'. David Ramsbotham says that, according to unofficial Prison Service estimates, there are about 1,000 corrupt officers out of a staff of 40,000. When he was Her Majesty's Inspector of Prisons he did his own counts by gauging whether prison officers on £18,000 a year could afford the cars in the prison car park.

It's more than good old-fashioned corruption; allowing in drugs has its advantages. A happy prison is a tranquil prison. As long as there's no trouble, why get too excited by a little bit of weed and a little bit of smack? By the same token, if a trouble-free jail means letting prisoners run their businesses undisturbed, then it pays to turn a blind eye. Jail is like any other society: people will put up with a lot so long as they're allowed to make a few quid.

Prison isn't cheeky geezers all having a jolly crime caper of a time. Cummines is at pains to point out what a brutal place prison can be. He should know because it was serious criminals like him who okayed and meted out the violence. Jails are hierarchical institutions in which the people at the top maintain their positions through violence and intimidation. A suspected grass might have his cell burnt out with a paint-thinner firebomb. A paedophile might be beaten with an iron bar in the showers. Weapons are easy to manufacture. Cummines carried a stiletto he fashioned by hammering a 6-inch nail into a blade with a cork for a handle. Cross him and he'd shank you. Cummines also kept one half of a pair of garden shears hidden in the prison bathhouse (Reggie Kray, another member of the food boat, had the other half) if something a bit bigger was required.

Category A wings, housing the prison's most violent criminals, such as Cummines and Kray, were especially dangerous. On the Cat A wing everyone carried a weapon and was more than capable of using it. Mindful of this, Cat A prisoners were always exquisitely polite. Forgetting to greet a prisoner was potentially a very costly mistake because, as Cummines explains, that prisoner was going to wonder why you didn't say hello. Hour after hour in his cell with nothing but gnawing jail paranoia to keep him company, he turns your solecism into a slight and then a threat. Does it mean you hate him? Does it mean you're going to cut him? Too dangerous to take the risk, so he decides to beat you to the draw and skewer you first. Next thing you know you've got a face full of razor for no other reason than you forgot to say good morning. People have died over nothing in Cat A. One prisoner wanted an onion for his spaghetti bolognese but the guy who'd stolen it from the kitchen had his own culinary plans. Sharing was out of the question so the dispute ended with one of them stabbed through the heart and the other serving life for his murder – all for an onion.

This foreshadows Ramsbotham and Cummines's point, which is that it's easy for prisons to be brutal and brutalizing places. For them the government's current policy of emphasizing punishment in prison is a disaster. Returning angry and embittered prisoners to society without skills or prospects is crazy because you're setting them up to reoffend. The cycle of prison and reoffending is a difficult thing to break; if you don't offer former prisoners the real chance of a different life then they'll keep committing crime. Leaving Cummines's office, I wonder whether Stanley will get stuck in this cycle. Will he end up one of the many thousands flitting in and out of prison, his offending and his troubles unaddressed, his potential wasted?

PART FIVE

Change

18. Clerks

'I said, right, you piss-ants, RIGHT,' barks Keith, the senior clerk, hands on hips like General George S. Patton, through the open window. Heads turn. Passers-by recoil. Two very junior clerks, beads of sweat trickling down their foreheads, teeth gritted, struggle to go further right, but the window frame, set in four floors of listed Georgian brickwork, is not playing along. The smallest clerk is lugging the air-conditioning unit. The other, following behind, grapples with a large pipe attachment, which he hopes he'll be able to angle at Keith's sweating frame.

'RIGHT, deaf aids. I want the cold air blown on me, not you two fuck-heads. I'm sick of watching the air-conditioning blow your hair around. Like a shampoo commercial, hair swishing around, getting on my tits. Lucky to have hair in the first place. I'm the one who needs cooling, not you two. Look at my armpits.' Keith puts his arms in the air to reveal two wet patches under his arms. 'Sweaty like a marathon runner's arsehole.' After a lot of heartache and shouting, Keith is finally satisfied. The air-conditioner is plugged in and a cool breeze starts to waft over him. 'There you go,' says Keith, settling into his chair, 'just like being on the pier at Margate.'

Clerks start young. Every year a new try-out fresh from school appears at chambers. They might be sixteen but with the ironed shirt and tie look more like twelve. I'm always convinced that social services will track them down and drag them back to the school they've bunked off from. The first test these baby clerks have is whether they've got the stamina. Clerking is hard work. They're given a trolley and for the first year do nothing but ferry towers of paper from one location to the other. Walk down to Ludgate Circus and you'll see them pushing case papers up the hill to the Bailey. Keith, as he likes to remind his juniors frequently, started out before the fax machine had been invented. 'My arse didn't touch the chair. You've got it easy,' says Keith as he dispatches an exhausted teenage clerk out on yet another hellish errand.

Clerking is a closed shop. Jobs rarely come up and then they're advertised by word of mouth. Sons and daughters often follow their mums and dads into the profession. It's a good career. You don't need any qualifications but if you work hard and bide your time, you can do very well.

Organizational ability and grit are important but to be a really good clerk you need subtler talents, too. You must be able to do three things well: flattery, threats and lies. Keith is blessed with an easy natural charm; he is only average at menace but what he really excels at is lying. The reason Keith is such a brilliant liar is that he only ever lies for a reason, so you assume what he says is true, forgetting that when you're senior clerk a minute doesn't go by when a well-placed lie is not a gold-plated requirement. Clerks are stuck between the suppliers of the work and the barristers and the only way to keep both sides happy is to play them off against each other.

The senior clerk must also keep the spirits up. Let's say one of the senior clerk's barristers calls. His practice is dying. Solicitors shun him. The murder case he had at the Bailey has been taken out of his diary and reallocated. He's got school fees to pay. He desperately needs a decent brief so he picks up the phone and asks Keith, man-to-man, 'Tell me honestly, am I over the hill?'

Keith has a choice: he can give speech A or speech B. Speech A is the truth and speech B is, well, bullshit.

A) Your practice isn't dying, it's dead. You lost whatever you had and you didn't have much in the first place. You've survived off other people's returns for years. Now that work is drying up across the bar I've got no more returns to give you. I've carried you for years but it's over. You're finished.

B) It's quiet everywhere. It's not only you. There are bloody good barristers kicking their heels. Things will pick up in a few months. I've got some good cases in the pipeline. There's private work (the prospect of which cheers up even the most depressed criminal barrister). It's coming, I promise you.

Which speech does Keith give? Speech B, of course. Why? Because it's loyalty, it's good manners and, most importantly, good business sense. Kicking a member of chambers out is basically impossible unless they do something depraved or criminal. (You can't rely on a barrister doing that. Admittedly, a few years back one young barrister obliged by getting filmed by the police bulking up a kilo of cocaine in his kitchen. 'Who is the Roman king, mate, me,' he exulted, 'I am a face and a half. We are making bundles.') You're lumbered with the chump so it pays to build his confidence and his hopes up. You don't want your barrister going to court feeling like a failure. Part of being a good barrister is being a good salesman. As a commercial law barrister I know says, 'It's all very well having a first from bloody Balliol but can you sell the fucking car?' Barristers who think they're washed up are never going to sell that car.

Clerks have their own difficulties. Take Keith: he's an old-style senior clerk who has had to adapt to a new way of doing things. Not so long ago, he ran chambers. Every big decision went through him. Best of all, he was paid a percentage of gross turnover, therefore earning more than most of the barristers – the going rate was between 2 and 5 per cent, not too shabby on a turnover of £10m a year. A few years ago Keith's pre-eminent position in chambers was superseded by a new overlord who went by the name of chambers' director. In terms of management, Keith, like all clerks, was a disinterested amateur: if the work was coming in, then chambers would look after itself. The new chambers' director saw things differently. He was a professional manager plucked from a sediment layer of management in some enormous company. He was steeped in systems, memos ('What the fuck was a "memo"?'), Power Point charts and cost savings. Keith the freewheeling Mongol chieftain was suddenly 1,000 years out of date. He had to relinquish chambers and take a salary. There was one very big consolation: he kept the clerks' room. This meant that he still had an absolutely central role in chambers because the clerks, and specifically the senior clerk, bring in the work. Nothing matters more to chambers than bringing in the work. Senior clerks live and die on their ability to keep it coming. A lot is forgiven if you can maintain the flow.

The classic example of this truth was Binnsy, senior clerk in a chambers up in Leeds and an old drinking partner of Keith's. Binnsy was a brilliant clerk of the very oldest school but you wouldn't want to spend a long weekend with him. His bullying, all-round vile behaviour and drunken outrages were tolerated because he kept the senior barristers' kids in private schools and their spouses in Tuscan villas. Life would not be the same without Binnsy so Binnsy was accommodated. When he punched a junior female barrister some years ago it was the female barrister and not Binnsy who left chambers. He was untouchable. He didn't just run chambers, he *was* chambers. The head of chambers, a very senior barrister, and the management committee, more very senior barristers, were just so much window-dressing.

Impunity is a dangerous thing because inevitably you go too far, and it was that which did for Binnsy in the end. Here's how it happened. One afternoon Binnsy takes two of his junior clerks to the pub leaving – a big no-no this – chambers undermanned. By evening, he's belligerently drunk and has been joined by a group of barristers from his chambers. Events are hazy but somehow Binnsy gets into an argument with the bar manageress and completely loses his temper. Allegedly he lunges across a table at her, bellowing like a bull walrus. The police are called, arriving as some barristers are pushing Binnsy into a taxi. Police enquiries reveal that the pub's CCTV camera has recorded Binnsy's performance.

There is, however, a chink of light. The bar manageress decides not to press charges, which means there won't be a walk of shame at a magistrates' court and certain dismissal. All the same there has been very major public embarrassment and chambers can't just shrug it off. So the powers-that-be – head of chambers and the management committee – conduct an investigation. Obviously they watch the CCTV but they also take statements. Now here's the interesting thing. The barristers who saw Binnsy in the pub are reluctant to put pen to paper because they're frightened. They know that, as senior clerk, Binnsy controls the work tap: he can turn it off in the same way that he can turn it on. Anyone grasses him up and Binnsy will take revenge by destroying his career. In response to the knocking knees and chattering teeth, the management committee prises the statements out of the barristers by promising them that no one's work will suffer. Meanwhile, an audit of chambers' accounts reveals that Binnsy has been spending thousands of pounds a month on taxis back to his house in Harrogate but hasn't kept any receipts. This massive figure doesn't include the thousands of pounds of receipt-less entertainment 'expenses', which he's also run up. The amazing thing is that chambers hadn't just let it happen, they hadn't even noticed.

In his meeting with the management committee, Binnsy pleads for forgiveness, asks for help with his drinking and hopes the job he does so well will still be his. The barristers whom Binnsy has favoured with the best work fight a rearguard action. Binnsy's future is put to the vote. The results are tallied. It's a close-run thing. Once upon a time he would have survived, but with less work around these days it pays to be professional and Binnsy is no longer an expense they feel they can afford.

Binnsy was not finished. He went to a rival chambers (taking his favourites with him), not as top dog but still a player. Ensconced in his new place he demonstrated his reach to those who were fool-hardy enough to make statements against him. They saw, as they had feared, their work dry up from solicitors who were more loyal to Binnsy than to them. Binnsy might have been gone but he was not forgotten.

19. Smoke in Your Eye

Wordless Will wasn't hanging about. When chambers turned you down for tenancy, the permanent job for which we were all competing, there was no point in lingering. The done thing was to vanish. Tenants hate the embarrassment of bumping into the also-rans in the corridor or the post room. No one looks forward to the strained smiles and meaningless 'best of lucks'. A few would be anxious that the rejected pupil might be able to tell that not only hadn't they voted for him but they had led the charge in rubbishing him in the tenancy meeting. It was common knowledge that the most smiley and solicitous tenant was the one who'd stabbed you in the back. Occasionally, the Judas' best line gets back to the also-ran. A friend of mine found out she'd been blackballed by a senior silk (now a judge) who'd said of her, 'More *solicitor* than barrister material, don't you think?'

It's therefore much better for everyone if you leave quickly. In some jobs there might be the slamming of doors, rages and the threat of employment tribunals but at the bar you exited like Captain Oates with an upper lip so stiff you could balance an emperor penguin on it. The really devious left with delighted smiles on their faces as though thanking the host of the best party they'd ever been to. Of course, they were the ones to watch, the ones whose hearts were filled with revenge, the ones who'd leave a steaming turd on the head of chambers' desk.

Harriet, cigarette in hand, watched Will from the other side of the room. He flicked open a black bin liner and swept the past eighteen months of his working life – notes, receipts, statements of earnings – into it. He moved on to his files, chucking them in too. A second bin liner held the small library of third-rate paper-backs that he'd accumulated for his train journeys to court. There was enough room in it for Will to tip in his wig, gown and the remnants of his gym kit. He was going up North. His girlfriend was a barrister in one of the big chambers in Manchester and they'd agreed to give him a try-out.

'You'll be all right up there, Will,' said Liam, trying to lighten the mood. 'Stress-free up there. You won't have to do a trial again. Not a proper one. It's all agreed in advance up North. Back and forth on counsel's row: one case you'll be prosecuting, the next defending. Funny handshakes at the back of the court and a wink to the judge to let him know it's all sorted. I tell you, there's more mutual fucking back-scratching at the Manchester criminal bar than there is in the most flea-ridden troop of baboons in all of Africa.'

'Yeah,' said Mamta, 'it's a total carve-up in Manchester. You'll crack three trials a week. Pocket £1,500 minimum. They give houses away up there. You'll be flush. Every other Friday, it'll be a weekend of Euro-bonk on the continent.'

Will wasn't that sad about going. It was Harriet and Jane that he minded about. They were his best friends and he'd miss them. The six of us – Will, Harriet, Jane, Mamta, Liam and I – realized that it was the end of an era. Once he'd finished gathering up his things he gave the girls a hug and shook Liam and me by the hand. He grabbed the two black bin liners and walked out of chambers look-ing like a member of the Serious Fraud Squad after a particularly successful raid. It was different for Harriet and Jane. Will had never persuaded himself that he was going to get tenancy but they had, busting their arses for two gruelling years with little more than black coffee and nicotine to keep them going but they'd been rejected all the same. Harriet and Jane would never show it, too polished for that, but we all knew they were devastated.

Harriet wasn't lingering either. She had lined up a pupillage at a heavy-hitting chambers up in Lincoln's Inn. Harriet being Harriet had a baby clerk from the new chambers on hand with a trolley to take all her stuff to her new home. She was to spend the afternoon in retail therapy. Jane didn't know where she was going. Somewhere would snap her up but first she needed a break. All her effort, all the sacrificed weekends and evenings had been for nothing. It was nearly too much to bear. She was mentally and physically exhausted and she knew she'd have to play the same guarantee-less game all over again. Like every rejected pupil, Jane felt used. A pupil's relationship with chambers is an abusive one. You need them more than they need you but you still commit in the hope that they'll love you in return.

After they had gone the pupils' room felt abandoned, as though we'd arrived at a top party half an hour after it had ended. One minute our friends, our comrades, had been there and the next they'd vanished, without leaving a trace. I sat on the table and watched Liam and Mamta console themselves with a succession of cigarettes.

'There'll be a new batch of pupils in a few months. More cannon fodder. Poor bastards,' said Liam, rebelliously flicking ash on the carpet.

'Course, you know what this means?' said Mamta. 'We're next — next for the fucking high jump.'

The three of us thought about this for a moment. She was right. We were next in line to be mown down by the tenancy committee's machine guns. It was coming up fast. The hard reality was all too plain: if they weren't going to take talented barristers like Harriet, Jane and Will, what chance did the three of us schmucks have?

There was a knock at the door. It was Araminta holding an A4 piece of card. 'Bad news, I'm afraid.'

She put the card on the table. It read: 'From the end of June this room will be NO SMOKING'.

'What do you mean, NO SMOKING?' Mamta asked, fishing another cigarette out of her handbag.

'It's not just this room. It's all of chambers,' said Araminta.

'What, no fags at all?'

'Yes.'

'Can't they make an exception for the pupils' room? No one gives a shit about us anyway. Why single out our lungs for special treatment?' said Mamta.

'It isn't going to be the pupils' room much longer.'

'What!' said Liam.

'Oh no, this room is going to be for tenants. The pupils' room is being disbanded.'

'B-b-but where will we go?' asked Liam.

'Haven't you heard?'

'Heard what?'

'You're to sit with your pupilmasters.'

Liam clapped his hands around his head and cried, 'Noooo, noooo, noooo.'

I didn't realize this at the time but the smoking ban and the demise of the pupils' room were the starting gun for change across the criminal justice system. It was a symptom of a general tightening up. Soon the smoking ban stretched to the cells at court. Not that things were getting any more efficient – it was the same old incompetence, only meaner. I should have seen it coming.

Once upon a time, if no interview room were available, the jailers would open up the cell and let you go in for a face-to-face chat with your client. Sitting in the cell next to your client as he ate a rank Prison Service Lancashire hot pot was proper camaraderie. You'd pull out a fag. They'd gratefully take it, have a few deep puffs and relax for a few minutes. It was a way to build a bit of rapport and a short respite from the stress they were under. There was a pay-off – you got better, clearer instructions. It was civilized, humane. Inevitably, they'd ask you for a few fags for 'laters'.

You'd scratch your chin, 'um and ah' a bit and then pass them the *whole* pack. Solicitors were very keen that we maintained their clients' nicotine habit. Let them know they were valued customers.

The tightening up was incremental but insidious. Initially, we were allowed to pass sealed packets of tobacco only to people in the cells. Security, they said. As if a barrister is going to pass contraband to a prisoner. Prisons are full of drugs, booze and illicit mobile phones already. They don't need any help from us. It was ridiculous. The next step, which didn't take long coming, was to stop any tobacco being passed whatsoever. The reason was of course that same lovely catch-all: security. I knew the real reason was administrative convenience. Fags were hassle.

A few months after the chambers cigarette ban, I came up against the logical conclusion of this step-by-step change in policy at Horseferry Road Magistrates' Court. To get into the cells you are buzzed through two sets of doors. This brings you into a reception area where you sign in. I had just gone through these formalities and was looking forward to seeing a particularly wretched false-passport holder when I heard a thud. It was coming from the cells. As I followed the jailer into the cell corridor the thudding, having taken on a metallic echo, got louder.

'What's that noise?' I asked.

'Cell three, sir. Banging his head on the door.'

'Why is he doing that?'

'Smoking ban, sir.'

'For Christ's sake, give him a cigarette.'

'I'd like to but we're not allowed. Health and Safety.'

I should have said, 'What about the health and safety of his head?' but I had arrived at my client. The man in cell three was now interspersing his head banging with shouts and moans. I lifted up the flap of the wicket in my client's cell door but instead of finding a hole I found a thick piece of perspex.

'Excuse me, jailer. Where's the wicket gone?'

'Filled them in.'

'How am I supposed to talk to my client? With a loudhailer? It's supposed to be a private conversation.'

'We've got interview rooms for that, sir.'

'They're full and there's a queue. Can you open the door? I won't be long.'

'Can't do that . . .'

'Don't tell me, is it health and safety? Is it security? Is it more than your job's worth?'

'Brainy lot you barristers.'

I turned back to the ex-wicket. My client's face behind the perspex seemed unnaturally large. I waved at him and smiled.

I looked at his charge sheet. Charge one was forgery. The passport, which no one disputed he was entitled to, had been properly issued and included his picture. The name in the passport was not the defendant's name. Using a different name is not a crime. In Britain you can call yourself what you like; if you want to be Prince Piss Face there is nothing to stop you. For something to be a forgery it must purport to be something that it is not. This passport was purporting to be exactly what it was. It therefore was not a forgery. The man behind the perspex was guilty of something, but deciding what to charge him with was not my job. I made the short journey to the Crown Prosecution Service's room, explained to the prosecutor the problem and asked him to review the charge.

'It's already been reviewed.'

'But you charged him with the offence last night. You haven't had time to review it. Let's adjourn for two weeks and you can think about an alternative charge, which he'll plead guilty to.'

'The charge was reviewed when we charged him.'

'That's not a review. A review is where you revisit the issue and consider it in light of fresh information, namely that the present charge is wrong in law.'

'I've told you. It's been reviewed, so that's that.'

I went back to the cells. The interview rooms were all full. Going past cell three on the way to my client, I could still hear the man banging his head. New jailer but same old line: they couldn't open the cell door. We shouted at each other like a couple of sailors rounding Cape Horn in a storm.

'Don't plead guilty.'

'What?'

'It's wrong in law.'

'You're right. Law has wronged me.'

'Say not guilty.'

'Not guilty,' he repeated, pointing at himself.

'But guilty of something.'

'Guilty?'

'Not guilty, guilty of something else . . .'

His eyes narrowed. I could tell what little confidence he had in me was now irrevocably gone.

Up in court, I begged for an adjournment but it was refused. He entered a not guilty plea. Back in chambers I drafted a written argument outlining why the forgery charge was wrong. I heard nothing from the CPS for weeks. Then a pro forma letter arrived on my desk saying that the forgery charge had been discontinued. Had someone 'reviewed' the file or had they found another word for it?

The non-review review was part of a target-led performance drive. It wasn't just the CPS; it was the courts too. They wanted cases to move more swiftly through the system. Efficiency drives are not a bad thing. Constant and often unnecessary adjournments do not serve justice. Think of the witnesses who pluck up the courage to give evidence and then wait for hours and days to get into the witness box only to be told at the last minute that the case has been put off. Back they come, often to go through exactly the same thing.

The problem with 'improving' targets is that it fails to take into account how the justice system really works. Trials are complex. They require lots of paper and people to be in the right place at the right time. Targets don't seem ever to address the inefficiency and incompetence in the system: probation reports are not prepared, the prosecution forgets to warn witnesses for trial, case papers aren't served, barristers (who never do anything until the last minute) haven't prepared the case properly, jurors get sick, and somebody doesn't get around to delivering the defendant from prison. Getting a trial up and running can be like trying to get two pandas to mate: not only does everything have to be in alignment but you also need to be extravagantly lucky. The authorities, gripped by the target frenzy, forget this. In order to hit the target, often the first thing to be discarded is rigour, which is worrying because it's the rigour that ensures fairness. I'm not just talking about fairness to the defendant but to everyone.

In recent years defence solicitors have noticed that increasingly suspects are being re-bailed and not charged, presumably so an unsuccessful prosecution or discontinuance doesn't spoil someone's performance target. Prosecutions are tricky and expensive; much better not to let them start in the first place. Serious frauds are now dealt with under the civil law because so few criminal prosecutions are successful. At the other end of the scale, fixed penalty notices (an £80 fine, which often goes unpaid) are used more and more, even for serious assaults. The crime can be recorded as 'cleared up' even though no finding of fact, let alone suitable punishment, has been made.

The CPS's core job is to decide which cases to prosecute and then to prepare them for trial. Its lawyers are on site at police stations to help advise police on what further action is required to make sure a case is ready for charge. In the last few years, the CPS has started a sea change by prosecuting more and more of its cases. The idea is that the CPS will save money by not having to pay the independent criminal bar. I should declare an interest. The CPS prosecuting cases in-house has been a disaster for independently employed barristers like me. Work that we used to rely upon has gone. As a consequence, there has been a stampede of barristers leaving the bar to work directly for the CPS.

Paradoxically, the CPS's determination to take on trial advocacy has undermined its ability to do its main job properly. The CPS is overworked and understaffed. I'll give an example. At the very last minute, a barrister friend of mine was instructed to prosecute a trial concerning drugs and firearms. The defendant had been in custody for nearly a year. My friend comes to court to find no DNA evidence and no evidence of drugs in the case papers. He calls the reviewing lawyer who is supposed to be coordinating the case but the reviewing lawyer doesn't answer. My friend, in a spasm of initiative, searches around the court's CPS room and in a closet finds big piles of case papers. 'Whose case papers are these?' he asks himself. 'Blow me, they're mine!' The trial is about to start and he hasn't had a chance to read them, let alone serve them (they are the prosecution's case after all) on the defence. Going through the papers he discovers he's sitting on an overwhelming case.

In court the judge decides to proceed with the trial. The defence argues that this newly found material should not be allowed to go before the jury, asserting that it's being served far too late for the trial to be fair. My friend counters that there has been no unfairness and in the interests of justice the material should go in. The judge, despite the prosecution's lateness, agrees. They have the trial: the drugs, the firearms, the bullets, some hollowed out for extra damage, are all presented to the jury. The defendant is convicted. My friend, having sketched this out to me asks, rhetorically, whether justice has been done? Without his prosecutor's wig on he thought not. The evidence he wanted to put into the trial was too late for the defendant to give his counsel proper instructions in response or to have time to decide how best to challenge it.

Fairness in trials is a balancing exercise. There is the understandable pressure to prosecute serious crime successfully but there must also be a countervailing impetus to ensure that the defendant is able to defend himself properly. In my friend's opinion, the judge's real mistake was that he was allowing the prosecution to get away with non-existent case preparation and non-existent service of the papers. Without sanctions, such as cases collapsing or defendants being bailed because their custody time limits have expired, then there is little incentive to do the job of prosecution properly. As for the CPS lawyer in charge of the case, he never turned up at court and never answered my friend's calls.

There are also many very able, dedicated people at the CPS. Over the years, they've sent me a lot of work for which I am grateful. I feel for them, too, because when I was seconded to them I saw the work they had to do. My main job was to prosecute their trials. As a warm-up, I spent three days at one of their offices, which was at the very top of a tower that rose out of a low-rise neighbourhood like a defiant middle finger. Its architectural statement – 'Up yours, South-west London' – was unmistakable. At the tower, files would come in for charges to be made, or to be reviewed or marked up for further action. There were thousands of them. It was dispiriting. If the windows hadn't been bolted shut I'd have jumped. Once I had got out of my training period, I was safely at court. The rule, however, was that if you finished before lunchtime, you had to go back to the tower to review files. I would do anything, *anything* not to go back to the tower. I even prosecuted this poor guy for some jumped-up possession of drugs offence so my afternoon would be occupied in court. There wasn't a jot of evidence. Two good things came of this: he was acquitted and I didn't go back to the tower.

Preparing cases for trial is hard, unglamorous work, and who can blame the CPS for wanting to go to court for a bit of cut and thrust? Why let those poncey briefs have all the fun? The truth is that until recently many CPS higher court advocates, or HCAs, as they are known, were those who couldn't cut it at the independent bar. Once you were in the CPS you got work because you were an employee rather than because you were good. The CPS nine-to-five work culture (don't bother calling after 5.15) is not well suited to the demands of trial advocacy. In trial, you have to prepare overnight for the next day and work weekends. People go to the CPS precisely so they don't have to work like that. It is a world of maternity leave, job shares, paid training days and 'sickies'. There's one charming CPS HCA who takes Wednesday as his day off, which means there's no way they can ever get him to do a trial. Another HCA who, when asked by a judge mid-trial to prepare a written argument for Monday, refused on the grounds that he wasn't paid to work weekends. At the criminal bar this is anathema. We're self-employed and if we don't work, we don't eat. More than that, being an advocate is a vocation, not a job. It pays to try to do it properly.

Many years ago, as a beginning pupil, I was packed off by my head of chambers for a Saturday-morning pep talk on the greatness of the CPS. It felt like being a North Korean foot soldier at a party rally. After the Bar Council's warm-up man had finished, a very senior CPS manager strode out on to the stage.

This was her opening gambit: 'If the CPS were an animal, what animal would it be?'

There was silence. No hands shot up. I didn't hear any little voices saying, 'Miss, miss, I know, I know!' Like any North Korean foot soldier worth his salt we knew this was dangerous territory. Get it wrong, and our chambers, which depended on this manager for work, would suffer. Wisecracks, to which the criminal bar is naturally predisposed, were especially *verboten*: word would get back from the overseers on the front row dooming our already slim chances of a tenancy. At the same time, no one could quite bring himself to toady with something sycophantic. I didn't hear any cheetahs, tigers or gazelles. The silence became embarrassing. Then the answer came to me and I whispered it to the girl sitting next to me.

'A warthog.'

'Why a warthog?' she asked.

'Because the CPS want you to think that they're full of vigour and fight, but we all know they'd rather be scratching their arses on a nice tree stump.'

In fact, this applies to the whole criminal justice apparatus but it's most true with the CPS. The CPS wants to be seen as tough and efficient but it isn't. It's overwhelmed. And getting a room full of people to chant 'we are cheetahs, we are cheetahs' did not suddenly make them all cheetahs.

What about the barrister class itself? In this new world of targets and cost savings, what was to become of us? More to the point, what was to become of me? Was the job I'd struggled so hard to get about to die on me like a terminally ill heiress who has neglected to put me in her will? It was time to turn to an expert.

I met Gleeful Bertie in a cellar bar north of Holborn, a bottle of tepid Chardonnay and a bowl of cocktail sausages (Gleeful's favourite food) at the ready. Gleeful, a specialist prosecutor, had come by his nickname because of the 'gleeful' way he went about convicting defendants. Nothing made his little black heart swell more than potting the crims. Once Gleeful had refreshed himself with some wine and sausages, he got down to business.

'You ask about the bar, Alex. Well, I'll tell you. The bar is roundly fucked.'

'Christ, don't say that.'

'*I'll* probably be all right, I'm senior enough. But babies like you ... It's going to be carnage. I've got something that underscores this truth,' continued Gleeful, reaching into a sinister-looking military rucksack lying by his feet. Out came a pair of battered army boots, 'No, not those,' and then, after more rummaging, one of his famous lever arch files. Gleeful had a file on everything. He probably even had a file on me.

'Here,' he said, pointing at a newspaper headline which read 'Legal aid millionaires: the dirty dozen revealed.'

'Yeah, so?' I replied.

'Look, don't you get it, brain-ache? We, the barrister class – toffee-nosed elitists who get criminals out of jail and back to preying on law-abiding citizens – are not loved. In the public's mind, we're one rung below benefit scroungers. And, to make matters worse, this headline insinuates to the tax-weary public that they're paying us top whack to do it.'

Gleeful was momentarily distracted by the cocktail sausages and I took my chance to ask a question. 'Is this legal aid millionaires thing true?'

'Nah, it's mostly bullshit. Majority of the people on the list aren't earning a million in *one* year. It's fees from cases being paid in arrears. What the article doesn't say is that these "millionaires" have been waiting two or three years to be paid and it's all arrived in one go.'

'I still don't understand your point.'

'That, Alex, is because you have the reasoning skills of a rhesus monkey,' he said, reaching for another cocktail sausage. 'Think it through. Such headlines divert attention from what most criminal barristers really earn, which is not very much. But there is a grain of truth to the headline because over the years a tiny minority of barristers have taken the piss with the legal aid system and made out like bandits ...'

'And screwed it up for the rest of us?'

'Oh well done, son! Two million years after everyone else, Alex McBride has come down from the trees to walk before us on his own hind legs. This headline is harmful because it reinforces the myth of outlandish fees, of barristers with not just their snouts but their whole heads in the trough.'

'Screws us politically, you might say?'

'Correct. How much do you earn?' he asked.

I told him.

'Good Christ, no one earns that little, do they?' said Gleeful, looking genuinely shocked, 'Look, the brackish dribble falling into your bank account makes my point even better than I do.'

'But no one cares about criminal barristers, you said so yourself, and let's be honest, who can blame them?'

'You're quite right there, old son. There are no votes in barristers. In fact, there are minus votes. Mustn't complain ...'

'Because whinging barristers aren't very attractive,' I said.

'I'm watching evolution in action. Once a rhesus monkey, then a savannah scamperer and now a hominid rooting for grubs with a bone. Whinging isn't only unattractive, it's ineffective. We should get tough but we won't. No one will go on strike cause they'd be worried that their rivals would steal their work – which of course they would. There's no honour among thieves or barristers.'

We refilled our glasses and ate a few more sausages.

'I don't care so much about the cuts in fees or the lack of work. It's the bar's cowardice that I really hate,' said Gleeful suddenly. 'Look at all those supine cunts running the Bar Council, kowtowing to the government, bending over, spreading their cheeks and taking another cock load of bad news from the Ministry of Justice. Hoping that if they rub along, they'll have their nuts tickled with a High Court judgeship.'

Gleeful was in full flow now. I ordered another batch of sausages to keep him going.

'I'll tell you what really pisses me off about the cuts though.'

'What's that?' I asked.

'They'll exclude bright kids from poor backgrounds from coming to the criminal bar. I thought the government was supposed to open up the professions. How does a poor kid do it: starting pupillage weighed down with tens of thousands of pounds of debt? The criminal bar is going to end up being a hobby for the wealthy, and,' he turned to look at me meaningfully, 'for those who can't get a job doing anything else.'

'Gleeful, you old flatterer,' I said, but he wasn't listening.

'It's not really the fees. What's killing the criminal bar is the squeeze on work. Solicitors' firms are so badly remunerated for preparing cases that they, like the CPS, want to keep the work in-house in order to earn the advocacy fee. There's nothing wrong with solicitors appearing in the higher courts. The risk is that a defendant doesn't have the choice that he should have when it comes to choosing his advocate.' He took a glug of wine. 'This is not to say solicitors are in any better position than the bar. They're facing competitive tendering and "one case one fee" payments rather than hourly rates. Many of them' (the estimate is a half to three-quarters) 'will go to the wall or simply stop doing legal-aid work altogether because it doesn't pay. Those that stay will play a volume game. They'll have more cases than they can handle and the first thing to go will be quality. In criminal justice, like anything else in life, you get what you pay for. Who's going to have the time to find alibi witnesses, investigate the issues or properly consider the prosecution case? We'll end up with the work being done not by qualified lawyers but by para-legals whose only advantage is that they're cheap.'

'Yes, but what about the criminal bar itself – my chances of continuing employment?' I ask.

'The great scarpering is going to continue: barristers off to the CPS or to solicitors' firms. Some will give up and go and get proper jobs. In the long run, however, it won't be the bar that suffers. The best advocates will continue as before but not in legal aid because well-remunerated private work will take up their time.'

'So I'll be all right, then?'

'Forget about yourself for a minute and consider who will really suffer. It'll be those who can't afford to pay privately, not to mention our much admired system of public justice. We'll have a two-tier justice system instead. The rich will get Rolls-Royce treatment from the best: everyone else will have to take their chances. You'll have outcomes determined by how much you can pay.'

Gleeful paused and smiled at me.

'Situations like this call for Samuel Johnson.' He dipped one of his long arms into his rucksack and produced another file. He flicked through the pages. 'Here's what he said back in the eighteenth century about lawyers and representation:

A lawyer is to do for his client all that his client might fairly do for himself, if he could. If, by a superiority of attention, of knowledge, of skill, and a better method of communication, he has the advantage of his adversary, it is an advantage to which he is entitled. There must always be some advantage, on one side or other; and it is better that advantage should be had by talents, than by chance.

'Why should the rich have the monopoly on the "talents"? Why should they buy their luck? I'm a prosecutor and when I prosecute I want my opponent to be at the top of his game. I want a no-holds-barred contested trial because that's the only way they end up being fair, the only way the right people go to jail and the wrong people don't.'

I thought about this as Gleeful started to pack up his rucksack. I looked down at the army boots. What was he going to do with those? Put them on his feet, was the answer. With the boots on, Gleeful's whole demeanour changed, he was no longer the wily prosecutor but a military man of action. Generous as ever, he paid the bill and strapped the rucksack on his back.

'What are the logical conclusions of these cuts? Are we trying to emulate the great state of Louisiana where public defenders are funded by speeding tickets? You run down legal aid like that and you're saying that the defendants in the dock are already guilty because they don't deserve a properly resourced system that will reach the right verdicts.'

I stood up as he left. 'Gleeful, boy have you cheered me up.'

'Any time,' he said smiling. 'Must go. Double-timing back to Putney. Parachuting out over Salisbury Plain on the weekend for some ops. Got some really nasty surprises for the boys.' And then, boots clattering up the stone stairs to the street, he was gone.

20. Going Guilty

Herbert and I sat knee to knee in the tiny annexe off the court's waiting room. The solicitor's rep, apparently entranced by his cuticles, had made himself inconspicuous by the door. I had given him strict instructions not to let any of Southwestern Magistrates' Court's denizens touch the door handle, let alone try to come in. Herbert stared at my left shoulder, his fatigued expression betraying his pain. I tried again, speaking very softly.

'The thing is, Herbert, the evidence against you is strong and you've got a near-identical conviction from only last year.' (He had put his hand down the front of a fourteen-year-old girl's pants and explored about with his middle digit.) 'If we go into court and call these girls flouncey little liars, the magistrates are going to take a dim view, a very dim view. They'll find you guilty and then blame you for making the girls (Raquelle, aged thirteen, and Rhona, fourteen) go through the ordeal of giving evidence, of publicly reliving the ordeal that they say you subjected them to.'

I stopped and looked meaningfully into Herbert's tired eyes. He blinked once. Did I detect a nod of his head? Was I making progress here? Guilty pleas from sex offenders have to be teased out. It's an emotional process, which often makes you feel more like a therapist than a barrister.

'I mean, you don't disagree that the girls were in your living room. You offered them alcohol and cigarettes?'

'They took those things. Drinking and smoking behind my back. They were my daughter's friends.'

'But your daughter wasn't in.'

Herbert thought about this.

'Raquelle says that when she was leaving, she bent down to kiss you and you slipped your tongue in her mouth and put your hands on her bum.'

'She kissed me. No tongues. My arms were around her waist.'

I retreated. Arguing the details was a mistake. It was the general thrust, the mood music, essentially not disputed, that the magistrates would be processing in a trial, and I knew that the melody I was hearing would finish Herbert. What was a sixty-year-old man doing surrounding himself with girls a quarter his age? What was he doing giving them drink? It was always only going to be guilty.

'My professional opinion, not my personal opinion you understand, is that you will be found guilty and you will be sent to the crown court for sentence and from there to prison. If you plead guilty, however, you're still going to be sentenced by the crown court but I think we can keep you out of prison. Your daughter has her exams coming up, doesn't she? She's going to need her dad.'

Herbert was close now. He could taste the guilty plea in his mouth. He was teetering. I could have pushed him over the edge then and there but my professional duty added a complication that I knew would make Herbert step back from the edge.

'What you have to understand,' I continued, maintaining my soft flat voice, 'is that when you plead guilty, you're accepting that you did it. You're making an admission. Saying guilty isn't just a technical thing, it's acceptance. You understand, don't you, Herbert?'

Herbert understood, his guts twisting ever tighter. He understood in the same way that he understood that prison would mean his daughter going into care and probably failing her exams. He loved his daughter. His wife, her mother, had died when she was tiny and Herbert had brought her up single-handedly. He'd done a good job. The daughter didn't know this but it was now payback time because her existence, her age, her exams would keep her old dad out of prison. Without her, Herbert would go the way of other second-time sex offenders with a weakness for teenage girls, which is straight to jail. For this little family affair to work, Herbert had to play his part and that meant pleading guilty.

Sex offenders almost never plead guilty. Facing up to your offending, admitting what you've done in this type of crime, is especially hard. Herbert's trade-off was the relief of avoiding prison versus the relief of saying to his daughter, 'Those little cows are lying.' Having to face your family is never easy, no matter how strong the evidence might be.

'What do you want to do?' I asked.

Herbert was shaking. 'I didn't do it but ...'

'It's not just a tactical move: if you plead guilty then you're accepting that you committed the crime, touched those girls.'

We sat in silence while Herbert thought about this. Then in a murmur I could barely hear, he said the word: 'Guilty. I'll go guilty.'

After Herbert's sentence date had been set, we said goodbye. As he was shambling down the stairs I spotted Liam coming up.

'Liam!'

He looked up from his papers. 'Want to play spot the flasher?' he said brightly.

'No one's going to pull their old chap out in the middle of Southwestern Mags, are they?'

'No, stupid. Spot my client, the flasher.'

'You're on.'

'Fiver says I spot him first,' said Liam.

'Done.'

We each slipped a £5 note under the cover of Liam's legal pad.

'Knee slap if you make an ID. No jumping up pointing and shouting 'Flasher, flasher.' It'll put him right off.'

Liam had cornered the market in flashers. His most celebrated case was known as 'Ongar's Frisky Fox'. The Fox had a very specialist interest. He'd lurk around the back of women's flats making fox noises. Apparently, they were very realistic. The woman would come to the window to see where the noise was coming from only to be confronted by the Fox with his cock in one hand and a cam-era in the other to capture her shock. Once he'd taken the photo, he'd give himself a stern telling-off. 'Put it away, man. That's dis-graceful behaviour.' The police eventually located the Fox's address. They paid him a little visit and found dozens of photo-graphs of shocked women's faces looking out of bedroom win-dows, except for one who had a big smile on her face. We all hoped the Fox got to keep that one.

We settled on to one of the waiting-room's benches, watching the stairs for likely candidates. Five minutes went by. The people coming up, part of the lunchtime rush, were all useless. It was the usual diet of South London kids practising their pimp rolls and coppers thumb-ing their pocket books. A huddle of policemen stomped up the stairs, late for their trial. I craned around to see who was coming up behind them but Liam had the better angle. He slapped his knee.

'There's my boy,' he said, standing up facing me, his back to the worried-looking man searching for his lawyer. Liam bent down to pick up his papers and whispered in my ear: 'Wrong face for flash-ing. Plainly a sex offender. Fiver says he pleads not guilty.'

'No bet.' Even I knew enough not to take that one.

He straightened his tie, and executed the discreet barrister call for his client perfectly.

'Mr Pinto? Oswald Pinto?'

Liam gave great barrister. He was reassuring and non-judgemental, as if he were treating Oswald for an ingrowing toenail rather than his predilection for masturbating in front of blondes.

Shaking Oswald's hand, Liam indicated towards me. 'This is my pupil, Alex McBride.'

I spluttered. Liam and I had been on our feet for eighteen months. Not being tenants, we were officially still pupils, but our pupillage year was long gone. One thing was for certain: me being *his* pupil was a preposterous lie.

'Liam, you cock nose,' I hissed but Liam drowned me out.

'Would you mind if Alex sat in? He's training, you see, and this is a way for him to gain a bit of,' Liam turned to me and grinned, 'experience. Anything said will of course be completely confidential.'

(Yeah, right. Whenever a barrister uses the phrase 'completely confidential' you can be pretty sure that your most intimate secrets will be exposed to the delighted hilarity of all his barrister friends in the pub. Your cringing shame will be the tears of laughter rolling down their drunken cheeks.)

I should have been irritated with Liam. I didn't want to hang around for his trial, but then I realized it would be a chance to see what one of my competitors for chambers' favour was like in court. I hadn't seen Liam in court since Skegness and I suspected he could teach me a thing or two.

It was, of course, much worse for Oswald. Things, ironically, had started so well on the day in question. Oswald was in his favourite bush bouncing on his toes while he watched the pretty blonde woman turn into the park. She was ready to be impressed and he was the man for the job. He checked the other direction. The path was empty. All she had to do was keep heading his way and everything would be perfect. She was twenty yards away, almost upon him. A few well-practised manipulations later and he was ready. As she reached the bush, Oswald leapt out, erection in his hand, and started to pump away. He was delighted by her shocked reaction, his body shivering with her disgust, hand whizzing up and down the shaft of his penis. Surprisingly, she didn't run or scream. Was she frozen to the spot, or just too well mannered? Either way, Oswald was having a ball.

'You should be ashamed of yourself,' said the woman. Oh, Oswald was, he was – blissfully ashamed.

'Stop that, you disgusting man,' she ordered.

For Oswald, it didn't get any better than this. Look how revolting he was with his big, attention-seeking cock. His hand was flying now, a blur of fleshy passion. This woman was the best ever, this 'flash' was the best ever – just a few more seconds and he'd be there.

'Put your penis away. I'm a police officer and you're under arrest,' said the woman, showing him her warrant card.

'Oh, shit.'

Oswald's sweaty fist stopped mid-wank. His eyes widened to the size of hub caps at the sight of the handcuffs the policewoman was producing. He was off, in a stooping run, encumbered by the difficulty slowly deflating between his legs. He got away but it wasn't going to save him. The policewoman recognized Oswald and knew exactly where to find him. She had had a clear view and her witness statement, recording the events in persuasive detail, sealed his fate.

Oswald was pleading not guilty, which pleased Liam no end. With a cod solemn expression on his face, he went through the damning features of Oswald's case. 'Okay, how do you account for the officer seeing your penis exposed in public?'

'I was caught short.'

'Caught short,' repeated Liam, noting it down in his legal pad. 'Right, but she says that your penis was erect. What do you say about that?'

'It wasn't erect. I've just got a large one.'

'Just got a large one,' repeated Liam matter-of-factly.

'One last thing, she says that you were masturbating your penis with your left hand?'

'Like I said, I needed a piss. I was cleaning my penis after urinating.'

'Cleaning my penis after urinating.'

'Got it?'

'Got it.'

The trial went pretty well even though the result was never in doubt. Liam was saving himself for a forceful closing speech at the end of the evidence. At least Oswald would feel his barrister had given him the best chance. He stood up and as though it were the most normal thing in the world described to the magistrates Oswald's 'call of nature'.

'Sir,' he told the chairman of the bench, 'Mr Pinto was in dire need. Preferring peeing in a bush to having it trickling down his leg, he nipped into the park. He found himself a bush and relieved himself. The officer saw Mr Pinto emerging from the bush. His penis was not erect. He just has a large one. When the officer saw him shaking himself off all Mr Pinto was doing was cleaning his penis after masturbating.'

Liam sat down with a satisfied smile on his face. The chairman of the bench of magistrates looked quizzical.

'Mr McLeish, you mean urinating, don't you?'

'That's what I said, sir,' said Liam and turned to Oswald to give him a big thumbs up.

It was hard to hear what Oswald was saying behind the reinforced glass of the dock but you could tell he wasn't happy.

After the guilty verdict, we couldn't get out of court fast enough. We sprinted to the train, laughing like hyenas. By the time we got on it, our laughter had subsided. Liam suddenly seemed melancholy. It wasn't like him.

'Liam, are you okay? Don't worry about Oswald. It was unwinnable.'

'I'm not worried about the trial. It's just . . .' He tried to smile as his voice trailed off.

'Come on. What is it?'

'There's no glow.'

'No glow?'

'When I first started being a criminal barrister I loved it. The challenge, the adrenaline, the battle – it was great. But the best thing was this post-trial glow, like a voice deep inside me saying, this work is the right work.'

'And now it's gone?'

'Yeah.'

'But it's going to come back.'

'No, it's not. It was the excitement of doing the job. The excitement has worn off. All I'm left with is the job and the life and I hate it.'

'But you're good at it. Better than me.'

'I don't care. I'm sick of doing it. Sick of the punters and their hard luck stories. Sick of the misery and sick of the stupidity. I know it's a laugh but I don't want to spend the rest of my life dealing with it all. I want a normal job with normal people. I don't want to spend my evenings and weekends scouring witness statements and police schedules for the elusive silver bullet that might, just might, if I'm really lucky, get my client off.'

'It's not that bad.'

'It is that bad. It's fucking worse – like standing under a waterfall of shit. Look at the bloody awful money. Look at the zero security and the terrible hours. I want a family and I want a life.'

'What about tenancy?' I said it as though tenancy were the cure to all ills.

'Fuck tenancy.'

We went back to chambers in silence, Liam thinking about escaping the bar and me thinking how disappointing my smoky, high-cholesterol life, which I loved, suddenly felt. I wished Liam weren't so persuasive. I needed reassurance. I needed comforting. This, more than ever before, was an Araminta moment. I pushed my way into reception, aching to see her. Ready to put my arms around her and hang the consequences. Sitting in Araminta's chair was a stranger, a temp.

'Where's Araminta?' I asked, looking alarmed.

'Who's Araminta?'

'The woman who is the receptionist.'

'Oh, she's got a new job. In Paddington, I think. Something in finance, more money, less of a commute.'

'But she didn't say anything.'

'People move on.'

I could have cried.

A month later I was back with Herbert for his sentence. His guilty plea and his daughter saved him from prison but his 'open door' policy with the local teenage girls was at an end. My open door policy with chambers was coming to an end too. They were going to decide my future in a month's time. Harriet, Jane and Will were gone. The pupils' room was disbanded. Liam had become semi-detached and, worst of all, Araminta had vanished without so much as a word. Even I was no longer sure if the barrister's life was for me.

21. The Great Rebalancing

The CCTV recorded the back-up unit's progress. They weren't exactly hurrying. Some officers jogged, others went the wrong way. A stout cop, bringing up the rear, stumbled on the stairs. The CCTV cut to another group of policemen who had a black man pressed face first against the wall of a pedestrian tunnel. There were too many to get a proper grip on him. They stood around as the man was pulled to the floor, handcuffed and taken away. What had he done to merit so many coppers? Mr V's crime was to busk in the tube without a licence.

London Underground will give licences to people with previous convictions only if they're 'spent'. The period before a conviction is spent depends on your sentence. If you've been sentenced to a period of imprisonment of thirty months or more, your conviction is never spent. Mr V, who finds it hard to cope in stressful situations, has criminal convictions for petty dishonesty and threatening behaviour but not for hitting anybody. He showed me the letter from London Underground telling him he doesn't qualify because of his record. Busking is a little job to make ends meet and Mr V depends on it.

When Mr V was arrested in the early spring of 2005, unlicensed busking, as set out in the London Underground Bylaws, was not an arrestable offence; a police officer couldn't nick you for it. If you were to be prosecuted, a summons was sent to your address. Common sense and police time dictate that buskers are usually moved along. Mr V is used to being told to leave stations and does so when asked. On this occasion, as the two officers approached him, he put away his guitar and tried to go. The police were not satisfied with this and asked for his name. Mr V has two surnames, his mother's and his father's. He gave them both. The police misheard and asked him to confirm his name so he gave his father's name, as it was the one on his birth certificate.

Under provisions set out in Sections 24 and 25 of the Police and Criminal Evidence Act the police can only arrest you for a non-arrestable offence if general arrest conditions apply. One of these is that they have reasonable grounds for believing that a name given is false. Before they can arrest you they must also ask for, and presumably check, your address. The officers failed in this instance to do so. Mr V felt wronged and humiliated. He refused to give his hands to be handcuffed. The police had other ideas. The male officer grabbed one arm, the female officer the other. Mr V wasn't giving up. A push-me pull-you struggle ensued during which Mr V managed to shake off the female officer. She panicked and pulled out her CS spray – never a good idea in an enclosed tunnel. The first time she sprayed him Mr V shielded his face with the peak of his baseball cap. The second time a gust of wind came down the tunnel, blowing the spray straight into her face, temporarily blinding her. Her colleague and Mr V were left tearfully bouncing each other off the sides of the tunnel. Having incapacitated herself, she radioed for back-up, whose ponderous arrival the CCTV had picked up. Mr V was charged with assaulting police officers and resisting arrest.

At trial I argued that the police hadn't had reasonable grounds for making an arrest as they hadn't asked Mr V for his address once the reasonable suspicion about his name arose. If general arrest conditions didn't apply, then the officers had no power to arrest him and their actions were unlawful. Mr V was perfectly entitled to resist their attempts to handcuff him. To my astonishment, the magistrates reluctantly agreed and the charges were dismissed. For Mr V it was a moment of triumph: he'd been wronged and the court made it right. The officers were dumbstruck.

The distinction between arrestable and non-arrestable offences is important because it regulates when a police officer can and can't arrest you. It's a statutory limit that ensures the police don't have *carte blanche*. Or at least it did. On 1 January 2006 the Serious Organised Crime and Police Act (pushed through Parliament on the eve of the 2005 general election) came into force. Buried away in Part 3 of the Act, Section 110 removes the distinction. The effect is that the police can summarily arrest you for any offence, even speeding. The reason for the change in the law was that the police found the difference between arrestable and non-arrestable offences confusing and therefore inconvenient. If I were representing Mr V today, he wouldn't have the legal protection he was afforded in 2005. Despite the behaviour of the police, he'd be guilty as charged.

Criticism moved the government to respond that the new rules would apply only where one of six conditions applied. One of these conditions was a catch-all. A police officer was entitled to arrest you in order 'to allow the prompt and effective investigation of the offence or conduct of the person in question'. No confusion now, the message was clear: nick whom you like. It should not be forgotten that an arrest is potentially a significant restriction on an arrested person's liberty: it triggers the power to detain that person for up to ninety-six hours, and to search his property.[1]

Mr V's story from the backwaters of the criminal justice system shows what can happen when safeguards are taken away. If you're living on the margins, leading a lifestyle that does not meet with the authorities' approval, or not toeing the line in a manner pleasing to them, it's easy to get pulled off the street. Section 110 of the Serious Organised Crime and Police Act wasn't the first sign of the pendulum beginning to swing away from suspects and defendants and towards the state but it is representative of a slew of laws changing the balance in the criminal justice system.

The Serious Organised Crime and Police Act and its older brother the Criminal Justice Act of 2003 point the direction in which change is taking us. These two acts have pushed beyond an earlier impulse to make the criminal justice system less intimidating and more user-friendly. This impulse had brought in sensible measures to ameliorate the awfulness of giving evidence in court. People who felt in fear were permitted to give evidence from behind screens, use pseudonyms or have their voices distorted. Child witnesses could have their evidence-in-chief taped and then be cross-examined on a live television link so they would not have to go into court. Alleged victims of sexual assault and rape could not, except in very limited circumstances, be cross-examined on their past sexual history. Other reforms that maintained the balance between prosecution and defence were also introduced, like permitting juries to draw adverse inferences against a defendant who fails to answer questions in police interview, and defence case statements in order to cut down on prosecution cases being unfairly ambushed by a last-minute defence.

Some of the latest reforms brought in by the Criminal Justice Act are not so much about improving the quality of witnesses' evidence as about upping the conviction rate. Hearsay evidence going before a jury is mostly uncontroversial, but allowing in a defendant's previous convictions, known as 'bad character', is not. The old common law rules had the benefit of being simple. A defendant's previous convictions could not be adduced in front of a jury except in limited circumstances. These circumstances largely depended on the defendant. If a defendant impugned another witness, for example, calling him corrupt or a liar, he 'lost his shield' and the prosecution could tell the jury about any relevant previous convictions. The incentive to not lose your shield tempered wilder defences.

The advent of bad character has generally been welcomed by the judiciary. The very senior judge I spoke to about it is convinced that bad character provisions are a timely and positive change. For him they are particularly useful where there is a strong case against a defendant but the jury is finding it hard to believe that the person sitting in the dock committed the crime. I am not entirely persuaded but I have to admit that, when prosecuting, putting in a defendant's bad character can, like placing a maraschino cherry on top of a gateau, round things off nicely.

Take the case of Malcolm. I was hoping my opponent would manage to steer him into changing his plea to guilty, but Malcolm wanted to fight on.

'Bugger won't plead guilty,' said the beleaguered-looking defence counsel with a weary sigh. I'd like to say I was sorry for him but all I felt was giddy relief that it was him and not me stuck with what's known in the trade as a 'no questions' trial. It's called that because the case against your client is so overwhelming that you can't think of any questions to ask on his behalf.

'Absolutely nothing to say. Might as well have brought my bongos,' moaned defence counsel, as the jury filed in.

Malcolm must have been wondering how it had come to this. He and his crew weren't slapstick junkies snagging themselves on windows and dripping blood (not to mention DNA) all over the place. They were professionals. They chose their targets intelligently: like the warehouse that they'd hit on a secluded industrial estate a few months back. He and his crew had come in over the roof, smashing the alarms and cutting the cables that connected the alarm system to the police station. Once that was done, they could work undisturbed. They dropped down into the warehouse, lifted the internal security doors off their runners and broke into the firm's store room. From there they loaded their Luton van with £90,000 of upmarket pens. Everything went beautifully, so beautifully that a few weeks later, employing the same strategy, they broke into a mobile phone company. They dismantled the company's delivery van's tracking device, loaded it up with £250,000 worth of mobile phones and were gone. Not bad, eh? Stealing the van to spirit away the phones. What chutzpah! What laughs! The plods would be left scratching their heads over such a bold coup.

Fast-forward five days and representatives of the local constabulary are closing in on Malcolm's premises. The gates to his yard are 100 per cent Gerrard's Cross stockbroker, but once you're inside it's 'Traveller Baronial' all the way. Neoclassical urns are juxtaposed with old generators and rusting cars. A squad of policemen head for the deluxe mobile home set in a little sea of concrete in the far corner of the yard. One of them is carrying a search warrant. Deep in his dreams, Malcolm hears the knocking. It must be something out on the road, he thinks, tucking the duvet up around his chin and slipping back towards sleep.

'Open up!' shouts a voice. Malcolm opens his eyes. 'Police! Open up!'

Malcolm, a moment ago dreaming cosily under his duvet, is now naked and cold and dashing around, hiding anything that might incriminate him. He has his work cut out: there is an awful lot to hide.

'Open up!'

'I'm just getting my jeans on,' says Malcolm, buying some time.

PC Mostyn watches through the window as Malcolm stashes two mobile phones in a cupboard. Next he tears the IMEI number, a unique number which identifies a mobile, off the Sony Ericsson box in which one of the phones has come. A few calming breaths later, Malcolm is holding the door open to an officer waving a search warrant while PC Mostyn makes straight for the cupboard.

'Whose are these?' he asks, pulling out the phones from their hiding place.

'Not mine.'

'Why did I see you hiding them in the cupboard then?'

Now that was a hard one. Realizing that the questions aren't going to get any easier Malcolm stops answering them. Another cop comes to the door to say that he's found the stolen pens in a

Luton van parked out in the yard. Lesson to learn? Never thieve something you can't get rid of. A police photographer arrives and starts taking pictures of the pen brochures piled up in Malcolm's kitchen.

Can it get any worse? Yes, it can. PC Mostyn notices that the hidden phones and the IMEI number torn off the Ericsson box tally with his list of phones stolen from the company. Malcolm isn't just tied to the mobile phone and pen burglaries: he is nailed to them.

Unhelpful as this all was, it didn't explain how the police had found him. Malcolm's mistake was the phone company's delivery van. The tracking device that he thought had been dismantled was in fact still working perfectly. It had sung like a canary, recording the route the van had taken from warehouse to Malcolm's yard where the phones were moved to another vehicle for transport to Europe (where they can't be blocked) and finally to Chertsey where it had been dumped.

During the trial, Malcolm did not give evidence himself. Instead, he got his dad, a veteran lag, to tell the jury that on the night of the phone burglary Malcolm had been at the family home tending to racing pigeons.

'Loves pigeons, your honour. Can't keep him away from them.'

There was just one little problem with this. In his prepared statement to police, Malcolm had neglected to mention any pigeons. His statement covered only the pen burglary. He claimed that three Irish travellers – Seamus, Logan and Francie – had threatened him and his family if he didn't let them park the Luton van in his yard. He didn't know what was in the van and he didn't know anything about the burglaries and therefore couldn't name anyone else who might be involved.

During a break in the trial, defence counsel buttonholed me. 'You're not going to put his "form"' (that's lawyer lingo for previous convictions) 'in, are you?'

Absolutely I was. Thanks to the Criminal Justice Act 2003 I am allowed to put a defendant's convictions before a jury if they show that the defendant has a propensity to commit offences similar to the one charged. Malcolm's 'previous' was littered with offences of dishonesty, mostly thefts and burglaries from industrial sites. Why was I being so mean when the guilty verdict was all but guaranteed? Because in law, as in crime, when you think you're away and clear you get cocky, and that's when disaster strikes. For as Malcolm well knows, there's nothing worse than blowing a sure thing.

Bad character is all well and good when the evidence is strong as it was against Malcolm but it is potentially dangerous when a trial is finely balanced and the result could fall either way. The problem with bad character in such a situation is that the prosecution is going to be much keener to put it before the jury because it might make all the difference between convicting the defendant and not.

A silk I spoke to gave an example of a murder trial she had defended where the bulk of the evidence against her client came from cell site analysis. Cell site analysis measures the rough vicinity of a mobile phone: if a person makes or receives a call on that phone, then by showing which transmitter was relaying the call you can plot that person's location to within a few streets. The prosecution wanted the defendant's bad character – possession of a knife – to be admitted into the evidence to bolster their case. She resisted and the two sides spent days wrangling over the admissibility of the knife conviction. The judge struggled with whether to allow this fact to go before the jury or not. In the end he let it in. The silk believes the knife conviction, which had nothing to do with the evidence in the murder trial, which was largely circumstantial, sealed her client's fate. The jury might have convicted without knowing about the knife, but with the knife it was a certainty.

This silk worries that changes to the rules on bad character have swung the pendulum too far towards the prosecution. A fair prosecutor or one who's not under pressure to get a result might not resort to a defendant's bad character to secure a conviction. But as the silk points out, the fairness of a trial shouldn't depend on a prosecutor's inclination but on even-handed rules which ensure someone is convicted on the evidence against them rather than anything they've done in the past. To do otherwise risks innocent people going to jail.

The Criminal Justice Act 2003 has eroded an accused person's rights in other ways too. It has brought in provisions for jury-less trials in complex fraud cases and where there have been attempts at jury 'nobbling'. The age-old rule of double jeopardy has also gone. A person acquitted by a court of law can now be tried again if new evidence comes to light. Control orders, used to restrict the movements of people suspected of terrorist activity, are made on the basis of secret information which neither the person subject to the order nor his lawyers are allowed to see.

There have been other changes that don't seem in keeping with the spirit of the criminal justice system. Police officers, CPS employees, judges and lawyers – me of all people – are now permitted to sit on juries. Judges and lawyers sitting on juries I suppose is okay but I do wonder about police officers and CPS employees, people, as Lord Bingham put it in a recent case on impartiality of the jury, 'professionally committed to one side only of an adversarial process'.[2] In law the test of an impartial tribunal is 'whether the fair-minded and informed observer, having considered the facts, would conclude that there was a real possibility that the tribunal was biased'.[3] Taking it a step further, how does it look to a defendant if the jury trying his case has coppers and professional prosecutors sitting on it? If I were standing trial, no matter what the law or the judge told me, I wouldn't feel that I was getting a fair shake. What if my defence criticized the police or questioned the integrity of a policeman? Few cop jurors are going to listen to that. The point is that it's not good enough for justice to be fair; it must also look fair. As a lord chief justice said back in the 1920s, 'it is not merely of some importance but is of fundamental importance that justice should not only be done, but should manifestly and undoubtedly be seen to be done'.[4] Having professional prosecutors on juries seems to be slipping from that benchmark.

One of the most shocking departures from the common law tradition has been the Criminal Evidence (Witness Anonymity) Act. This Act was passed to negate a House of Lords ruling that the use of anonymous witnesses – which a prosecution of a gangland killing had relied upon – whose evidence 'solely or to a decisive extent' led to the conviction of a defendant, did not meet the standards of a fair trial. The legislation was a knee-jerk reaction, putting the desire for convictions above fairness. British courts haven't used anonymous witnesses since the Star Chamber Court was abolished in 1641. It is a fundamental principle of justice that you know who your accusers are. With faceless witnesses, how can you check whether they have got something against you or an interest in getting you convicted? Anonymity is a perjurer's dream: you can say what you like about a defendant and there's no comeback. Without knowing the identity of a witness there's no way you can properly cross-examine, no way to test that witness's evidence properly. The defendant is left, in Lord Hewart's famous phrase, 'taking blind shots at a hidden target'.

We're told that many serious gangland and Trident (that's black on black) crimes would never come to court because witnesses would be too frightened to give evidence. I understand this. It is a serious problem. I'd certainly think twice about giving evidence against a gangster. Inconvenience, however, is not a reason for limiting someone's ability to defend himself. IRA terrorists didn't manage to intimidate people into not giving evidence. Witness protection programmes ensured that they'd be safe. Other jurisdictions, including the International Criminal Court, have opted not to go down the anonymity road.

The most worrying aspect of this sort of legislation is the loss of nerve. Our rush to embrace anonymous witnesses is representative of a failure of confidence in our justice system. When we come up against an obstacle or a difficulty in criminal trials, the default reaction is to legislate it away without considering how it could damage overall fairness. The final result has become the main concern and the means of getting there a distant second. Whittling away a defendant's protections might make us feel like we're getting tough, or making things work better, but in reality it degrades the safeguards which help stop innocent people from going to jail.

We have to decide what in the end is more important, acquitting the innocent or convicting the guilty? To answer this question properly you have to ask another question first: what is more offensive to the notion of justice, to see an innocent person go to jail or a guilty person walk free? Lord Denning once said, 'It is better that some innocent men remain in jail than the integrity of the English legal system be impugned.' I think that's a disgrace. The integrity of the English legal system, of any legal system, must be based not on holding the line but on fearlessly battling for the fairest result no matter who ends up looking bad in the process.

Epilogue

'Who the fuck are these people?' I asked myself.

They are the tenancy committee, that's who the fuck they are – the deciders of my future. I'd never seen any of them before, let alone done any work for them. I hadn't expended any of my pupil's capital covering their bums with kisses. Could I make up for lost time here and now, I wondered? Logistically, it would be difficult. They are one side of the mahogany table, under which I'd spent so many happy hours fast asleep, and I am the other. The most junior member of the tenancy committee halts my panicked thoughts by getting down to business.

'Right, we want you to do the plea and mitigation we've asked you to prepare as if you were in court. Pretend I'm the judge.'

'Okay.'

'I've put a few googlies into the papers. Let's see if you spot them.'

'Fu ... I mean right.'

'Fuck' was bang on. I was never going to spot any googlies – or any flippers, doosras or chinamen for that matter. Any guile in his bowling and my stumps were going to get flattened. It was too late for regrets. What was it that my pupilmaster had said? 'To get tenancy here, you have to be indispensable.' It was an impossible bar to clear. No one is indispensable. Even Jesus Christ found himself being let go. Still I should have followed my pupilmaster's other, more practical piece of advice, 'Find out who is on the tenancy committee and do work for them.' Too late now.

I looked across the table. The committee had arranged themselves around the room like upper-class sadists posing for a group photo. I droned through my plea and mit, looking out for signs of how it was going. The junior tenant playing the judge was impassive; in fact no one said anything at all. I thought it might be one of those mental health tests where psychiatrists sit in silence as you, the subject, gabble your way into a straitjacket. They didn't even ask me any ethics questions about what I'd do if I were offered illicit cash.

Q: Your client hands you an envelope stuffed full of £50 notes. What do you do?

A: Er ... shove it down the front of my trousers.

Q: A solicitor offers you £500 not to mention a mistake to your client. What do you do?

A: Blow it on tarts and coke ... no ... give it to the donkey sanctuary.

Fifteen minutes after the interview started it was over. On the way out, I passed Liam and Mamta, waiting in the stairwell. They looked as sick as I did. After we had all done our turns, the tenancy committee would consider our applications and make their recommendations at a full chambers' meeting where our candidacies would be put to a formal vote.

It can take a good three hours before you're phoned with the result, which left me with a dilemma. Do I hang around chambers telling everyone what a brilliant performance I gave or do I disappear? The latter option seemed the best. The problem I had was disappear where? Traditionally, you found a quiet pub and got drunk. I didn't fancy a drink. I felt restless. I might have gone through pupillage with Liam and Mamta but I wanted to face my fate alone.

I decided I would take a turn around 'Law Land' – Temple, Lincoln's Inn and Gray's – it might be my last chance after all. I walked up Middle Temple Lane, imagining what a formal chambers' defenestration would be like. Would the tenancy committee dunk me in tar, roll me in feathers and then run me straight into the Thames on a rail? Maybe they'd be more site specific: the stunt judge from the tenancy committee with a bunch of hard-kicking hangers-on booting me down Middle Temple Lane as someone shouted 'Fuck-up' over and over again in my ear? Somehow, evaporating like the forgotten man seemed the worst humiliation of all.

At the top of the Lane, I went through the little black door cut in the arched gates and stepped out on to Fleet Street. From there, I crossed over and turned up Bell Yard towards the southern entrance to Lincoln's Inn. In the autumn's early evening light, Lincoln's Inn was as beautiful as ever. The wide-faced buildings looked down at me with gentle discretion. I maintained my northerly progress, past the old fifteenth-century hall, and underneath the chapel in which John Donne, the poet, as Dean of St Paul's, gave the first ever address in 1623. I cut right on to Chancery Lane, crossed over Holborn and walked into Gray's Inn, past its garden, and out through a little used side exit. I found myself in Bedford Row, Law Land's last outpost. I walked along the terrace of eighteenth-century charcoal and red-bricked townhouses and turned into Theobald's Road, where the legal hush gave way to police sirens and traffic.

I looked at my watch. Only half an hour had passed since I'd left chambers. I remembered Fryer's Delight, a rather good fish and chip shop but fifty yards away. Luckily, there wasn't a queue so I ordered plaice and chips, two pickled onions and a Tango and slid into a booth. I put my phone on the table and began to eat. An hour passed, and then another. My phone stayed silent. Just as I was beginning to think that the meeting and the decision were all a practical joke my phone jumped into life, vibrating across the formica table top. I could see my pupilmaster's number flashing on the screen. I knew I wasn't the best barrister in the world but I hoped luck would intervene. If I couldn't rely entirely on luck then surely the sympathy vote wouldn't let me down?

I let the phone ring three times before picking it up. I wanted to appear casual but my cracking voice gave the game away: 'He-ll-o.'

'Hi, Alex.' My pupilmaster's voice was grave. 'Bad news, I'm afraid.'

We had a brief conversation — something about the end of the world not being nigh. I hung up and stared at my phone. How should I mark my failure, I wondered? Duct-tape two large slices of pizza to my temples and dunk my head in a bucket of shit? A text message from Liam arrived. 'Sheep or goat?' it asked. I texted him back, 'I'm Billy Goat Gruff.' 'Me too, thank Christ. Boarding my flight to Greece,' came his reply.

What about Mamta: she was suspiciously quiet. I texted her that I was out, but I got no response. Thirty seconds later the phone rang. Mamta was in a noisy pub, surrounded by happy voices. 'I'm a tenant,' she said breathlessly.

I walked out of Fryer's Delight feeling that I had been left behind. Mamta was drinking champagne, Liam had escaped, Araminta had disappeared without a word and was probably right this minute in the arms of some investment banker. What really got me was that I hadn't even had a proper last day at the bar. Hadn't gone out with a bang. I could've leapt up on to the table that separates the barristers from the judge in court, bladder brimming, and pissed all over them. Instead I was going out like a weepy kid not picked for the football team. I crossed into Lamb's Conduit Street, self-pity eating away at me.

'Who's that over there?' said a familiar voice.

'Oh, it's only fucking Alex,' said another.

I looked up and saw Jane and Harriet sitting at a table outside a pub. They were wrapped up against the chill, smoking cigarettes.

'Hi,' I said, trying to smile

'They've chucked you out, haven't they?' said Harriet.

'How can you tell?'

'You've got the same expression that I had. Lingered for days.'

'Do you want a drink?' asked Jane.

'I bloody would.'

We both looked at the empty bottle of wine on the table. I was about to say something but at that moment Wordless Will came out of the pub carrying a fresh one.

'Will? Aren't you supposed to be in Manchester?'

'It didn't work out, not even with his girlfriend,' said Harriet.

Will got me a glass and poured out the wine. I looked around the table at their bright faces and realized that I was in the alfresco version of the pupils' room. It was just like the old days. Jane was curvy and beautiful, Harriet was wearing her red Mac 'Most Wanted' lipstick, and Wordless Will ... well ... he was standing up holding his glass in a toast.

'To the pupils' room,' he said, 'I hope none of us ever gets out.'

We did. But it took a while.

Notes

Part One

1. Middle Temple Lane

1. J. H. Baker, *The Common Law Tradition*, Hambledon Press, 2000, p. 14.
2. Ibid., p. 12.
3. R. G. Hamilton, *All Jangle and Riot: a Barrister's History of the Bar*, Clarendon Press, 1986, p. 60.
4. Ibid., p. 66.

2. Meet the Clients

1. Horseferry Road was renamed City of Westminster Magistrates' Court in July 2006.
2. Bow Street Magistrates' Court closed in July 2006. It is now a hotel.
3. Under the Criminal Justice Act 2003, a DTTO is now called a Drug Rehabilitation Requirement or DRR for short.

Part Two

5. The Unlikely Story of Trial by Jury

1. William Blackstone, 1765: iii.379; iv.350.
2. J. H. Baker, *An Introduction to English Legal History*, Butterworths, 2002, p. 72.
3. Julius Marke, 'History in the Law Books', *New York Law Journal*, 1992.
4. John Langbein, *The Origins of the Adversary Criminal Trial*, OUP, 2003.

5. J. M. Beattie, 'Scales of Justice: Defense Counsel and the English Criminal Trial in the 18th and 19th Centuries', *Law and History Review*, 1991, quoting W. Hawkins, *A Treatise of the Pleas of the Crown* (1716–21) vol. 2, p. 400.

6. Sadakat Kadri, *The Trial: A History from Socrates to OJ Simpson*, HarperCollins, 2005, p. 92.

7. Langbein, *Origins of the Adversary Criminal Trial*, p. 49.

8. Beattie, 'Scales of Justice', p. 225.

9. Ibid., p. 227.

10. Langbein, *Origins of the Adversary Criminal Trial*, p. 254.

11. Beattie, 'Scales of Justice', p. 241.

12. Ibid.

13. My emphasis.

14. Langbein, *Origins of the Adversary Criminal Trial*, p. 307.

15. Leon Radzinowicz, *The History of English Criminal Law*, vol. 2, Stevens & Sons, 1956, pp. 326–32.

16. Ibid., p. 317.

17. Albert Alschuler, 'Plea Bargaining and its History', *Columbia Law Review*, 1979, vol. 79, no. 1, p. 10.

18. J. R. Spencer, 'Accusatorial and inquisitorial: the history of criminal procedure in Europe', p. 10.

19. Alschuler, 'Plea Bargaining and its History', p. 11. Despite repeated calls to the Ministry of Justice, they were unable to produce a UK figure. It is likely to be in the low single digits.

Part Three

8. The Evidential Burden

1. Metropolitan Police Service crime statistics, 2007–8.

2. Andrei Semikhodskii, *Dealing with DNA Evidence: a Legal Guide*, Routledge-Cavendish, 2007, p. 89.

3. Graham Cooke, 'Evaluating DNA Evidence', in *Rook and Ward on Sexual Offences: Law & Practice*, 3rd edition, Sweet & Maxwell, 2004, p. 592.

4. Ibid., p. 595.

5. Ibid.

6. Detective Chief Inspector Mick Neville, head of the Visual Images, Identifications and Detections Office, Metropolitan Police.

9. Identification: 'I'd Know Him Among a Thousand'

1. For the full evidence of the two Beck trials and the later commission of inquiry, see *The Trial of Adolf Beck* by Eric Watson, William Hodge, 1924.

2. Valentine & Heaton, 1999.

12. Cross-examination

1. Prec. Ch. 531-532, 24 ER 238. Quoted by Lord Bingham of Cornhill, the then senior law lord, giving judgement in *R v Davies* [2008] UKHL 36, para. 5.

2. J. M. Blumenthal, 'A Wipe of the Hands, a Lick of the Lips: the Validity of Demeanor Evidence in Assessing Witness Credibility', *Nebraska Law Review*, Vol. 72 (1993), p. 1165.

3. Jill Hunter, 'Battling a Good Story: Cross-examining the Failure of the Law of Evidence', *Innovation in Evidence and Proof*, edited by Mike Redmayne and Paul Roberts, Hart, 2007.

4. J. R. Spencer and Rhona Flin, *The Evidence of Children*, Blackstone Press, 1993, p. 272.

Part Four

14. Bias

1. Roger Hood, *Race and Sentencing*, Clarendon Press, 1992, p. 7.

2. Ibid.

3. See Richard Rovere, *Howe & Hummel, Their True and Scandalous History*, Strauss Farrar, 1947.

16. Doling it Out

1. J. H. Baker, *An Introduction to English Legal History*, Butterworths, 2002, p. 514.
2. Ibid.
3. Sadakat Kadri, *The Trial: A History from Socrates to OJ Simpson*, Harper-Collins, 2005, p. 98.
4. Leon Radzinowicz, *A History of the Criminal Law*, Stevens & Sons, 1956, p. 168.
5. Ibid., p. 172.
6. Ibid., p. 174.
7. Andrew von Hirsch and Andrew Ashworth, *Proportionate Sentencing*, OUP, 2005.

17. Bird

1. Prison Reform Trust Briefing, December 2008.

Part Five

21. The Great Rebalancing

1. J. R. Spencer, *Cambridge Law Journal*, 2007, p. 283.
2. Taken from Lord Bingham's judgement in *Abdrikof* [2007] UKHL 37, that turned on the jury which included a police officer having to choose between the evidence of a police officer and a drug addict defendant. Were the directions of the judge to the jury to treat all witnesses in an open-minded and impartial way enough to cure the unfairness? The House of Lords thought not.
3. *Porter v Magill* [2001] UKHL 67, para. 103.
4. *R v Sussex Justices, Ex parte McCarthy* [1924] 1 KB 256.